Horses in Her Hair

Horses in Her Hair

A GRANDDAUGHTER'S STORY

Rachel Manley

KEY PORTER  BOOKS

Library and Archives Canada Cataloguing in Publication

Manley, Rachel
Horses in her hair / Rachel Manley.

ISBN 978-1-55470-052-3

1. Manley, Edna. 2. Manley family. 3. Jamaica—History—20th century.
4. Sculptors—Jamaica—Biography. 5. Artists—Jamaica—Biography.
6. Jamaica—Biography. I. Title.

NB311.M36M35 2008   730.92   C2008-901753-6

ONTARIO ARTS COUNCIL
CONSEIL DES ARTS DE L'ONTARIO

The publisher gratefully acknowledges the support of the Canada Council for the Arts and the Ontario Arts Council for its publishing program. We acknowledge the support of the Government of Ontario through the Ontario Media Development Corporation's Ontario Book Initiative.

We acknowledge the financial support of the Government of Canada through the Book Publishing Industry Development Program (BPIDP) for our publishing activities.

The author gratefully acknowledges the excerpts from *Focus*, the Jamaican literary magazine.

Key Porter Books Limited
Six Adelaide Street East, Tenth Floor
Toronto, Ontario
Canada M5C 1H6

www.keyporter.com

Text design: Marijke Friesen
Electronic formatting: Alison Carr

Printed and bound in Canada

08 09 10 11 12 5 4 3 2 1

For Uncle Douglas, my lifelong friend and safe harbour.

Mythology

AT HER VAST FUNERAL, I felt my grandmother puckishly near.

The funeral—held at the solid old Kingston Parish Church—was one of the largest in Jamaica's history, some said almost equal to Bob Marley's. Although that's probably an exaggeration, it was certainly bigger than her husband, Norman's, and maybe even her cousin Bustamante's. Both men were towering political figures, each in his own right larger than life. Norman Manley, considered by many to be the father of Jamaica's independence, had been premier for almost a decade. His cousin Alexander Bustamante, as charismatic as Norman was statesmanlike, had also been a national leader. He had split from Norman's party soon after its inception in 1938 and started one of his own, becoming Jamaica's first prime minister after Independence.

Between them, these men had created two tribes and perhaps instigated the argument that continues to define and shape Jamaica's politics to this day. And Edna Manley—my grandmother—what had she done? What had she done to deserve such an outpouring of grief and affection and emotion? There is no simple answer to this

7

question, nothing that history books can easily explain. Looking for meaning in Edna Manley's life is baffling if the conundrum is approached head-on. She was always more in the weave of life than in its embroidery. She saw the world in terms of the symbolic, most things open to her interpretation. She understood and lived her life between its lines rather than according to an accepted script. Edna, cousin to both Norman and Bustamante, crept between the starker realities to claim another role—a role, some say, as mother of Jamaica's artistic soul.

As I look back now, the funeral crowd seems larger even than the one for Michael Manley, my father, and Jamaica's most contro-versial prime minister. Others disagree. It may have been my own sense of hollow desolation that made my father's funeral feel oddly sparse—void of either sorrow or a definable shape of loss. For when I think of it, there *was* a massive crowd, dense but somehow fes-tive, slightly frantic and still drawn to a lingering charisma that had become an entity of its own. I remember their excitement and, inexplicably, thinking of children hitting a piñata. I saw a sea of people but, as always with Michael, I watched at a diminishing emotional distance. It felt as if I, not my father, were absent.

But I was lodged at the heart of my grandmother's funeral. My grief, drenched and laden, had a shape, and its heft and logic made sense of the years.

I wasn't aware of her presence in the church. She hadn't been a great churchgoer, and may have found this part of the goodbye ghoulish. But we were there, each of us, her sons, her grandchildren, her poets and dancers and singers and dreamers—to a large extent all beings of her imagination—whom she had inspired and influ-enced by her unshakable belief. We were performing for her as usual—our poems and songs and eulogies—like children staging a concert for an adoring but invisible parent beyond the footlights.

But once we were out in the sunshine, walking slowly up

towards Heroes Park after the service, I am sure she was there. She would have found that fun. It would have been like hitting an election campaign trail again. She might have avoided the morbidity of a service, but she was too curious to have missed the rest. She would have wanted to know what we all wore, how we behaved or misbehaved, what cock-ups there were; she would have been demurely touched by the attendance, but more interested in whether we remembered to look after this one or that one, her perennial list of waifs and favourites.

We trailed behind the cortège towards my grandfather's tomb where the government had arranged for her burial beside her husband. He was interred in the special plot reserved for national heroes—Garvey, Gordon, Bogle, Nanny, Sharpe, Bustamante, and Manley—each beneath a monument.

The artists, those from the island's cultural green time now very sad, grieving their late muse and mentor, had seemed an unlikely team to carry the casket out of the church—a bewildered and shaky bunch of old men far from their Jamaican Camelot, emerging into sudden afternoon brilliance. Among them two of Jamaica's pioneer poets, George Campbell and Mike "M.G." Smith. George and Mike had grown up like sons in the Manley family. George was the sensitive, nervy child who had lost his father. Mike had lost his mother at birth and would be forever marked by that scar. Even when they were boys, Edna had recognized in each the soul of a poet to be rescued. Over the years they had become part of the corps of young artists and writers to claim a distinctly Jamaican legacy.

George, a frail figure, was now distraught, and his knees suddenly buckled under the weight of the sturdy coffin. Despite nearly dropping the beloved cargo, the artists recovered from that momentary slump, completed the brief mission, and handed their charge over to eight immaculate soldiers who carried the coffin up to Heroes Park.

Edna was a sculptress. Because she so loved wood we wanted to bury her in majestic mahogany. The highly polished mahogany box looked almost too pristine compared to our well-worn, familiar dining-room table, or Edna's carvings, or her husband's rustic pieces of domestic carpentry, and I hoped she wouldn't find it too ostentatious.

While my father was busy organizing the details of an official funeral for a national hero's widow, his only sibling, his elder brother, Douglas, had been designated along with me to choose the box. My friend Kyk drove us downtown to the funeral home, to the same undertaker who had buried my grandfather.

We entered the dingy parlour through a small pair of heavy iron gates that had recently been added for protection, for by 1987 not even the dead were safe from crime in Jamaica. The place felt makeshift, a conversion of an old garage or storage yard. A short, middle-aged lady with an amiably round face suggesting a certain malevolent mischief waved us into the cluttered room to look at a variety of options.

"See what you like," she said rather loudly, as she slapped, then rubbed, a nearby coffin like the flank of a favourite horse. Her jovial familiarity with the paraphernalia of death was disconcerting. The light was gloomy but not in a subtle, reverential way—more that of a stuffy, windowless place. The uncovered ceiling bulbs made the display more macabre than solemn.

"These are not real wood," I said.

Whereupon my uncle and I, standing on either side of a large, ornate, white casket, embarked on a brief but ghoulish discussion of his mother's dread of maggots. I pointed out that wood might attract worms.

He looked across at me. "But the worms aren't in the box— they're in *her*."

We die with our maggots inside us waiting to hatch, he said.

"Like bringing weevils home from the shop in a flour bag?" I asked.

"Something like that."

He always enjoyed irreverence.

Kyk and I started to laugh, because there really wasn't anything else one could do—about the maggots or death or Doug.

We inspected a variety of coffins with gaudy satin linings, plump satin pillows, and lids displaying religious paintings of the Lord and His angels, or Jesus neatly hanging on a cross, presumably for the dead to contemplate.

"I can't see Mother staring at this for eternity," Doug said, peering at the Last Supper.

"We really want a genuine mahogany coffin," I explained to the lady.

The mortician was discouraging. Mahogany was rare and very expensive, she explained. "Just for heads of state."

We looked at each other. We had never thought about the cost, probably because my grandfather's funeral had been paid for by the government and now, by the laws of the land, his widow's would be too.

"Well, we want mahogany," Douglas said with finality, and the lady bristled, seemed to grow in the chair, and wrote with such haste that it made me wonder just what she had noted, and what in fact one could do to the dead if one wished to be unpleasant. I asked her what Mardi should wear. I planned to bring down an ankle-length silk plaid skirt with a long-sleeved blouse, an outfit she particularly liked. Although she had lovely calves, she had decided after eighty to cover what she could of her myriad age-spot freckles.

"And I will bring a pair of flatties," I added confidently, looking down at my shoes.

The lady shook her head and pointed in short jabs at the ceiling. Apparently I had committed another faux pas.

"*They* don't wear shoes up there," she said.

My grandmother had ugly bunions and always wore closed-in shoes. I had recently bought her a pair of soft black leather loafers with tiger faces.

"Why not?" I asked.

"They'd make too much noise," she said, and lifted her chin as though to heaven.

"Well, Jamaica will find her footsteps comforting," I reassured her, and the following day I sent down the shoes, which now I could only hope she was wearing.

I proceeded up the street a few steps behind my father and uncle, Mike falling into the procession beside us. I can still remember an uneasy sense of floating along in disbelief, everything seeming either unreal or too real. Like all children raised by grandparents, I had been indulged, made to feel special in their world, and had lived in dread of this moment. I could hear my grandfather's regular admonishment, a Biblical quote: *That which thou hath greatly feared, hath greatly come upon you.*

He had died sixteen years earlier. I never felt his presence at his funeral—though his memory is the largest part of who I am—or anywhere again, not even in a dream. Now I was nearly forty and my grandmother had gone as well. But I'd kept bumping into her since arriving from Canada. In fact everyone kept bumping into her. She had died in her home, next door to my father's house, with her Walkman over her ears playing Quincy Jones's "Amazing Grace." My father was jogging around the Mona Dam at about the same time, and suddenly found himself bursting into that song, though he's not a man usually given to singing. In the following days, incidents abounded—lizards dropped from the ceiling onto food trays or plopped on tiled floors, and even got tangled in the housekeeper's hair. An ailing vulture took up residence in one of my father's flower-beds.

"Oh, for heaven's sake," said my father who thought it all a load of superstitious rubbish, "why on earth would Mother choose to come back as a vulture? Or as a lizard, for that matter?"

But all these things were seen by the rest of the family and the staff in his house as signs of the matriarch's lingering spirit. Next door, the poor, who had always made their way up her driveway seeking her help, still arrived, as though on a pilgrimage, collecting in small clusters; too loyal to transfer the honour, to ask a favour of anyone else. They appeared stubborn and outraged at her passing. Maybe theirs had always been ultimately a quest for her blessing, for the chance to feel better about themselves. In these faces were the subjects of her sculpture—Miss Aggie, Solomon, Nugget, Shook, Fitzy, ever-ancient Ernest. On the short, steep driveway that day they appeared lost and out of context.

Now along the crowded funeral route people were standing in doorways and leaning out of upstairs windows, and as in all things Jamaican, there was the blood-beat of music emanating from every-where. Suddenly there arose a crowd-voice singing, each syllable sin-gled out and snarled with gusto as though affirming us as we passed:

You wrong fi trouble Josh-u-a, you wrong
You wrong fi trouble Josh-u-a, you wrong
For Josh-u-a is a li-on
And li-on will devour you
You wrong fi trouble Joshua, you wrong.

"What's that song?" asked my husband, a Canadian journalist who didn't quite understand the Jamaican dialect.

I was about to explain that Joshua was the people's name for my father when they were fond of him, as they had been in the early seventies when they elected him to lead the country, and that this had been his election song, when Mike, who was probably slightly hard of hearing, pre-empted my answer, replying sagely, "It's an old Yoruba dirge."

I opened my mouth to speak, ready to correct Mike's inaccuracy for everyone's benefit. In an instant, though, I changed my mind and stifled a laugh. *An old Yoruba dirge.* Now *that's* Edna, I thought. It's not the answer I'd give, it's not actually correct, but it's an answer. It's not factual, but it's a thing that could be. Should be. I mean, why *not* a Yoruba dirge? Better than an old English song about dashing away with a smoothing iron, or something Scottish about the bonnie banks of Loch Lomond. It might even be more apt than a traditional American Negro spiritual. Listening to the crowds that day, I knew they were celebrating my father again, and when you came to think of it, how different was that from grieving for his mother? If they had been mad at him, would they have deemed her the mother of the nation and come out in their hundreds of thousands to pay their respects? They probably would have—she had earned that in her own right—but maybe they would have been quieter, perhaps even sullen, making sure he received their message. They certainly wouldn't have sung *his* election song. Father, mother, and son were part of a tribe, popular or unpopular; they were all a single entity, related to a point where their margins blurred. So the people sang for him and it was for her; the steps he was walking, hadn't she walked before for her Norman? Hadn't they all walked this path, struggled for their country's right to be born, died in its arms, been despised or applauded so many times?

Everything had merged into Mike's Yoruba dirge, breaking away from the buildings like a volley of shots, clean syllables like a twenty-one-gun salute to the grand old man who had reluctantly entered the fray for them, and the fiery son who had brought

Babylon down on their heads. He'd brought it down and even got caught for a bit in its rubble, and here he was coming back to honour his magical, mythical mother, the improbable matriarch of the nation, an imposing but slender white figure who had sat on the long-ago, here, now, and forever Kingston wharf and fed the strikers in 1938, when everyone had just said enough to colonialism, and history was throwing up its unique opportunities; his mother the sculptress, whose bronzed, emblematic sculpture *Negro Aroused* now stood there in that exact spot overlooking the harbour, Jamaica's very own Statue of Liberty.

Edna would have said that Mike was right; that it was indeed a sort of Yoruba dirge, in the sense of all the senses and every sense. And even if it was a casual, fanciful invention—showing perhaps that Mike, who always had an opinion, didn't quite know what in this particular case he was talking about—she'd have said it was okay because it was the poet in him, and so like life, and so like Mike.

At that moment Edna was there. She was there in the way that she had always been there—a spirit swooping in from another world on a brief foray. How else could she have invented that whole iconic system of deities that governed her work and our lives, many of which now stood, magnificent, in our National Gallery?

Her mortal remains seemed almost incidental as they were about to join her husband's in the dignified monument sunk in the earth, its marble crowned by a carved star.

The park was now a forest of people, almost dark if you looked down at your feet, and the crowd's tramping seemed to come up from the ground as it converged tighter and tighter around us. In the shoulder-high wall of Norman's circular tomb there was a gash where they had entered to dig the new grave. A steep path, muddy and treacherous from many previous days' rain, led down to the reopened crypt, and the gouged corridor appeared in danger of collapsing.

We edged our way closer to this raw side entrance. The crowds bore down on the family and my youngest sister, Natasha, was inadvertently thrown against the hot exhaust pipe of a motorbike that was skidding along in the surrounding field of slush. People were screaming at the man to move but he couldn't get out. Someone rescued Natasha, but my sister Sarah started to panic as we all crammed into the narrowing tunnel. I remembered Mardi's advice to me as a child when I'd accompany them on election campaign trails, and the huge crowds would scare me.

"Look up," I shouted to Sarah through shoulders and arms and shirts and bosoms, myself looking up at the relief of sky overhead.

I don't know if she heard me, but there in a dense, deeply still blue sky, with only its inner equations of substance and volume, was a single white cloud. A wisp. A simple, impressionistic brushed drawing of a horse's head with its eye staring wide open through its forelock, and a single raised hoof, as though the creature had paused for a moment rearing up for us, before journeying on.

My grandmother's *Horse of the Morning*.

She's got away, I thought.

⚜

I grew up with a life-sized torso of a mahogany horse looming over my childhood. It was there in my grandmother's living room, seven feet tall on its plinth, when I lived with her; and it was there in my father's house when, later on, I went to live with him. It had been carved by my grandmother out of Guatemalan redwood, one leg gingerly raised, its long face resting on the knee, its mane tossed up, its eyes staring down at me like lit globes below the tower of its forehead. It was called *Horse of the Morning* and it had been a wedding gift to my father and mother.

When my father returned to Jamaica from England in 1950 it was waiting for them, but their marriage had ended and so he came alone. When my grandmother died at eighty-six, my father gave the horse away to the National Gallery. He felt no one person was entitled to own this sculpture—it belonged to the people of Jamaica. When my mother heard of its fate, she remarked dryly that it wasn't his alone to give away. It had never dawned on me to resent his gesture until then; but as the only child of their union, and despite the logistical reality that it was too large to fit in any home I have lived in since, after that I did.

It was the sort of grand and selfless gesture that I had come to realize was expected of the family. Despite our teetering finances, the folly of his generosity never struck me at the time. I always knew that Jamaica was entitled to whatever we had worth giving. It went without saying. A generation before, it was common knowledge that my grandfather was the best lawyer in Jamaica, if not the English-speaking Caribbean. And yet when he eventually retired from politics the world discovered that he was broke, having given almost all his money to build a political party. When I was growing up the talk was always of public service, and I assumed that this was the family business. Around our dining table, Jamaica was not just our homeland, it was our cause.

I think my grandmother probably had this in mind when she named the work Horse of the Morning. I mean, she didn't call it something universal like Pegasus, or familiar and predictable like Brown Beauty. It was named for the morning of Jamaica's birth, its dream of independence, with all the struggle and challenge that such a name implies.

It's therefore not surprising that any thought of a horse brings both my grandparents to mind. There were stories of my grandfather as a boy galloping full tilt along mountain trails and through startled rural villages. He was a reckless rider and liked speed in anything he did. They always owned horses, and my grandmother rode every day until she was nearly seventy. In fact, both their homes were discovered on weekend rides. They loved horses, and long before I came into their life they owned a thoroughbred called Roysterer who was a Jamaican National Derby winner. I remember Edna thundering through our pasture at Drumblair, her majestic bottom (her husband's pride and joy) lifting and falling firmly like a very big, very slow bobbin. Looking back now, it's as though even Norman was one of my grandmother's horses, brittle and fast, proud and nervous, tentative and independent. The vulnerability of something exquisitely pure, her enduring fascination.

Since we were nearest in age, I grew up with my cousin whom we called Little Norman—my Uncle Douglas's elder son—under Edna's supervision. The only children in a family bent on changing the world, we were often thrown together, odd reminders of less sublime domestic reality. This Norman has made a way of life of resisting the expectations that his famous name evokes. Today, his cellphone rings "Rule, Britannia." He takes a firm stand on that watershed in history that defined his namesake, cussedly insisting that Jamaica should never have followed Norman Manley into independence.

Little Norman declares himself uninterested in "all that artyfarty stuff," a term that covers the other strand of our legacy—poetry, theatre, classical music, and fine art supported by both grandparents, but generally associated more with Edna. So I found it unusual when recently he paused beside a reproduction of a large watercolour Edna had painted in the eighties, shortly before her

death, that hangs in the entrance to my Toronto home. It was originally called *Woman with Horses in Her Hair*. Its size, she said, did not
reflect burgeoning ambition, but failing eyesight. Large work was
easier to see.

Norman gazed at the young brown woman rising from the
curling, white-crested, breaking wave of the sea, on her face an
expression of unabashed expectation, her hands outstretched to
heaven, and lifting from her hair the heads of three ghostly white
horses—the embodiment of our grandmother's three recurring
themes: water, the horse, and identity.

"What do you think she meant?" he asked.

I watched him stare curiously at the picture, so near to it that
he appeared to be reading it like a book. "I think it's a self-portrait,"
I said.

He stood back and gave a surprised, mocking toot of a laugh,
almost like a rebuke.

"But that can't be *her*. This woman's *brown*!" I found his comment interesting, for I would have said the main difference was
that this woman was *young*.

"Well, she always thought of herself as brown. Her mother was
mulatto; she just came out white like her father. It happens." I was
also thinking of myself, who had come out with little of the
Manley colour. My grandmother would often explain that we were
quadroons, as though we belonged to some rare, select sect.

"Did she? . . ." he mused, and now his smile was gentle as he
looked fondly at the picture. "I loved the old girl, you know.
Though I think she was a bit crazy. But she really loved horses.
Remember she'd let us ride—you always got the bigger horse! I'd
whip my old mare to go faster when Mardi couldn't see—none of
that trotting for me—and once when I fell off, I remember her rubbing me all over with prickly-heat powder!"

It was the sort of odd, impulsive thing our grandmother would do with us, as though she had never raised two sons and was now making up child-rearing as she went along. I thought about how, despite her avowed lack of interest in small children, she had taken on the bother of us when, after both her sons divorced, she realized we needed a grandmother.

"So what does the picture signify?" My cousin wore a familiar expression—a moment's bemused, almost embarrassed attention before, predictably, his restless spirit darted away.

"I think it's about her death," I said, but tried to modulate my voice, hoping his interest would remain for a while longer. "I have a theory that she saw herself as emerging from her life, which is water—the ocean—and the horses are her freedom in the spirit world—her death. Maybe her philosophy of life."

He squinted down at the bottom of the picture, where its official name—the result of our grandmother's confusing tendency to rename her work—had been printed.

"But it's called *Birth*!"

"Maybe that's her point. That death is birth?"

"Oh," he said, and shrugged. "No beginning, no end." Recently he has turned to Buddhism, and may have found some correlating position in this.

The horse was Edna's symbol. To her it represented ultimate freedom. As a child I never thought to question her passion for horses, real or metaphorical, rearing their heads above our stormy life. I understood this with simplistic faith, in the way children do. In one form or other horses inhabited our world—in the stables, whinnying their equine commands, banging their hooves against the paddock doors, or standing at somewhat insolent attention for us to ride; galloping under my purposefully crouched grandmother through the tall green grass. They rose over my youth in mahogany or chalk, charcoal or wash, shining, iconic.

But if the horse was my grandmother's symbol, the sea was her Piscean element. I knew this all my life without really understanding why. It wasn't until I visited Cornwall in 2000 that I realized that my grandmother had come from the sea.

Part One

I

Horses and Water

And as always as a background to all things, the ever-changing sea—
tameless and primeval. Elemental.

—Edna Manley: *The Diaries*, early August 1969

THE SEA WAS THE BLOOD OF CORNWALL, Edna said. This was the sort of vivid image she'd leave in my mind, the sort that is probably responsible for my lifelong tendency to think in metaphors. She was born next to water. Not the water I had known in the Caribbean, warm and buoyant, mindless, resilient and forgetful. Edna was born in England, another island. Our stories begin with our earliest memories. And hers were of St. Ives, on the cold, opaque northern sea that pounds relentlessly along the Cornish coast, where her family relocated shortly after her birth.

It's an odd twist of fate that I was also born there. In 1947 my father, Michael, Edna's younger son, needed Latin to qualify for entry into the London School of Economics. He rented a seaside cottage in St. Agnes in order to study, taking along my pregnant mother and her five-year-old daughter, Anita, from a previous marriage. I was delivered in a nursing home in the neighbouring town of Redruth, and spent the first six months of my life there. It was a life that, like my grandmother's, began with the sound of the sea, and the stroll of beaches under my father's long feet as he smoked his pipe with tobacco from an assortment of old cigarette butts, and carried me through the ripping breezes practising his Latin conjugations, "*Amo, amas, amat,*" and later, when I could clutch a toy, "*Puella pupam portat.*"

When we moved to London later that year, for it was growing cold, I was already claimed by Cornwall—a birthright only my conscious mind would forget. I would be faced with this birthright fifty-five years later when, in 2000, having decided to write this book, I applied for a fellowship to do research on my grandmother's life, and returned to Cornwall to retrace her footsteps and, coincidentally, my own.

Whether from ruin or survival, the seaside town of St. Ives gazes out across the St. Ives Bay towards the Irish Channel. At England's southerly tip, it seems to yearn for the source of its ancient Druid past, ignoring the immediacy of a battering sea always at its hem. Perhaps the soul of that county, a small country of its own, is more driven by history and mythology than by any current political reality.

Life on this knuckle of cliff is lived at the edge of time. The village, strung along taut fingers of rugged hillside, has long since turned its back on England to reach for the elements, each small home defiantly lit at night against danger, pressing against its neighbour to gain a view of the sea's parade. And all around this stubbornness, the sea extends itself, connected and absolute. Rocked by the wind's uncertainty, lichen from overhanging rock hovers over a million conversations of water. But for all its force, no gale disturbs the salt-starched bushes further up the cliff, pillars of longing and regret, their windblown heads forever looking back towards the mainland of their home.

It was a hundred years after my grandmother had been there, and I stood awed by time and my tenuous connection to the place. I watched a single gull float overhead, buoyed up motionless, balanced in the jaws of the wind; over the centuries they must have learned that the bird that coasts can float upon the storm.

I think bodies of water must be the subconscious mind of Earth, holding its memories and secrets, its profound inner musings. That must be why writers like the anonymous author of *The Seafarer*, or Homer and Hemingway, Melville and Twain, and the Caribbean poets Walcott and Vincent-Brown, are affected so by them.

I fear being submerged in deep water, but beside it, sometimes upon it, I find myself in bigger voice and wiser mind, watching its endless obsession with itself, its capacity for nervous stillness infinite, its mutterings and tut-tutterings under the pier, its puckering flirtations at midday, its skin basking lavishly in sunset like some gleaming rich woman who could have any man she wished. Standing watching the bay, I wanted to live in such a place and wake every morning to its certainty and modesty of secrets, to its paradoxical immodesty and nakedness—its eternal choreography. It is, after all, not painful to be mortal beside such immortality.

I am not sure what informs our sense of legacy, of tribe. I know that Cornwall was always within me, whether St. Ives, the landscape of Edna's childhood, or St. Agnes, that of mine. I remember things I cannot source with any certainty; perhaps they are from Edna's words. Fifty years later I found things that before had been no more than essence in me. The relation of man and water in such a place is almost inevitable—the presence of water like a temperament always to be considered, the enigmatic surface of the sea, its buoyant simplicity, its terror—faces that would be reflected for me later, when I joined my grandmother on the rough side of

Palisados road, or opposite in the dark, quiet water of the Kingston harbour, or sometimes faraway in the playful, transparent water of north-coast Jamaica.

People are said to come "from" somewhere, as though they sprouted from loam. I realized I was now looking at my grandmother's youth. This was where she had come from. This Cornish cantankerousness, this cussed refusal to conform, this capacity for longing rather than belonging—this was her loam.

Her father, Harvey Swithenbank, my great-grandfather, became the junior minister at the Wesleyan Methodist Chapel in St. Ives in about 1902. He was the son of a well-off wool merchant, born in the north, in Yorkshire. But Harvey spurned the family business and chose the life of a cleric. In the final decade of the dying nineteenth century, his church sent him to Jamaica as a missionary. There he served for seven years, as long as it takes to fully change the cells in a human body. He returned to England with diminished health, a mulatto Jamaican wife, Ellie, two island-born daughters, and his wife's trousseau of solid middle-class silverware and Jamaican mahogany. Back home in Yorkshire, two more children were born in quick succession.

Ellie's fifth pregnancy, with her third daughter, was peripatetic. The family accompanied Harvey on his pastoral service south to Hastings, north to Hexham and then, hoping warmer weather would stabilize his failing health, on to Bournemouth, Dorset, where Edna was born. Her first cries would split the seam of midnight that joined February 28 to March 1, 1900. No one has ever been quite certain of the date of her birth, whether it was the end of one month or the beginning of another, grey hares or white rabbits. In later years Edna, a spinner of legend, claimed that her birth, haunted as it was by what she interpreted as magical mixups, was actually the twenty-ninth, and for that reason quartered her advancing age. But despite the fact that she had deftly slipped an extra February 29 into our collective intelligence, when the family checked the records of the calendar, 1900 was not a leap year.

Shortly after Edna's birth, Harvey was offered the position at the church in St. Ives, in Cornwall, the neighbouring county. My grandmother grew up surrounded by Celtic lore and feral Cornish beauty. The androgynous Cross of Iona with its mysterious womb-like belly, which may predate Christianity, was so much a part of Celtic art and the Cornish landscape that it was probably more familiar to her than the old rugged cross of her father's church.

It's strange how fate conspires to help us when we are in search of answers. At around the time I was leaving for Cornwall, a friend sent me *The Mabinogion*. I discovered that like the Bible it comprises many storytellers, and each story may have been retold over and over through time. The tales of *The Mabinogion* are told by the Welsh, descendants of the Celts, and are a mix of Celtic history and culture, legend and apocrypha, probably truth and untruth, understanding and misunderstanding. They are magical tales that echo Arthurian England, with all its romantic flair and idealism, its honour and heroism. It was there in St. Ives, in Celtic mythology, that I found the source of my grandmother's famous horse.

I started reading, and found much of the allegory and animism of my grandmother's expression, the alchemy of mundane into divine, the combination of myth and reality. The name of one of *The Mabinogion's* mythical figures, Epona, means "Divine Horse." Epona was half woman, half horse, and, like a mermaid, had a human torso. The legs of a horse made her faster than a man. Epona is said to have been conceived when the god Stellos, who hated women, mated with a mare.

The names and the myths differ somewhat, but in all of them this figure is half woman, half horse; to the Celts she is Epona, but to the Welsh this figure is Rhiannon. "Rhiannon" comes from "Rhiain," which means "maiden" and "Annwn," which means "Underworld." Sometimes this figure is a king's wife who, having lost their infant son, Pryderi, lives out her punishment banished from the royal court in this hybrid form. Even in England, she is found in the nursery rhyme "Ride a cock horse to Banbury Cross, to see a fine lady upon a white horse."

The mythological stories that grew out of the land and local experience were powerful, and often more colourful than Christian accounts. Part fairy tale, part landscape, how easily they slid into my grandmother's consciousness. Each tradition would name these ancient figures variously as the goddesses of animals and asses; of horses and horsemen; of fortune, fertility, and the newborn; of the Underworld and the dead. The birds of Rhiannon were the messengers of hope and bliss and forgetfulness—totemic birds that sang their way between worlds, as did these very myths.

It's said that the custom of the Grey Mare still continues in Wales. Every year, between Christmas and Twelfth Night, children set off on a hobby horse, a mare's skull fixed to a beribboned stick, knocking on doors and posing riddles that, wrongly answered, ensures entry into that home for the Grey Mare, who may then have to be bribed with treats.

But the most vivid legend that Edna passed on to me in my childhood, was the story of the white horse of Portwidden. In the nineteenth century a man called Birch owned a magnificent white horse, flowing mane and flying tail coming alive with her excited gesticulations each time my grandmother repeated the story. He was the delight and pride of his master who loved him dearly. At the end of each afternoon Birch would ride to Portwidden to bathe. But one stormy evening a current swept Birch away, and his horse just stood there on the shore waiting for his master who never returned. Only a ghostly presence remained, sometimes seen at dusk riding on a white horse.

The myths drift like kites.

When I remember Edna as she stood in the Blue Mountains of Jamaica fifty years later, naming the peaks and creating her personal carved pantheon, I think of her father, Harvey, attempting to replace the Celtic gods with Christ for his parishioners. Maybe, despite all his years studying theology, he wasn't sure himself. Unlike some of his fellow ministers who saw impediments to spreading Christ's word, perhaps Harvey believed that the marriage of old and new ideas would ensure a natural transition. He was an ardent theologian and would have been aware of how Christian and pagan rituals can intertwine. Like the Virgin, the Lady of the Horses was the mare of sovereignty who lost her foal. He was found in a stable, as Christ was in a manger, surrounded by lambs. Christ's totem was a lamb, Pryderi's a foal—the grey mare was banished from Bethlehem's stable for a more important birth. The thought of that infant would have brought Harvey full circle to Jesus.

Celtic and classical, pagan and Christian, probably intertwined in Edna's imagination the way they did in Cornish life. But beneath all this a deeper tide flowed without ambivalence, with the peaceful assurance of sleep. It was the abiding presence of her mother. Although Ellie settled in her marriage and would never return home, she could not forget Jamaica. And her homesick nostalgia was imbibed by Edna. The Caribbean beckoned to her in the arms that held her as a small child, in her mother's beige Caribbean skin, her gentle, less angular features and soft brown eyes and the wave of her hair. It was there in the nut-brown arms of a Dominican nanny who helped out for a year, who'd sing old Negro spirituals that rumbled into Edna as she rocked her. It was there in the way both women sat too close to the fireplace and pulled their shawls ever tighter around them; it was there in the way her mother shuddered at the cold northern water of St. Ives. It was there, Jamaican lore, in Ellie's evocation of the mountains and rivers, the blue sea and old pirate town of Port Royal; in the *Grimm's Fairy Tales* laid aside to make room for another adventure of the mythical island spider Bro' Anansi; in the Sundays that never passed without a fond account of saltfish and ackee with boiled green bananas, and at Christmastime in the description of glasses of cold, deep red sorrel, till the ginger and colour of this dark, sweet, unobtainable drink became the flavour of longing. And though Edna could never say how she knew it, she had always known the warmer Caribbean Sea pounding like the memory of sound in a shell deep within her.

How like life, that our stories are so often half-truth from half-truths, a garment of scraps and rags.

Among the few impressions of the small seaside hamlet of St. Ives engraved on my mind, images my grandmother shared with me so vividly that they could have been my own memories, was a stone tunnel she remembered as too narrow for more than one person to pass through; they would walk single file, the walls high and the darkness pockmarked with peepholes. It led to the beach. Edna was always hoping to see Birch's white horse there. One day, emerging at the bottom into the sudden brightness of sunlight, the sea a hundred yards before her, she saw what appeared to her to be, even retelling the story years later, a thousand horses storming over the sand from where she never knew; looking back, she assumed that in the summer months their grooms probably rode them to the beach so the animals could swim.

Horses in water are beautiful, terrifying creatures. She watched them swimming, their necks lifted above the waves, their huge shoulders, muscles oaring them along, their restless ebullience— Biblical beasts she heard of in her father's readings at church on a Sunday, from the book of Habakkuk, as otherworldly there as they were on land:

> *Were you angry with the rivers, oh Lord, was your wrath against the streams? Did you rage against the sea when you rode with your horses . . . churning the great waters?*

Her other vivid memory was of her father organizing the townsfolk during a shipwreck off the coast. I hoped to track down both the landmark tunnel and any documentation on the shipwreck.

I would wake early each St. Ives morning and "meet the dawn," hoping to relive Edna's youth in just a week. As I gazed through my third-floor window in the small hotel above the town, the world that was lost each evening would revive layer by layer, the roofs in moss pretending to be hilltops, the walls masquerading as beach, green seeping out of black rocks like a sweetness of sloping land-bones. The unlit windows like missing teeth, the chimneys with their waking breath of smoke, froth returning to a single wave far out, each sneaky light offshore quietly shutting down, till the daylight came in as a silverness setting things up again, each house in its place, walls leaning out to look at the sea— some with plumply thatched roofs like fat cheeks—the white-washed brick waking first, before the muddy and the grey, the cobblestones threaded just the right way, the arms of the coast stealing into sight—*we are all right, we are all right*—the peninsula returned under the watchful eyes of its coast guard station.

"Fishermen leave before dawn," I could hear Edna say, as she would in Runaway Bay, Jamaica, as though theirs was some grand calling, their tiny lanterns bobbing in my mind like lost stars. By the time St. Ives awoke, these early fugitives would be carried away by the sea.

On my first day, as The Island came into view, I remembered my grandmother's description of the village looking like a mother trailing a small child. Now from my perch I recognized the wayward peninsula extending from the long curving underarm of Porthmeor Beach, its wider tip like an atoll just off the shoreline. To me it appeared to be dragging the town behind it, a sticky albumen eye attached by its thread to the yolk of an egg. At its summit a tiny fisherman's chapel had been restored after one of the wars. In the early twentieth century, who knew if it was a church, a rock, or a ruin—a tiny consolation of faith and shelter, or grass grown over, some state of roofless semi-collapse binding its broken walls? But there before me the picture took shape, colour bleeding up through surfaces as though conjured by magic.

Aided by a small guidebook, I picked my way carefully down the steep hillside, the narrow roads threading through the shops and houses of the busy summer town, wondering what my grandmother would think if she could see this modern tourist trap. It is curious how tourists can make landscapes similar—it could have been any small, ancient cobbled European town now beset by visitors gazing equally intently at historical sites or plastic souvenirs, bargaining with locals selling mementoes in stores or sidewalk stalls. In the distance the beach, with its ritual clusters of lounge chairs and umbrellas, suntanners and sandcastlers, could have been anywhere in Sussex or Malta.

My handbook explained that the town divided itself, as towns tend to do, into two areas, Upalong and Downalong. Predictably my hotel was in Upalong, and now I descended to the seaside part of Downalong, which extends between the harbour, Porthmeor Beach, and The Island. It said that fishermen lived with their families here, in among what was still a maze of tiny streets, sudden passages, and unexpected courtyards. The smell of fish, explained my booklet, was stronger in the Downalong streets than in the harbour itself; it came from the vast pilchard cellars, from the barking houses used for tanning nets, and from the smokehouses for curing. The more well-to-do houses of Upalong could catch the smell on the breeze in the morning through an open window. I imagined Edna, always an early riser and a great lover of fish, which she insisted was good for the brain, opening the window to let in the sound of the distant surf, faint, salty-fish perspiration drifting up from the streets and the sea, and her mother, Ellie, closing them again with an islander's instinct to protect against salt and corrosion.

Harvey and his family had lived in the junior manse. I found it, one of a row of grey stone homes on the side of a hill in Upalong, its twenty steps rising to the front door as though out of my grandmother's memory. It was a narrow row house, and indeed it would have been a squash to hold a family of seven. Farther down the town was a labyrinth of cluttered alleyways and steep stairways, leaning houses, rugged walls between whose crude stones the mortar snaked like veins, laundry drying on lines or fish destined for export hung in the sun on hooks from the walls, old stone gateways, overhanging upstairs windows that looked curiously down.

Everything led to the quay, sloping towards a watery destiny. The seine fishermen unloading their catch in the autumn, cleaning the ling cod right there on the beach—the bits of skeletons and scales, the cloying tenacity of stench, the pungency a complex curiosity. The fishermen's small anchored craft would ride the back of the water like saddles on the wake of each new swell, swaying to the memory of their journey. Boat by boat they'd arrive, the fleets of mackerel and pilchard luggers loading or unloading their cargoes at Smeaton's Pier, the seine boats arriving from Porthminster, stuffed to pot-bellied, silvery shining. Later, the fishermen would saunter along the narrow quayside, caught between the walls of buildings and an unprotected drop into the menace of becalmed harbour, the glug of water against rocky siding, the ground beneath moving like a small boat in danger of capsizing, disappearing into their lodges or the Sloop Inn, their voices rising like one giant conversation. On its graveyard shift, the tide would come in delivering the village its fish, watering down the sand, cleaning its mouth, salting the air to recede slowly as the little town awoke.

I crossed the road towards the beach, and quite unexpectedly found myself staring at what I was sure must be Edna's tunnel, its walls probably not as high or its pathway as long as she remembered, but with the peepholes she had described. Again I felt the wonderment of standing in her shoes, though soon I was mostly aware of holding my guidebook to protect my head, with so many pigeons swooping down around me to land on the little eyelets or waddle down the musky steps, and I wondered if there had been such an abundance in Edna's days, or whether this also was a consequence of tourism.

Time hadn't stood still, I was sure, but maybe I'd returned to it. My grandmother wasn't here anymore, but I'd entered a landscape where there were places she had lived and loved, walls she had touched.

Emboldened by new certainty, I was determined to find proof of the shipwreck. It would probably be harder to prove. I crossed the small town and entered the local library armed with only a single but solid detail about a night with a shipwreck on the rocky coast. I hoped to look at microfilm of old newspapers that might have reported it. I was sent upstairs to the records department, a bright room with many windows and an oddly low ceiling for a public building, which gave me the impression that this research area had been created by reclaiming an attic. There were half a dozen librarians shuffling and reading papers while sipping their tea, completely ignoring their visitor. An air of easy, cheerful camaraderie hummed along with the lines of fluorescent lights, diminished by sunlight pouring in through pigeon-mucked panes and slanting across the walls and desks.

"I believe we have a whole box on shipwrecks," said the relevant clerk, whose interest I managed to attract despite a highly trained indifference. "Which century did you say—this past one?"

I remembered that my grandmother said she was about five or six years old, and her age was also the year.

"Yes," I said, "1905 or maybe 1906."

I followed him to the far side of the room, where he pulled out a large green file box labelled "Shipwrecks 1900–1910," which he placed on a table before me, offering me a seat. The box was almost empty.

"And what would your interest be?" he inquired, his nosiness disguised as punctilious British formality.

I told him my grandmother's story about Harvey Swithenbank. "She grew up in Cornwall," I said, but didn't mention that she was born in the next county. I was, after all, Mardi's granddaughter, and facts were useless if they had to be exact.

"Actually *I* was born here," I added.

I didn't think I had said it very loudly, but I was suddenly aware that the room had gone quiet, its hairs standing on end. A common head turned to look at me. They appraised this member of the family with surprise and the fierce curiosity of recognition. Soon there was enthusiastic handshaking as I tried to explain my connection. They nudged me with questions, and I said I had been born in Redruth, in a nursing home, whereupon they argued among themselves, someone pointing out that St. Agnes had not always had its own nursing home. A mere half a year was apparently enough to establish my credentials as a Cornish national and create a bond, so I proceeded to tell them what I knew from my grandmother's story—my great-grandfather's moment of honour and recognition for a heroic performance at a shipwreck in St. Ives a century before.

There are moments when the past improbably returns and stands there right in front of you in black and white. In this case, something as invisible as a kernel of family legend. It may be smaller than you imagined, or shabbier—less romantic for its reality, but no less significant. That's how I kept feeling that morning. I retrieved a brown manila folder labelled "1905" and opened it. I immediately saw a picture of a schooner (clearly marked "scooner"), *Enterprise*, which had gone down in 1905. Here before me was a small, flat-looking ship, not particularly glamorous, with two upright sails and another trailing it like a perky tail, destined to be broken into smithereens on the rocky coast, a fragile yet eternal testament to my grandmother's early world. It could have been a model ship in a bottle on some traveller's shelf. It was a simple black-and-white outline, but it represented an event that had tested her father, and had brought a previously skeptical community to respect a stranger who had until then been the unproven junior minister for the local Methodist Church.

For tenpence a sheet I copied the pages, and then searched the rolls of microfilm for old newspapers. Sunday services were announced in September 5, 1905's paper, at the Wesleyan Chapel, evening at four, Rev. J. Swithenbanks. Maybe they got his name wrong, but *The Summary* announced a six PM. Sunday service presided over by Rev. H. Swithenbank, February 11, 1906, at the Wesleyan Chapel.

I also copied a short announcement of Harvey's appointment to the St. Ives Wesleyan Circuit, noting that it was initially met with regret for they had wanted "a son of the soil." Although the congregation would have welcomed the junior minister with due courtesy, he had evidently embarked on his duties in the shadow of local disappointment. His arrival coincided with the passionate work of the Cornish Revivalists, who wished to preserve their Celtic nation with its ancient language and customs intact.

All I had after a morning at the library were these few small details. The key to half of my grandmother's psyche lay with her father. But what more could I ferret out of this place about this man? How to begin to uncover his life, when I wasn't even sure where to find his grave?

2

Harvey

If a girl who turnip cries
Cries not when her father dies
It is clear that she would rather
Have a turnip than her father.
> —Anonymous rhyme often quoted by Edna

FAMILY HISTORY IS LIKE SCENT THAT LINGERS. Blood is lasting; defining markers endure.

What did I know of Great-grandfather Swithenbank? I knew him through a funny little nursery rhyme he used to recite to Edna, the nearest she ever got to worship, clasping her hands as if in prayer, extending the two index fingers, and repeating it for my benefit as he had done for her.

Here is the church, here is the steeple,
Open the doors and see all the good people.

And I'd watch her strong, veiny hands that had shaken and battered all day, clutching the mallet and some tool against a large log
of wood, the fingers now entwined each with its twin, as she con-
centrated on the task and whispered with her light, indefinite,
thready voice, which had that old-age tremble:

Here is the parson walking upstairs,
Turn him around and he'll say his prayers.

And following his long-gone example, she'd wring her joined
hands inside out and wriggle her thumb in its fleshy pulpit of
digits, her head cocked to one side, no doubt listening attentively
for the father's prayer she remembered clearly.

I knew him through countless reiterations of a joke he had
told Edna: The bishop was coming to visit a parish and stay in the
manse. The minister kept coaching the young servant boy to take
water to the bishop's room each morning, knock on the door, and
announce, "'Tis the boy with the water, my lord." On the morning of the visit, the boy turns up at the door very nervous and
knocks. "Yes?" says the bishop.

"'Tis the Lord with the water, my boy."

I knew him through our walks in the Jamaican mountains. My
grandmother would commandeer my hand and re-enact her own
six-foot father swinging her hand to order a march as though to the
thump of drums:

A soldier was drunk and he packed up his trunk and he left, left . . .

And she'd grasp my hand as though gathering loose ends and we'd
proceed, left foot first, repeating the ritual fifty years later. I remember her telling me that when she was a child, his was the only
hand she ever held without protest. I suppose she thought being

led showed weakness—too great a concession to make to her large and encroaching tribe.

"And what about your mother?" I'd ask, as I knew she was still alive then.

"Oh, she loved your grandfather," she'd say with pleasure and certainty, as though this was paramount in the equation of who this intangible great-grandmother was.

By the time she was nine they were a family with nine children. Edna always claimed to be squashed in the middle at number five, but I notice that my Aunt Vera's family tree has her at number six. With only a minister's salary and accommodation, the family lived at close quarters. Ellie would urge Harvey to take Edna off for walks or to accompany him to service so as to get her out of the house, where she was restless and, if she couldn't go outside, often disruptive, not liking the others to touch her pencils or crayons or drawings or some bird or insect she was nursing. She would pound on the piano if called away from practising her scales to help around the house.

"And do you not think he was right?" she'd continue, and we would skip once to repeat on the right leg and change step, she tactfully allowing me to catch up. I liked changing step. I enjoyed the bump in the middle, the small, exhausted huff my grandmother made on her hop to alter her stride beside me. She would laugh as we landed together and we'd look at each other with satisfaction, as though we had come through something important. When we went uphill she walked faster, and when we went down I did. For her the roles had changed since St. Ives, through generations of nature's age-old democracy.

Driving through Trowan and Trevalgan, or Trevegia and Wicca, even as far as Zennor, along the narrow coastal plane through stone-fenced fields and farms, I probably passed those walks she took with her father—Harvey and herself coming upon the surprise of an unexpected Jack and Jane wall, stone-fenced fields, empty acres of wind-groomed marram grass, routes that would take them near ancient grave-mounds, landscapes still peopled with the abrupt figures of prehistoric Druid stones, with texture she could feel with her spirit as much as her hands. Slim, long-legged, sharp-featured, and strikingly pale, Edna, who often behaved like a poltergeist indoors at fifty or five, would smooth out and settle, probably finding her gait at her father's side. I could imagine her alone with him out on those moors, moving into a treasured separateness with its own calendar, horoscope, and map, the infinite possibilities of the world beyond family; outdoors was her world of escape as a child. She would return home exhausted and somehow exorcised.

Whether through this medieval landscape, Harvey's thundering sermons from the pulpit on a Sunday, or her mother's nostalgic musings on her lost tropical paradise from which she was always waiting for news, waiting for letters, longing for red pea soup with hot pepper or a visit from her nephews and nieces, waiting and longing, the world grew on Edna in a series of symbols and impressions that she interpreted through the zodiac of her personal universe, pilfering this world for stage-props to establish her cosmogony.

Mothers we do not see, do not need to see. They are in us, we are in them. Fathers we have to meet. Maybe we view fathers the way we see the mountains and the land, the world outside and beyond. Harvey, whom Edna was destined to lose too soon, would have been the time-worn, maverick cliffs whose vantage point enabled her to see beyond the early womb of family, the anchor from the span of whose tethering rope she peered at the suck and swell of water; her foundation; her bony armature; the still, fixed centre of her soul; the listener; the back of the spoon in which she found her unique truth reflected.

To Edna, Harvey's bright blue eyes, which she had only dimly inherited, must have seemed like Cornwall's summer skies. These eyes reflected amusement and interest from which she seemed to derive—even at a young age—confidence, clarity and self-image. They became very close, and maybe he sensed that this unusual child was easier to recognize through difference; that she lived almost as if beneath the skin of things.

And perhaps, in their special relationship, Edna's was the only route Harvey took that didn't go via God. As he hankered after some invisible voice, Edna hankered after him, and her interruptions were probably as real and as present as a swell of swift, acidic flavour in his jaw, often providing the true trial on earth for dogged, devoted, downright British Isles Harvey.

It was only when I saw a picture of Harvey that I realized whom Edna looked like. She always thought of herself as the dark child, the Jamaican of the Swithenbank tribe, but in the picture they all looked very fair, like their father.

Although she'd describe my great-grandmother to me, Edna couldn't evoke a clear picture of Harvey Swinthenbank, because he had died when she was only nine. He became a kernel of sadness so intense that much of the rest of her childhood faded out of focus in her memory. She would have been too young for anything but loss to have a language or a shape, so Harvey took on legendary proportions in her consciousness, and later in mine, as an absent fathering, tall and shadowy, my grandmother meeting his memory with surprised, childlike bursts of rapture as it emerged around some corner of her heart, leaving her fleetingly empty as it receded into ghosted disappointment. I knew he was her early sadness and I equated it with a familiar bulb planted in me, an inarticulate heaviness that weighed within me each morning when I woke. It seems, in families, the wheels keep coming round.

⚅

There was something inevitable about Edna seeing Halley's comet twice in one lifetime. The ancients believed that a comet was a harbinger of good or evil. Halley's comet, whose appearance was first recorded in 240 BC, was there at the fall of Jerusalem in 66 BC, and appeared at the eve of the Battle of Hastings in 1066. King Harold of England regarded it as a bad omen. On the other hand, the victor, William the Conqueror, saw it as a favourable sign. Mark Twain, who was born in 1835, when Halley's comet was visible in the sky over Missouri, predicted in 1909 that he would die the following year, when it was next expected—as indeed he did.

In 1910 Hawaii was expected to be one of the best viewing spots on earth, so an observatory was built at Kaimuku. And while travellers gathered from all over the globe to see the celestial body, many Hawaiians sold their possessions and awaited the end of the world. In England, comet pills were being sold to counteract the effects of cyanide poisoning, for the earth was expected to be brushed by the tail of the comet, which contains cyanogen gas. Children were reportedly returning home from boarding school to be with their parents in case the end should in fact come to pass.

My grandmother always believed in omens, and feared things that might go "bump in the night." But she recalled little anxiety in Cornwall at that time but her own. This westerly outpost was open to the full blast of the most volatile elements, so there was characteristic Cornish indifference to the hubbub. People around her were viewing the coming event with the unemotional shrug they accorded other varieties of natural phenomena, all of which could and often did become nasty. Their world had never been safe, as every fisherman, farmer, and miner knew only too well. And if they were to go about seeking sinister signs there was no end to the omens they might find. Bad things happened all the time. Fate, they felt, needed no encouragement to be harmful. And they were certainly not going to build up any star bigger than it deserved.

In September 1909, Harvey was promoted by the church to the position of Callington's circuit superintendent. The family moved to this inland town near the border with Devon, a breezy enclave caught between two desolate, wind-torn dominions, Dartmoor and Bodmin Moor. Maybe accepting the post was unwise, as Harvey's life had increasingly become a series of truces with his health, and his new workload was far more demanding and required a lot more travel, much of which was local and had to be done on foot.

From the moment the family arrived in Callington, Edna felt a sense of dread at the approach of that ominous comet. It became a drum roll in her psyche. She missed the coastal frenzy of St. Ives, the hiss of opposites meeting, the freshness of smell, the expectation of the surf's recurring voice, a familiar undulation that had been her metronome; she missed this chorus of the earth's performance. Fifty years on, whenever we went to the sea, she would embrace it all over again with the joy of recognition, as though remembering that early shock of desolation she had once felt without it.

Callington felt sterner beneath Edna's shoes, more substantial and yet less giving, without the hack and spit, caress or lick of the sea. Despite the endless wind, which was often cruel and combative, she had entered a landscape hard as porphyry, more dense, things demanding to amount to more. People went about their business as though walking against wind had steeled their resolve. Whatever had been fluid and shifting settled into solid, concise form. Harvey had slipped his familiar definition, no longer the passionate, romantic figure ministering with his worn black Bible and trailing gold ribbon. His disappearances now were long and unpredictable, and he came home loaded down with bagfuls of administrative responsibilities. A no-nonsense practicality seemed to replace the nebulous, unpredictable drift of Edna's earlier youth. In this new world, in its certitude of shape, in its accountability, the family had left St. Ives behind, its legends and rumours and landmarks slowly receding in her mind like a haunting fairy tale.

"No point looking back like Lot's wife," her mother would always say, though one could take that advice from her with more than a grain of salt.

"Tragedy is the refusal to accept reality," Edna would say in turn to me, generations later.

The past, though tempting, was now inaccessible, and Edna, by instinct a survivor, listened to her mother and waived the prerogative of looking back, not content to become its petrified ghost.

Ellie probably had little chance to make much of Halley's comet, her time filled with predictable, life-affirming domestic chores. This comet, with all its exotic notions, would have seemed as unnecessary an indulgence as the breast of chicken for which her daughters vied. Ellie was happy to eat any part of the bird that was left after the family's bids went in, savouring little scraps of carcass held daintily to her teeth. And no matter which scientist claimed what star, she was content just to live under heaven.

Harvey's promotion provided the family with a manse. Called "The Retreat," it was a house large and deep enough for sleepy verandahs and indefinable shadows where Edna would often find her mother on a lounge chair as though dreaming of sunshine; there was a new composure within inviolate boundaries through which the family could roam without forever bumping into itself. Within the high walls lay a garden into whose life Ellie joyfully disappeared, at last free of that unquenchable cold and the salt-voice of a northern sea—and free of the jostling elbows of neighbouring houses.

Edna was now perhaps the middle child of nine, and always

spoke of herself as such, embracing the myth of claustrophobia—being squashed between forces, and feeling marginalized by a large family—yet set apart by a restlessness and imagination that seemed to be shared by none of the others. It seems that her youth was already a struggle for sufficient freedom and space for the familiar to become distant enough to loom emblematic, like planets in the sky, or totem poles. She needed a place where she didn't have to wade through the everyday but could know each thing in essence, its symbol at the core. She craved her own cosmos, one she could shape out of intuition and imagination, and now she hoped she had found such a place.

At first, like a landed sailor, she was off-balanced by the rhythm of the sea still in her legs, but soon, with characteristic curiosity, she became distracted by the possibilities of the large house. She found an asparagus bed in the garden, which she considered exotic, and at the back of the building she was thrilled to discover a second staircase that she probably saw as a means of escape—hers was now a family with alternatives. Beneath the main staircase she found a storage cupboard containing a stack of life-sized cardboard cut-out torsos. The previous superintendent had used these to line the pews of his church on Sundays when the congregation's turnout was small. She decided to repaint them, even though she was sure her father, who had packed the church in St. Ives each week, wouldn't need them. But most of all she was impressed by the fact that "The Retreat" was a house with a name, a tradition she would adopt for herself later on in life.

Fifty years later, as I rummaged through the dusty cupboards at Drumblair, the family home in Jamaica, I found albums and envelopes filled with old photographs, newspaper clippings, and magazines, but only one picture remaining of the whole family together. Ellie had assembled all eleven members for their first family photograph, taken in the garden of the manse. They were arranged by a local photographer into a composition, the family gathered around their mother, who sat on the lone chair, with the baby, Mona—just a bundle of christening frills—taking her turn on her mother's lap.

As I looked at each Swithenbank face, they settled into a vivid, lifelong memory. No other family photo exists, that I know of. Bound with Edna to a unique moment, they were stranded like all memory in my subjectivity, these images combining to form my only visual impression of my grandmother's childhood.

Ellie appears more a thereness than an anchor, the matriarchal vine surrounded by her circle of blooms, most of her outreach invisible. At her left shoulder stands Harvey. Six foot four in his dark suit and clerical collar, he towers over the family with his head slightly cocked to one side, a hovering presence waiting politely to be released, looking quizzically at what would have been a hooded figure behind the camera. Beside him, the tall and humorous Nora, Edna's favourite sister. On Ellie's lap the swaddled infant, who was born in that house and contracted meningitis. She narrowly escaped death after a bonfire of three feverish weeks, and was henceforward cursed and blessed as the Piggy-Whidden, the weakest of the litter, remaining the baby of the family and always having a wide-eyed expression which, from the single time I met her, left an impression of surprise or naivety belied by years of shrewd comments on the family and current British politics in her letters to me.

Leaning over Ellie's shoulder is my grandmother's favourite brother, Leslie, whom Edna would point out in the picture—the one who loved to read and once announced to her that he had one hundred books. Beside him Gladys, whom Edna called Swiddle,

plain, outspoken, and very what she called "Yorkshire." I remember two things said about her—that she always took charge (my
grandmother by nature would resist), and that she tended to think
out loud.

Edna sits at the front of the picture between her beloved
youngest brother, Ralph, and Winnifred, about whom I know
nothing except the fact that she died of TB as a young adult. Leaning sullenly into his mother with what I assume was a burdensome,
envious neediness is Harvey Jr., who once fell in a nearby river.
"Harvey's fallen in the wiver, fallen in the wiver," Edna would say,
mimicking Ralph, who couldn't pronounce his R's and had sought
rescue for him. Young Harvey was her lifelong nemesis, whom I
grew up despising without ever really having any reason but my
grandmother's sibling antipathy, which she never explained—perhaps
because it was so long ago she couldn't remember.

Directly in front of Harvey, Lena, the eldest, is kneeling,
steadying herself on the arm of Ellie's chair. She forms the outer
edge of a triangle with the figures of her parents. At fifteen, six
years older than Edna, Lena appears to look out with quiet confidence, and I remember the story of her standing in the middle of
the breezy main street in Callington campaigning for a woman's
right to vote. I have always thought it interesting that of those
sisters Lena, not the maverick Edna, saw her identity in her gender,
as though this, her half of the human equation, contained her,
explained her, encompassed what she was, and if she could just
make that space everything she needed it to be, why then. . . .

Edna was never against votes for women, never against the
suffragettes or her sister Lena, but all her life she felt very shy about
feminism, to which she used to refer vaguely as "this whole femi-
nist business." But then she was always cautious about anything
that involved a crowd and a movement of common intent and the
combined show of struggle. How could everyone think exactly the

same thing? she wondered. She would have the same reaction years later, visiting China, when she could not imagine being harnessed into a team to sculpt a communal piece of art, glory of the state or not. She said it reminded her of the three-legged race in kindergarten. The next time Lena congregated beside the road with the activists, Edna chose to take another path home. In some ways this incident defined both sisters.

After a week in Cornwall, retracing my grandmother's journey from St. Ives to Callington, I found the garden in which that photograph had been taken nearly a hundred years before. The building still stood near the Methodist church but had been converted into some sort of school, which was closed for holidays. I never saw inside and I was glad for that. I wanted to think of it with the possibility of my family within. But in the garden, though I found no asparagus bed, there was a small, slimy pond that momentarily burned with the promise of a goldfish breaking its surface like a subconscious memory. My grandmother had said that her mother always fed the birds—as though it explained her own similar devotion—and I wondered if this had been a bird-bath in Ellie's brief time here.

The minister I located at the church had no idea where my great-grandfather might be buried; he wasn't from Cornwall and had never heard of him. But he suggested I come back the next morning, when some older parishioners were meeting for what he called "a social" at eleven. Someone might remember something useful.

The following day I went to the bustling private room behind the chapel. It was a mostly female group, the more elderly members smiling sweetly or glaring suspiciously at me from the circle of iron chairs. The younger ones hushed babies; the middle-aged kept the little gathering going, passing round homemade cakes and biscuits and pouring cups of strong tea and weak coffee with snippets of gossip in short, harmless volleys. No one had heard of Great-grandfather Swithenbank. When I was about to leave, an ancient lady bent almost double shuffled in, heaving herself forward on her walker and ignoring a younger female companion who made a show of hovering attentively.

"Ah," said the parson, "now here's someone who may be able to help you," and he shouted at her by her name, which I now forget, as though she was hard of hearing. "She is the oldest member of our congregation," he explained to us in a whispered aside.

"In the *parish*," the old lady corrected him.

When she was settled in a chair with her tea, the pastor sat next to her and explained my mission. She had that opaque stare of the blind who seem to be seeing things inwardly.

"Harvey Swithenbank," she mused. "I remember the name well . . . some said . . ."

The room around us paused with village anticipation.

"What did they say?" I prompted her.

"My mother said there was never anyone like him. She spoke as if he was a saint. So fine an orator." She savoured her tea and her wrinkled mouth trembled to produce an affectionate smile. Her face, like a fruit on a branch, slightly bobbed as though in the breeze. "Sometimes he spoke his words on thunder . . ."—her old jaws chewed slowly at her thoughts—". . . sometimes on streams of milk and honey." Her false teeth were not in sync after she managed the murmur of the word "milk."

I thought of my father, whose charismatic speeches had held the attention of an island for at least a decade. I had naturally assumed that this gift came from his articulate father, Norman.

This stranger, who had never known my great-grandfather, had lived with him through her mother's story, one that, with all its implications, delivered him fiercely and intact to me that day a hundred years later.

⚏

The parson sent me on to the town hall, where the county's burials were listed. The registrar was a cheerful man, young enough not to seem sinisterly familiar with the dead. He jotted down the name and the date I gave him and went to fetch a large leather-bound ledger from an adjoining room. He checked the pages, running his finger down and muttering, "Swith, Swithen, . . ." as he went, as though perhaps he could tease the name out from its hiding place. No luck. He fetched another book, and another.

"Was he born here?" he asked.

I summed up the details I knew.

"A Methodist!" he exclaimed. "That's different." And he set off in another direction. He returned bearing two well-worn record books, the same shape as the ones before but far less grand in appearance.

"In those days the Methodists were buried in unhallowed ground," he explained, and located the year and the entry with my great-grandfather's name, where it had sat all these years, waiting patiently to be located. He jotted down his brief instructions, which I took with me to the nearby cemetery.

It was cool for a summer afternoon, and the wind was blowing in from the moors. I walked up the gradual sweeping rise of a modern highway, and the cemetery was on the right, behind a modest stone chapel that one had to pass through. It was dank inside, and dark, seeming no more than a covered path, with many candles lit at a low altar for the spirits of the dead—no more than a brief archway through which to pass from one world to another.

Graveyards remind me of orphanages and prisons. One enters expecting some deep sorrow or remorse, expectation or explanation to express itself, but there they are, busy with their own timetables and rituals. I looked across at a great plantation of headstones, each occupying its plot, straight or drooping, tidy or untidy, intact or crumbling, each serenely marking a bygone life. I walked through the even rows of this democracy cheerfully attended by wildflowers and patrolling birds, imagining my grandmother coming here, a child at nine marching for a last time in memory of her father (*and he left, left*), and I did a small skip, being careful not to step on the bright yellow dandelions that smiled valiantly from the grass on behalf of the departed.

I found Harvey's grave. He was in section B, row seven, space nine on the opposite side from the hallowed ground. The graves on the unhallowed side did seem less grand in size and ornamentation, but a general state of wear and tear was common to all. They were all ancient, many sinking or leaning, the names on some barely visible where the wind had worn down the past. His was on an aisle. The stone was broken like the crust of one of my cakes from the oven, the circumference intact but the middle split and sitting sunken, impaled but alone, like an ill-constructed patio my father had had at the front of his first house. It felt immediately familiar.

I stood in front of my great-grandfather, a child who has been summoned and waits to be warmly greeted. I gathered a few small pebbles for my siblings and sons and stuck them in my coat pocket. The headstone with its dedication was shaped like a church window, intricately sculpted around the edges like one of Ellie's elaborate doilies that my grandmother used to use to line her trays:

In loving memory
of Harvey Swithenbank
(Superintendent of the Callington Wesleyan Circuit),
who was called to higher service
Nov 18th 1909, aged 44 years

and below that, in italicized print, Harvey's last pledge:

I know in whom I have believed.

The words at the bottom of the stone belied the stoic Ellie:

This stone was erected by his devoted and sorrowing wife.

Although she would never see it again, a carved hand, closed but for the index finger pointing from the apex of the stone to the sullen heavens that day, remained engraved in her mind, the haunting reminder to Edna of the higher service to which her father in his sacrifice, and all sorrows and sacrifices, now belonged. He would hallow that ground.

Sorrow and Sacrifice. Sacrifice made and Sorrow endured. Words that matched the pewter sky. Sacrifice by her father, by her mother, sacrifice made of Harvey by the church, sacrifice made of Ellie by Harvey. Sorrow that went sorrowing on, its present participle continuing forever and ever amen bound in that moment of stone at section B, row seven, space nine. The sum of a man.

※

I had found my great-grandfather in Callington years after my grandmother was gone. A glimpse of his spirit gave me a chain of custody to retrace who he was to Edna the child, who she was to my father, and who my father was to me—who fathers are to their children, and how absence magnifies any parent—how in the cycle of life ancestors invisibly pervade.

But for my grandmother, Callington would remain the place where she lost him. Within a year of moving there, Harvey had returned to the manse one morning at dawn like a tattered eave off the roof of the world. Edna could hear deterioration in his jagged voice. She knew he had caught a fresh cold over an old one, could feel his chill in her own being, feel fear like a breath passing over the shameweed fern, *Mimosa pudica*, that chastely folds away its leaves. She knew he had crossed the family's danger line.

Swithenbanks have weak lungs. But to my grandmother, her father's lungs were bearers of gladness, messengers of melodic psalms and fulsome sermons she was able to hear over any storm of wave-blasted Cornwall, over the squandered, meaningless noise of her never-ending family; from those lungs came the only language she was able to understand.

"*Goodness must be practical. Goodness is a doing thing. It's activism,*" he'd say.

"Now, if he had gone for a *birth,* . . ." Ellie had said grimly.

Weeks of praying and gathering and listening in sleep and worrying and more praying. Ellie like a bat to and fro through the room, all the children muted and shadowy, unbelonging substances in the gloom of their home.

"Ellie, my dear, I am struggling to live for you and the children's sakes."

"He is the most patient man I ever saw," observed the junior minister from his church, making notes of his final conversation with the dying man.

"Jesus is precious to you now, isn't he?"

"Precious, so precious," said Harvey, his long hands pressed together facing each other in front of him, as if motioning a completion of goodness to a congregation.

"You are not ashamed of the Gospel of Christ?"

His short answer was the signature of blunt testament left at the end of his world. "Never less," he said, and from his memory the words of Saint Paul to Timothy: "*I know in whom I have believed.*"

Ellie summoned the children to tell him goodbye.

Edna would always remember the moment. Her father lay out of reach of anyone's call, and all she could hear was him gurgling occasionally in between such preparatory stillness, a father beyond even his own meditation or prayer. He was dying from duty, from visiting an old woman who as far as Edna was concerned had carelessly chosen to die during a storm three hard miles away.

He had left in his long grey coat and galoshes, left, left into the mud and puddles, the wind and the night.

The room was bathed in a strange light that Edna would remember as blue, but that wasn't true. There was no colour, just the presence of light. The scene before her appeared pale and still, almost shrouded, a cataract that kept Edna separate. The shape on the bed covered by sheets, plane upon plane, a flat bas-relief spread like a lesson she would learn and relearn.

Love turned to stillness like marble, a still figurehead, her companion on so many walks, the tender voice of the preacher to whom she didn't always pay attention on Sundays, with his lessons and stories. Above the metronome of his words, left right or right left, his silent, mocking twinkle, a hand holding hers, now here in this last room. With growing horror she watched him, the tender voice already arranging itself in her memory into the peals of an echo, the pleats of a robe, a long grey coat now folded away like his heart and his mission and passion, folded neatly in light that was not really blue but sepulchral, somehow, to this child of nine.

Light translucent, transcendent, all of the things in his sermons that seemed too high to reach, things on this world's uppermost shelf, but Edna loved them, whatever they were, whenever he spoke.

Outside, Halley's comet appeared to pay its respects to the young century. In the room, its light reflected blessings of angels now come to collect him, and the glow of her father whose holiness had begun to escape. Harvey was preparing to flee the mortal coil, which wasn't coiled but lying straight and resigned, undisturbed by his wife or the undertaker as long as he was able to offer those brief little rasps.

His friendship remained in the billows of his breathing, all he had left.

"Oh, the power and the glory and the wonder of it all," he abruptly proclaimed, sweeping his frail hand towards the window where he saw Halley's comet shining like the beacon of his redemption.

"See God's angels come to collect you," said Ellie, with a look of pride that Edna remembered as infuriating.

"It's only the *comet*," Edna said, horrified at the implications of such a misunderstanding.

But he couldn't hear. He was already marble, or bone or stone.

"The manse has to be vacated for the next Superintendent." Ellie wrote to her sister, Margaret, in Jamaica, as though all of her heartbreak, and everything she had ever borrowed for happiness, were explained by this one simple sentence. And by the spring of 1910 the family had moved back to the coast, to a smaller home in Penzance.

Before leaving Callington, Ellie placed a headstone where Harvey lay in the public cemetery on Kendall Green. Edna remembered that her mother had appeared calm as she busied herself with practical details in the wake of Harvey's death. The Methodist Church had provided for his burial, and offered a brief, dignified acknowledgement of his life—his name engraved on a simple cross. Ellie decided to erect what she considered a more significant headstone, perhaps compensating in grandeur for what he'd been denied by location.

"If I have to sell the silver, . . ." she declared to the children, and made the execution of this project her top priority, paying many visits to Harvey and to the local stone carver, as though mediating a discussion between the living and the dead.

Just before they finally vacated the manse, Edna recalled the children all accompanying Ellie to a small, informal unveiling of what appeared to her to be a towering headstone. She remembered the day for the darkness of the sky, its almost overwhelming reflection of irrefragable bleakness, for it would rain for the rest of the day, pausing only for the moments they stood there in mud to honour the dead, sunlight appearing from nowhere to reflect off the grey.

3

The Days of Love and War 1914–1922

August 1914, as anyone alive then can bear witness, was a month of
such magic in Cornwall that one could almost have predicted after
this—the deluge. Into this glory walked Norman Manley.
                    —Edna Manley: *The Diaries*, early August 1969

MY GRANDPARENTS HAD MET BRIEFLY in the summer of 1914, the year
before the Great War, at Ellie's new home in Penzance, when Edna
was fourteen and Norman was a brash young twenty-one. The
meeting is as indispensable to our family lore as is the lower limb
to access a favourite plum tree. Norman arrived from Jamaica to
enter Oxford University on a Rhodes Scholarship, and to join his
siblings, Vera, Muriel, and Roy, who were already in England. They
had each turned up, one at a time: first the eldest, Vera, a formidable short-haired beauty, to study music; then her petite sister
Muriel, always shadowing Vera with her long brown plait of hair,
to study medicine; and finally the youngest, Roy, a handsome and
charming teenager who wrote poetry and wanted to be a playwright,

joining his sisters to attend a public school in London after their mother's death left him orphaned. They lived in London but travelled down to Cornwall for holidays to stay with their aunt, Ellie.

With the arrival of each new cousin Edna became yet more intrigued with the faraway island they had left behind, with the sunshine they brought with them in their handsome brown faces, the sisters' so like her own mother's but darker, Roy's even darker but with finer features. When they spoke she could imagine islands where people sang so much that the rhythm of the music stayed in their voices even when they talked. They lifted their sentences so prettily, as though always asking questions, a sort of mocking amusement in their tone that never seemed to become serious even if what they said was stern. And yet it wasn't strange to her; just a familiar whisper, a tentative edge of her mother's voice that now she heard aloud.

Norman was the last to arrive. With the recent loss, his mother's memory had galvanized him to recant a rebellious youth and settle down to study. But if mending his ways was inspired by his mother's passing, his choice to study law at Jesus College is not surprising, his litigious father being famous for dragging even the most insignificant issue to court, and sometimes on to the Court of Appeal. As a college athlete, Norman was one of the fastest in the world. He had set the schoolboy record of the 100-yard dash in ten seconds flat in Jamaica in 1911, and he would hold it for forty-one years; the following year he ran the 220-yard in twenty-three seconds, then almost an Olympian time. He had recently survived a near-death struggle with typhoid fever. After a period of intense study, he had won the Rhodes Scholarship. By the time he arrived to visit his aunt in Penzance, he was already a legend in the family.

Without her father in her life, Edna had become a defiant, wilful teenager, a tomboy who liked the outdoors and was more

comfortable with animals than people. She was happiest on holidays, mucking out the stables on neighbouring farms, grooming the
horses, or astride a saddle tearing over the moors. She too was
building a legend, hers one of rebellion at West Cornwall College,
a nearby boarding school where the Methodists had arranged a
place for her. Ellie was often called in to see Miss Hanna, a strong
but empathetic Irish headmistress with a sense of humour, whose
lot it was to negotiate with this fiery, imaginative student. Edna's
pranks included knotting together the girdles of her housemates,
jovially whipping them naked in the showers with a wet towel,
escaping school whenever she could, and lately, when there had
been a fire upstairs and the damaged second floor was declared out
of bounds, climbing through the hazardous building to check out
the forbidden area for herself. The floor gave way and Edna fell
halfway through the collapsed ceiling of Miss Hanna's office, and
was stuck there with her long legs, unmistakably Edna's, dangling
over the headmistress's desk.

Miss Hanna introduced Edna to William Blake—his poems and
his art. Within the pages of every library book she was able to
locate on this artist, she pored over his thoughts and images. She
liked the dichotomy in his world. She found in it a mix of human-
ism and animalism, his simple division of his world into good and
evil as innocence and experience, the ease with which he spoke
through either words or drawings. She studied the drawings and
tried to relate them to his poems, and vice versa. She became fascinated with his 1808 drawing of Death's Door, perusing with sadness
and horror the old man with a cane at the open-mouthed tomb of
death as though driven there by a high wind in a storm. Above the
tomb a young, strong naked figure of a man was sitting looking up
to the heavens, with one knee drawn up as though he was getting
ready to rise. This, like Halley's comet, she supposed was meant
to represent the resurrection.

In the foreword of one book she found a story of Blake's life, in which she learned about his background and the outrage he felt at the plight of the poor, especially as conditions worsened during the onset of the Industrial Revolution. Blake had grown up near a workhouse for orphaned and abandoned children on the grounds of Paulett's Garden, Coventry, where these disenfranchised souls were treated disgracefully, half-starved and beaten, usually worked to an early death. In 1767 an Act of Parliament was passed that gave rise to a wonderful facility near his grandparents' home that welcomed these children into a rural setting and taught them to read and sew. These stories reminded her of the poverty she had witnessed in her own young life on the docks of St. Ives, or in the families of miners in Cornwall, and the fundamental goodness of her father's work in his endeavour to help.

Edna was on holiday when she was called inside to come and meet her cousin. She resented the interruption. It was a glorious summer day that she remembered as "full of sunshine and running." And there before her stood Norman. She always described their first meeting the same way—Norman standing in front of the empty fireplace with his hands in his pockets, swaying, handsome, faunlike, and smiling mischievously. She studied him for a moment and was met with a mocking smile. Though she was only fourteen, deep within her "something stirred and died."

"Can you do this?" he asked, and horrified her by yanking from his head a handful of his hair, which, unknown to her, was thinning due to his recent fever. Then they went in to dinner and Ellie asked him which cousin he liked the best. I am surprised he answered her, for he always used to tell me that comparisons were odious. But he looked across the table at the oblivious Edna and whispered, "I think the plain one with the spirit."

And then he left for university, and the war changed everything for everyone. In less than two years Norman and his brother had joined the army and been sent to the front, as had Edna's brother Leslie, and her sister Lena's husband of a few days. And Edna, having abruptly decided to study art when she failed her music exam, at age fifteen would board a train headed for London, leaving forever Cornwall of the wild moors and rugged Celtic beauty, its mysterious seeds safely sown within her.

If you asked my grandmother what she did during the war, she would tell you she broke horses to be sent to the front somewhere in France. They would be ridden by soldiers who fought and survived or died there—some of them people she knew, members of her own family. Though she lived through the loss of her special brother, Leslie, and her cousin Roy Manley at Ypres, and Lena's husband of only a few months at the Somme, it was the horses she always seemed to regret the most, maybe because their fates were the only ones for which she felt responsible.

War is usually about freedom. Man's freedom. Whether freedom under threat, or the vision of it that men hold for themselves and interpret as an oasis on the horizon, or its blunting and shaping into army discipline, Edna believed that one way or another war had to do with freedom's loss or gain. That everyone construed freedom differently—came to terms with unbelievable personal loss, found extraordinary courage, changed, compromised, bled, sorrowed, mended, kept faith, adapted to war, in the name of freedom.

It has been said that for every three men in the First World War, there was one horse. Many aspects of war depended on the breaking of horses. At the remount depot in Wembley, Edna would come to realize with sadness that whoever, for purposes of war, had to break a horse, that purest of freedom's engines, was in fact betraying the animal. Horses were trained to be instruments of man's arguments, whatever their premise, in a battlefield of slush filled with the filth of slaughter, to be shaved for mange only to die from pneumonia, the filigree of their lower legs buried in mud to catch gangrenous dermatitis—possibly to be blown sky-high. If they were so lucky as to escape, they were not returned home to a hero's welcome for fear they might bring disease, but kept in Europe and sold to carters or butchers for slavery or meat. Mankind, who fits so perfectly into the small of their backs, was now reneging on a trust—their treaty of mutually beneficial compromise.

They say a million and a half horses were used during that war for the cavalry alone. Many others hauled guns and supplies to the trenches. Half a million horses died in the four years between 1914 and 1918. Many of these had been brought from Canada.

The forewoman at the depot was a Canadian. "I'm the donkey of the pack," she'd joke, with a self-effacing humility Edna never trusted. The woman had married a Scotsman who had enlisted and was said to be fighting at the front, and she always seemed to be waging her own battle on behalf of her horses, and saw all the English grooms and stable workers as part of the enemy, members of a European conspiracy to make slaves of a breed who were proud and free in their homeland. One night she had too many beers and told a group of the grooms that she resented her husband offering his life for a country that treated the Scots as second-class citizens.

By the time the Canadian horses reached Wembley they had already been through hell crossing the Atlantic. The forewoman had been deeply affected by an incident at the beginning of the war, when eight thousand Canadian horses were said to have been delivered to Plymouth, nearly a thousand packed into each ship for the twelve-day voyage. They were a tried and trusty breed whose blood had been shed in ample practice during the Civil War in

America and the Boer War in Africa. No proper preparations met their arrival at Salisbury Plain. They had to be tethered to trees or vehicles by odd bits of rope or straps, without any shelter, in high winds and continuous rain. Many died.

Weighing only ninety-eight pounds, Edna was put in charge of seven half-broken Canadian horses she was the first to try, her bony knees grimly dug into their sides. Seven horses that she would care for throughout the bitter winter of 1917, rolling bales of peat for their bedding, mucking out their stables, braving their walleyed fury to place more feed beside these already overfed, underworked, overwrought animals. Horses she would get to know at the end of a rope as they circled her round the training ring in their ritual dance of defiance, both of them waiting for the moment maybe weeks later when one would stop and acknowledge the other, reluctantly concede to the presence of resolute patience, accept the paradoxical treaty of friendship and bondage. Edna was breaking her natural friends of innate freedom to send them to certain death in France—often slow death, by hunger or thirst, engulfed by the heavy quicksand of mud, the slow cruel emptying of the body by cold, or, less likely, by the listless thud of shrapnel disappearing into their hide. By weaponry was a kinder way to die. The Canadian forewoman told them how one night her husband's horse was so cold that he gave it his own blanket, and in the morning the blanket was gone. The horse had eaten it just to produce body heat.

Edna took care of the horses for a few weeks, fed them and made them warm, rode them, respectful of their single-mindedness, their valiant hearts, whose gladness men had stolen as raw material for their own courage. In a war of betrayals and inhumanities, this period was just another stage of their journey on the road to hell, and she knew that this was no more than a hiatus of care to prepare the animals for an awful outcome.

Years later, she heard about a man who killed himself fourteen years after the war. He was a carter. His wife confided later to a grandchild that he had been depressed over the fate of those horses for the remainder of his life. His own family had never believed him. They had thought he was crazy. My grandmother told me that it was difficult to explain to anyone who didn't love and work with horses. But she understood. It was a sadness that had not ended for her at Wembley.

The forewoman never allowed anyone else to check the mail at the depot. She collected it herself from the box at the entrance and sorted it. The others had to wait till she got around to it, and if she received a letter from her husband, they would have to wait even longer, till she'd read and reread it, before she passed out the remainder of the mail.

"Hey, we've all got people there, you know," Edna would grumble.

So when they heard the knocking at the door that night, it was the Canadian woman who answered. She turned to them, all waiting with dread lest the telegram bear their name. But it was the Scotsman who was dead. They all tried to hide their personal relief as she fell weeping into someone's arms, the telegram crumpled between her and another's shoulder. Then, pulling herself together with a cup of tea, with everyone gathered around her, she turned to look uncertainly at Edna.

"*Well, there are other men in the world, I said. It was like kicking a dog,*" she wrote to her cousin Norman, with whom she had started a steady correspondence. His first letter had arrived from the front when she was still in Penzance, and she had slept with it under her pillow every night until the next one came, starting a relay of conversation. "*And I don't know why I said it. Maybe because she wept in front of everyone. Just something in her manner struck me. I don't know what. I am ashamed of how cruel I am. But yesterday there was an air-raid over*

Harrow," she went on, though she always had difficulty forming these sentences to him, for she had no clear picture of where her cousin was or how in this terrible war he would receive them, or even if he would.

> *Many of the girls are sick and absent, so I was riding one horse and leading two others when all hell broke loose . . . aeroplanes everywhere and bombs dropping and all the horses bolting. There was a woman walking with a small child and a pram ahead and they were in panic. I decided to let go the two leads and just jump the bloody pram. I knew the horses would eventually gallop back to the stables. The fore-woman, who naturally despises me anyway, was furious with me. Why come back without the lead? she asked me in an acid voice.*

And then Norman's first dark letter arrived. His younger brother, Roy, who had joined the army underage to be with him—following his hero as always—had been killed in the preparation for the great offensive at Ypres. It was June 1917.

> *Edna, Roy is gone. It all seems so pointless now. His death was in character. He was rushing out to rescue a fallen comrade. An ironical footnote—the soldier he rushed out from safety to rescue, and carried back to the dugout when he himself was hit, was actually long dead.*

> *Nothing in the terrible years of this war, its human toll, its unspeakable horror, has brought home to me the utter waste of life and talent and youth and hope and love and purpose as this; my limp brother. It all seems suddenly pointless.*

Soon after that her favourite brother, Leslie, was killed. And at the end of the spring the depot was closed. The war was winding down.

After the depot closed, Edna worked at the War Office for a while, sharing a room in a London hostel with her sister Lena, the heart-broken war widow. Edna could hear her sister's muffled sobs under the partition, but pretended not to, finding any excuse to leave. She had difficulty dealing with outward shows of emotion. She loved to go to the zoo and draw the animals . . . lions, tigers, and wolves; the solemn monkeys who looked at her as curiously as she looked at them. They were always themselves; they didn't have the artifice to be anything else. She had no training, but her empathy and their authenticity drew them to the page. She was still deter-mined to study art but she had no money, and her mother advised her instead to teach, which she didn't want to do.

London had become like a nagging mother. She felt the pressure of its gaze everywhere—Ellie, the War Office, Lena in tears. She felt surrounded once again, as she had in her childhood, needing to cope with people, to keep them politely far from her dreaming, thoughtful centre. It always made her talk too much, try too hard. She needed to get away. At the War Office, bored with the bureau-cracy, Edna chose the occasion of a visiting dignitary to make a dramatic entrance; sliding down the banister, falling at his feet as he stood with the welcoming party at the bottom of the stairs. She was fired.

Edna took the first job she saw posted, for a team of young workers to pull flax in Norfolk for the summer. The war effort was a big pair of jaws eating up everybody's wool and their men and their hearts and their spirits, and now their flax. Flax was needed to make aeroplane wings. Harvesting was gruelling, back-breaking work—they had to pull up the entire flax plant, stalk and all; nothing was to be wasted—but at least it was on a farm. The experience steadied her. Far from the family and London, Edna drew comfort from the infinity of flat monotony surrounding her. She enjoyed the continuity of the predictable routine of rural life, each day the same, nothing letting her down. She always loved watching clouds. Perhaps she gained perspective seeing them drift like continents moving towards each other, meeting and fitting seamlessly, their masses melding into one. Would European enemies do the same one day? Australia and Asia? Each continent drawn like a puzzle piece to the mate of its shape? Would the distant Caribbean be squashed in this reunion, or sit like a cluster of tiny moles on the newly assimilated body? With her cousins now in England, her aunt and Roy already dead, what was left of her legacy in that island of her imagination? But she was certain she'd see her mother's homeland one day.

Love had brought loss and grief and dislocation. It required the offering of sorrow and the humiliating rituals of sympathy. In a perverse way, in this total anonymity she felt released into serene, unimpeachable freedom.

After the flax season, Edna took a job briefly as a gardener with a family in Ditchingham. Here she found herself squatting anonymously within the safe parameters of upper-class grace, where war was discussed by country gentlemen only after dinner, over fine port. She stayed in a large, airy room over the stables, and spent her spare time drawing again. Determined to find a way to go to art school, she wrote a letter to a wealthy uncle, her father's brother in Yorkshire, asking for financial assistance. She enjoyed the feeling of having disappeared, knowing that to the world she now inhabited she was safely invisible, until one morning her employers accused her of having an affair with the chauffeur and fired her.

"But we were just out chasing rabbits," she protested.

Ellie had moved to Neasden, in London, during the war, and

Edna now took refuge with her. A letter was waiting for her from her uncle, who granted her request. She was overjoyed. She enrolled at once in Saint Martin's School of Art, where she studied for the next two years. She also took an occasional class at the John Cass Institute, or Regency Polytechnic, and three nights a week she took classes taught by the animal sculptor Maurice Harding. This was her favourite course.

At Saint Martin's she had a Scottish teacher, McCrossen, with a thick brogue. He had a very structural approach to sculpture and used to tell her, "If you look at a curve, every curve is a series of planes, or flat lines. Look after the planes, lassie. Look after the planes and the curves will look after themselves." She felt she was his favourite student. Probably because she worked so hard, and because he had once come in and found her still chipping away at eleven at night, having persuaded the watchman to let her in.

"You know, mi lassie," he said, "you're a lass after mi own heart. You love to work."

After the war ended in 1918, Norman returned to England, exhausted of mind, and one day found himself in the library at Oxford writing meaningless phrases. A further breakdown of every shred of his being found him alone in London on his knees, staring up at a fractured black obelisk of ancient Egyptian art in the British Museum, thinking that he might be looking in a mirror, that he might have fossilized. He wondered if he had actually died and not realized it. Having no idea where he was or how he had got there, instinctively searching for answers and safety, he bought a one-way train ticket to his aunt, Ellie, in Neasden.

Neasden. To reassemble his pieces in the very place his aunt had relocated to in order to reassemble her own. He would reunite his being to its shadows now cast eerily against the walls by the light of frugal candles, his hands reflecting their ghosts, as though amid the impenetrable silence of his being he was attempting to regain life's attention. And Ellie, who looked so like her older sis-ter, Margaret, was the closest Norman could come to finding the comfort of his mother.

By the time Edna came to visit, he had already ridden out his pain for six weeks, in some ritual exorcism of nightmares often witnessed by Ellie in the cocoon of her spare room. He would see a flash of light before the noise came, and dreaded what might be revealed—a scrap of ragged flesh lost in the unaccustomed earth, or a limb or a glimpse of bone—too many fragments of too many people to retrieve or do honour to, the good earth like a steady friend, there and unconditional. Ellie would sometimes see him oh so softly conducting with his hands, as though hearing music. Their shadows traced meanings over the walls, small pigeons flut-tering. His long brown fingers, that neither Oxford nor war and the laying of guns with his cockney buddies way behind the trenches had managed to subdue or coarsen.

The first time Edna saw Norman after the war, he was in the guest room at the back of her mother's row house in Neasden. She found him on a cot, lying flat on his back. War had attempted to break him in a way that neither the loss of his mother nor typhoid fever had done. It had forced him to a stop, and he didn't know how or what to mend. He didn't stare at the ceiling, or shake in the way Edna imagined a man would shake with shell shock. His hands were neatly folded on his chest, and his eyes closed as though he were asleep or resting in meditation. It was his quietude that struck her. Whatever pain or fear he endured was a sinking stain that deepened within him. As Edna knocked gently on the open door, he turned to her quite naturally and smiled a familiar, friend-come-to-me smile. He was relieved to see her, as though she had come back from a world he had thought might not exist anymore.

She brought one of her drawings to show him. It was a lion on its haunches, thin with a straggly mane.

"Hardly reminiscent of empire," he said, with a wry smile whose softness and sweetness convinced her that his anguished spirit would yet survive. He looked gaunt enough to model for her anatomy class.

She told him about a small plaster figure she had made in school, a lion over an eagle. It had won a prize. She had overheard her teacher say to someone, "The German eagle and the British lion—it would make a fabulous war memorial."

In time the days they spent together would grow in confidence, and he would quicken in recounting trivial, irreverent moments that dispelled the dread of his thoughts, for the vignettes were incidental, but they were spoken in a tone used to the rhythm of bathos. They wrote each other notes, and sometimes she imagined she was hearing his thoughts seeping in through his words, and at other times it was his words interrupting his thoughts, leaving her unsure of what was spoken or unspoken, or what had been written, all of which together became a growing conversation between them.

In between the deafening artillery I'd grab the moment of silence to treat the fellows to a few bars of Madame Butterfly.

But he now knew that war was not the death or the cannons or the guns on battlefields trudged through waxy sludge, or the stretchers lying ready next to the pre-dug graves; war wasn't your brother's weight in your arms.

While this Catholic was saying his rosary beside me in the trench, I
was reciting my high school football cheer . . . Hash and Roast Beef,
Mince and Pie . . . N-O-M-E-R-C-Y.

War was the damp of the trenches at night, the mass of
humanity upon humanity; the disappointed energy of hunger, the
cold that becomes a concentration, the smell of each other inside
and out, knowing oneself and every brother in each private phase
and at each daily stage of his humanity, knowing this all the time,
knowing how he whimpers or shudders or curses, how he misses
his mother or hates his father, how he beats up his girlfriend, how
death pales like a star at morning in the face of his heartbreak over
a penpal he has never met who won't write again.

More importantly, in French towns liberated from the Boche, the chaps
and I were liberating Veuve Clicquot.

Knowing this over and over, knowing it all the time, knowing
the words of prayers of imperfect stutters like comforting traces of
moss on long-ago walls, leaving all that they knew of each other
there under the snow, and yet taking it with them as they moved
ten more yards the following day, each carrying maybe sixty
pounds of ammunition on his back, stepping over the hand or the
leg of a man. A man. A man like him. That was war.

In the weeks following her arrival, he often spoke to Edna
about his late brother, Roy. It seemed to comfort him in unexpected waves.

He wrote poetry and charmed the ladies. He had such a fine mind. He
intended to make writing his career and spent all his spare time when
he was not talking to people writing short stories and scenarios for
Cinema. I have never in my life met anyone who found it so natural

and habitual to get in touch with perfect strangers . . . and to get lost
in a talk in which they revealed themselves . . . for him every walk in
the city was a potential short story taken from life.

But mostly she saw he brooded. There would be no point in
telling her the depth of pain, the emotional weight of a small piece
of shrapnel lodged in his brother's heart. Dawn had broken on July
27, 1917, and Roy was one of the dead. They buried him, wrapped
in blankets, along with the thousands of others that day in one of
the pre-dug graves that had been prepared beforehand in this indifferent landscape. Roy had followed him through the days, through
the Porus red fields and the logwood green hills of their youth,
always trying to run as fast or jump as high, always so generous
with brotherly pride; followed him even into this damned war.
Jamaica and his departed mother seemed so far away; all Margaret's
endeavours to put them through school, her farm and her jellies
and sewing each evening, her unsuccessful trip to America to work
with the U.S. Postal Service, her own small postal agency in Porus,
her struggle to manage the farm and grow more pimento, to teach
the field hands and domestic help to read and sign their names—
all her hopes, her courageous defiance of a petty society whose
comforts she had every claim to, her dignity and even her early
death in 1909 when she was only forty-four, which had brought his
youth to a sudden stop, all had come to this: a limp conclusion of
the family's flesh in his arms.

Instead he must speak of life.

Roy and I were walking past an auction house one day and they were
having a sale. So we went in. We didn't understand the procedure, so
every time the auctioneer nodded in our direction, we politely nodded
back. Turns out that we had purchased a large consignment of alarm
clocks with every last penny of my Rhodes' allowance. We had to hire

a barrow to transport them along the Embankment and dump them
into the Thames.

The offensive continued after his brother's death. Was it four
weeks or six that they struggled on in that quagmire, battalions
retreating or regrouping, men stepping over fallen men, cursing,
wailing, then falling, men advancing, men retreating, their eyes
always on guard, noticing the pattern of the bullets coming over
and over from the same place, theirs being similarly noted by the
enemy? He could not remember how long. But he knew that he
had fired his gun relentlessly for forty-six hours before the end
finally came, knowing the persistent impatience of that clattering,
battering sound as it ran through his shoulders and back would
never fully quit and leave him even if he survived. But he assumed
the final unavoidable conclusion would be death, more predictable
than imprisonment, more tolerable than the close smell of trenches,
more endurable than winter, safer than life, than the labyrinth of
its nightmares afterwards.

I will never forget four a.m. . . . . when all the thousands of guns we
had laboriously assembled opened fire at a precisely timed second . . .
how the world can dissolve into one vast sound like a great wave
drowning every feeling and every emotion and nothing exists except
the unbroken sound broken every minute by the vast roar of your own
gun, and punctuated constantly by the staccato tattoo of dozens of 78-
pounders, pounding a practised roll—but mostly just sound that you
could feel, that enveloped you and bore you up.

Despite himself, Norman had survived. The Red Cross collected him in a fever, the fever of the endless humanity stuck in
those troughs, the subterranean world of nights beneath ground
level with only his flashlight and his small copy of Browning that

he'd take out of his knapsack, the smell of feces and urine and old food and white men's sweat, the smell he remembered from a roof full of scampering rat-bats and mice, sometimes the acrid smell of fading noxious gas.

Norman had opted to remain a corporal, even when offered a promotion to officer's rank. He felt the sharp edge of formidable British bigotry far more dangerously, though less visibly, from higher ranks. You knew where you stood with cockney foot soldiers, and if you worked well together they accepted you. As a mere corporal in the infantry, as a gunner, he would now be rewarded with a simple military medal, instead of the more prestigious Military Cross.

Rats are curious creatures. They would be still when the guns were blazing and the trench was shaking, and then as the dust settled and the air went quiet they would suddenly skid across the ground and disappear again.

"Sleep now, Kid," Edna cajoled.

Edna stayed in Neasden to be with him, cheering him with her lighthearted stories. She had met a Guatemalan art student nicknamed Gherke in her anatomy class. With her Spanish R's she could roll out Mr. McCrossen's instructions "the brrrreastbone is connected to the thorrrrrrrrax," and she'd tell him her stories that made him laugh. Before class one day, they had set up the skeleton so that its upper limbs were hitched over its head, and as soon as McCrossen touched the ribs, an arm fell on the Scotsman's head.

They took long-legged strolls together, learning to laugh again and setting the course for his recovery, weeks of music and theatre, of poetry and art galleries. Then Norman set off alone for the New Forest to walk in the healing company of ancient trees, before returning to Oxford. Edna returned to London, resolved to do whatever it took to dedicate her time to her art, with no other thought or plan. "You'd be wasted on teaching, my dearest," Norman had told her.

After more weeks of letters coaxing and sparring, delighting, gently disappointing and forgiving, she awaiting his wisdom, he outwaiting her coquettishness, both staking out territory, Norman wrote to Edna: "*I know my destiny awaits my return to Jamaica.*"

This was the start of a conversation that Edna longed for but would at times mildly resist, for as they grew closer it seemed to imply her presence with him there.

"*If you ever hear me say I am going to marry and have a family, shake me till I wake, Norman!*" she replied. She had always seen life in terms of her work, and had never thought of marriage or bringing up children.

And then a little later she wrote again: "*I am working on just understanding the aponeuroses. I am rereading books on trees. Isn't it strange how a book can gobble up all your attention and energy and yet you forget? Dear old storky man, I am so afraid of talking of love . . . I have spoilt so many things by talking too much!*"

There gradually emerged a chiaroscuro of their joined features, substance and shadow. They had fallen in love. Beside him, giving him comfort, confidence, and delight, was the otherness of this special woman Edna. He knew he must turn and follow these filaments of light away from the dark place.

Edna derived perverse pride from the fact that her small rented flat in St. John's Wood squatted above a fish shop. Norman became a regular weekend visitor from Oxford, and he would take her out for a square meal of roast beef, her favourite. The visits became islands of healing, their life together a work in progress, words spoken on weekends, or written in finger-webs linking them through letters when they were apart. Sometimes Edna couldn't remember which was which. Did he write or did he say, *I want to dance a fire dance with you*—or did they indeed dance a fire dance? As always, the lines between what was spoken, written and lived blurred in her mind.

You are stealing surely into me, Edna, wrapping yourself around every corner of my heart. You are always there to meet me on the platform, giving that little quick-step run with your shoulders shrugged up, or walking back to the flat with me, your face firmly forward with a shadow of uncertainty lest I turn and kiss you suddenly beneath the lamps.

To which she replied:

I feel the same old thrill at waiting for the post man I feel the same little skip of joy when I meet you—I can't make myself take it as a matter of course. As I go to sleep at night I still whisper "Goodnight Kid dear" & slip your letter under my pillow only I don't let myself think of you during the day now except as I write you—because it is better so. I'm a terrible all or none person I haven't altered only I'm often afraid to let it show—so I keep it to myself—& when I run to the door to meet you I laugh & say nothing . . .

Whenever he returned to Oxford, the familiar disorientation he had felt in the trenches descended over him again—so much so that he'd taken to sleeping on the floor so as not to wake falling out of bed, startled from the grim dreams that housed his battle-field, as if the world he knew, and how he knew it, was slipping away, his old certainties fading like his assumption of empire, and by reflex he'd wake up to catch them. Around him the grey light of night hung eerily cracked in the icy surface of the window.

By now they both knew that after his degree Norman would be returning to Jamaica, and Edna would be going with him. But they were both afraid to tackle the subject with the family. They worried about the issues they felt sure would be raised by Ellie— the question of cousins marrying and the question of race. Edna wrote a letter to Vera explaining her feelings and their conundrum, and Vera replied with somewhat restrained warmth that Edna had chosen well, but warned that if she hurt her brother she would never be forgiven by either her or their sister Muriel. Vera would always rub Edna the wrong way, and Muriel would always try to remain neutral. Vera felt it wise not to tell Ellie till their last school year was over, but also reminded her wryly that her aunt couldn't bring up either issue without offending her nieces and nephew.

Edna had always loved that brownness of her cousins, a legacy she longed to claim for herself. Norman was a handsome man, and as they strode down the streets together, if people stared, she assumed they did so with admiration, and she squeezed the arm escorting her with pride. Bodies were elemental things for her. They were the magic of nature with its millions of accumulated conclusions over generations. They were family stories and countries' histories; they were each their own proud nobility, capable of the god-force of creation, receiving the past through each unique union, rejoicing in assembling a new combination of truths and sending it on through time.

So when faced with the question of colour as a problem in the possibility of their union, Edna's response was predictably fiery:

"*The coloured race can never die*," she wrote with characteristic fervour in a long diatribe to Norman, who was always touched by her almost crude naivety.

*The coloured race has to go on now. White people are going to be forced
to accept them when they see them develop superior intellects. I want
to do my share towards helping on and improving a new race. We are
both intelligent . . . maybe we will produce that indefinable thing, a
genius. I don't want him to be white, I want him to have your own
beautiful brown skin and I want him to grow up proud of his race,
prouder than any white man. Wild blood and northern civilization
will make him able to cope with anything! I am proud of my mate and
proud that somewhere I have coloured blood in me. I want a sturdy
brown baby like you, but with my love of laughter and fun.*

But the longer Norman lived in England—maybe just the longer
he lived—the more colour dragged out its implications before him.
In his childhood he had never had to account to others or question himself about who he was. His mother had owned the modest estate they lived on, and employed the people who worked
there. Unlike his sisters marooned in their home, Norman had
mixed in with village life. The Manleys were coloured, and
although his mother paid a high social price as the fair-skinned
woman who had married a black Jamaican, her children lived in
their world as the shapers of their own destinies.

Norman had grown up within these limits as someone who
mattered, and how much he mattered was determined not just by
his mother's authority but by his own personality, his physical
strength, and his mind, which he could use as leverage to his own
advantage as much as he chose to. He was not vulnerable to any
chance wind save the whimsy of fate. So the concept of inferior-
ity had not dawned on him. And if he felt superior, it was by way
of education and comfort, not in any way related to shades of
colour.

As a child he had unconsciously associated his mother's and
sisters' fairness with their femininity, as though they were paler,

more delicate flowers in the field of life. His father, his brother, and he were dark. It was these strong, self-sufficient women who always believed in him, and had been the quiet source of his strength and self-esteem. This was what he probably needed from Edna, who was even fairer than his sisters though strong as walnut, filigreed as fern, and as flexible and indestructible as the rubber of its stem—yet, enduringly, an unworldly waif.

By nature Norman was little affected by what people thought of him. He always knew who he was and in what he believed; he was prepared to stand up for his views. He never had the least notion of white superiority. The only superiority he accepted was excellence, an attitude he probably got from his mother.

All this was challenged by England and the Great War, which made many colonial subjects think about the meaning of Empire. Norman had to face the issue of race. In England, other than the times he spent with Edna and Ellie and his sisters, he felt chained to his difference, always just a queer foreigner behind an immovable barrier.

"You know, colour meant nothing to me before I came to this country," he once told Edna.

"Colour shouldn't be allowed to be a man's destiny," she said. "Why, it's just a shade of meaning!"

"Destiny is sometimes who we are left to be when cornered," he surmised.

Despite the Rhodes and lately his medals, he was treated differently. He might be educated and have all the attributes that England strived for, but he was still coloured.

So he would find himself thinking over and over about those war years. Norman and Roy had begun to realize that it was a white man's war; that it really had nothing to do with them. It was an argument between white men about land. But what had been the point of thinking about it then, as the war raged around them?

They were like miners trapped; vibrations of outrage might bring the roof down, or disturb Norman's carefully balanced sanity. But now, his brother sacrificed for their cause, the memories bore down, and sometimes he shared bits and pieces of them with Edna, who listened with growing alarm as the true nature of the world in turn bore down on her and she couldn't find a way to rearrange the facts to make it any better for him.

But the facts were inescapable, and damning. Members of a volunteer regiment, the British West Indies Regiment, had not been allowed into battle. Instead, they were used as labourers. And they were just blown up as labourers, not as soldiers. Some might say the same earth takes the blood of all.

"The British don't want any checkerboard army," said an English soldier everyone called "Owl" because he slept with his eyes open. "At least they aren't cannon fodder like us!"

The British officers thought the blacks should never be used in combat on the European front, though they were sent to aid in the war against the German allies in Egypt and Palestine, where it was deemed politic for them to fight what was considered by them in their bigotry to be a lesser race, there being "little to choose between antagonists."

Many Jamaicans hoped that if they could prove themselves equal—not just in strength and dexterity, but in character and mentality—to any soldier on the imperial battlefield, and in patriotism and courage equal to any British heart, conditions at home might improve. Even the black nationalist Marcus Garvey advocated support of England, romantically hoping that loyalty would win black Jamaicans recognition and, arising out of that, political rights and equality. In the hearts of a few was a soldier's idealistic dream of fighting for king and country, but in most who lived as second-class colonial citizens fated to cut cane for nine pennies a day, there lay only the hope of escaping poverty. As simple as that. So they joined up. But some were rejected right there at the depot in Jamaica, for being too black. They'd be too conspicuous, it was said. Also, the English thought they might be laughed at by the Germans.

Although the British army had established the West India Regiment in Britain's Caribbean possessions, Jamaicans who were accepted to enlist as professional soldiers were mostly fair-skinned, educated young men from the more affluent middle class. For all intents and purposes, it was an all-white regiment. The local army officers refused to recruit poor black rural farmers now volunteering for war. The British military traditionally thought that guns in the hands of black men would be a major mistake. Maybe they worried they would rebel. At first the generals believed the war would be over in a matter of months; these black volunteers would not be needed. But as the conflict dragged on, bogged down in trench warfare, the British needed more and more soldiers to feed the costly war. Illness, injury, and death decimated the ranks, so the Colonial Office had to accept any man who was willing to serve. When the case of these rejected volunteers was brought to the attention of the future King George V, on his advice the British West Indies Regiment was formed as a strictly volunteer group. This mostly inexperienced band of well-meaning, black rural farmers was enlisted only for the duration of the war; they would not be allowed to join the regular West India Regiment as professional soldiers in the British army.

The first contingent, of more than a thousand black soldiers and twenty-five white officers, set sail for England in March 1916, wearing light khaki tropical uniforms. German U-boats added to the danger of crossing the Atlantic. But every Jamaican who left to fight that war, whether motivated by patriotism, curiosity, adventure, or opportunism, was a willing volunteer. The ship ran into a blizzard and was forced to detour north towards Halifax, when the soldiers had their first experience of snow and frostbite. Their ship's quarters were unheated and they had to shovel snow overboard from the deck. Some literally froze. They froze because in a most bizarre twist the officers refused to hand out their consignment of winter clothes, which was there aboard the ship, deciding instead to wait till they reached Halifax, by which time it was too late. Half of them were already dead, and many survivors suffered from frostbite; some required amputations in Canada. The survivors were sent to the Bahamas to recover, and some were seen crawling down the gangway on arrival.

Everything was hushed up. Nothing official was said. But rumours abounded, and news of their fate quickly filtered through to the front in letters and messages from family to their soldier sons and husbands, and through lively Caribbean gossip. The callousness of the story was unimaginable to Norman. All around him was war, but this was different. This he considered tantamount to murder.

Then more news arrived, this time about an incident in Taranto.

Everyone agreed that the British West Indies Regiment had won a gallant, a brilliant battle in Palestine. They had shown great restraint and discretion, refusing to slaughter forty frightened enemy soldiers they found lying beneath a bridge, hiding. They accepted their surrender, and sixteen men were decorated for bravery.

After the armistice, more than eight thousand Allied troops were assembled in southern Italy at a small town called Taranto, to return to England. Amongst them were members of the British

West Indies Regiment. The British wanted nothing to do with them. They endured awful living conditions in their camp. They were not even given the sixpence-a-day raise of their white counterparts. They complained but were ignored. They were stranded there long after the war had ended, unable to leave, while the rest packed up to go home to "Blighty." The volunteers were virtually kept prisoner in their barracks and used for cheap labour, totally frustrated and, worst of all, shamed by having to do menial work.

By December their dissatisfaction reached boiling point. On top of being made to do laundry for the white soldiers, they were asked to clean whites' toilets. So they mutinied. All hell broke loose for three days. They attacked their officers and unit commanders, who sent a telegram asking for additional white troops. This request reached general headquarters, and four days later the entire regiment was disarmed. The 48th British Machine Gun Battalion was mobilized and put on standby.

England was sensitive to any insurrection, given the revolution in Russia and the triumph of Marxism. The world order was changing, old systems falling, and the proletariat were on the march. So the mutiny at Taranto met with immediate and severe punishment. Many of the volunteers were court-martialled, accused of sedition. One was executed by firing squad. It was even suggested that the volunteers serve more time as punishment.

The War Office eventually repatriated the men in September, ten months after the war had ended. The stories leaked back to the Caribbean islands, and to West Indians living in England. Rumours abounded. Norman heard that cruisers had accompanied the soldiers to Jamaica, Barbados, and Trinidad to prevent possible unrest. The local governments were warned about their returning heroes; being well trained and politically aware, it was thought they might be a threat to national security. "The black man has come to think and feel himself as good as the white," a secret Colonial Office

memorandum of 1919 stated regretfully. There was news that some
of the non-commissioned officers from Taranto had formed a
Caribbean League, whose mandate was to achieve self-determination
for Jamaica. Demobilized soldiers in British Honduras had raised an
insurrection, and in Trinidad incited a postal strike. When they
docked in Jamaica, instead of celebratory fanfare, the soldiers were
made to remain on board for twenty-four hours before disem-
barking, while authorities tried to encourage some of them to emi-
grate to Cuba, Venezuela, or Colombia where they were told there
were better job opportunities. They nearly mutinied again. They
felt disillusioned, betrayed, and abandoned by an empire for which
they fought so valiantly.

And each new story cast a new cloud over the West Indian
soldiers at the front.

Norman knew that these stories were not limited to Caribbean
experience, and throughout the British Empire there were similar
tales. This he would always believe was the true fuel for the wild-
fire of nationalism that would spread through the British colonies
far and wide, and would light within his own heart something—
a way of seeing the world—that perhaps hadn't been there before.

Both Edna and Norman had been hurt by life, he by a scattershot
of continued loss, she by a single early lethal shot. But beyond all
this, each saw the infinite possibility of the other. Edna helped her
cousin reconnect to the world; he helped her chart a course
through the edgy turbulence of her restless personality, encouraging her to use its friction to ignite her work.

For Edna, belief made things too solid. She wasn't even sure life
was meant to be believed in. She liked to be surprised by a moment
and to capture it. She saw everything as nourishment, as mulch to

help something else grow. She was now the healing spring. She was both a child drawn to the mystery of Norman's stillness, and a mother to his wounded soul. She sensed his strange loneliness, like that of some faraway mountain, and saw the appreciative yet dignified way he responded to her tenderness. Bringing him into the light had become part of her own recovery from great loss, and from a subsequent youth of intangible anger. Something profound linked them, and she wasn't sure if it was the people they shared and had lost, the legend that the life one saves belongs to one, his recognition of her individuality and talent and hers of his intelligence and worth, or the gentle, comfortable fact that the man she loved was her family, her cousin.

Friendship never came easily to Edna. Something about the smudging of boundaries made her resist the intimacies it required. The old feeling of resentment from the days of her childhood haunted her—of being invaded, of emotional or domestic demands she couldn't meet, of recognition she didn't want to keep fighting for, her sense of space compromised in her large family by people and more people. She threw herself into her art, and became fascinated by animals in the wild. She wrote to Norman:

> *There is something basic I find in the animal kingdom I do not find in man. We have lost something lean and basic which is to do with survival. I can't explain, but when I stand looking at these animals in a man-made zoo, they are looking out at me from their own country inside their heads. They are not adapting or becoming spoilt by materialism or life simplified around them. They haven't lost their spirits or compromised their souls, and I do believe they have souls. The jungle and its rules are still there looking out from their eyes . . . in the stillness of their gaze and the tail's tension remains the rule of the hunt, who is whose prey, the distances they keep, their totally focused judgments based simply on survival. They are essential. In their kingdom there are no fat cats.*

Edna received five pounds for her plaster *Lion and Eagle*, her first sale. The lion roars victorious as it pins down a flustered eagle as its prey. She sent the full amount to her mother. She modelled a *Lone Wolf*, a small plaster figure on its haunches, its head thrown back as though baying at the moon. Both are modelled emerging from their sculpted base of rugged landscape. And then she started her *Panther*, which she worked on mostly at night, using gaslight to provide the shadows of a jungle. Later she got Norman to borrow a camera from the university and photograph the piece, warning him to pay close attention. On the back of one photograph he wrote, "*I wish you sureness to your hands, fire to your brain, and loneliness to your heart.*"

"*You make this all sound so primal, so unspiritual somehow,*" he mused in a letter to her some time afterwards, used to observing her abrupt about-turns of mood, like a farmer calculating the weather:

> *A man's spirit is first touched with awe and wonder. Passion starts to rage, and out of that passion is born the spirit of fatherhood. It is never a desire for offspring . . . but a queer complex clutch at the heart that makes your love for your girl seem ever so vast, so full of worship. That love, while it is the mania for reproduction, also purifies a man's soul and makes it tender. Even a lone wolf must have his mate.*

They worried a path across the landscape of their differences, Norman introducing her to George Bernard Shaw and Samuel Butler, while he settled down to read Edna's great loves, D.H. Lawrence and Thomas Hardy. She was angered by satire, and though skeptical of the power of romanticism, for her he opened himself to the lure of its pages.

"Internalize," she cautioned him.

"Externalize," he cautioned her.

"*Men wrestle with barren ideas like mountain climbers. And when they are*

clutching at rock face they hear their mothers or their wives call out calmly, 'Supper is ready, dear,'" he wrote to her.
"See . . . we do externalize!" she replied.

"Remember that you have your art—the peace of self-forgetfulness is self-
expression, a fertile, loamy plain."

On a visit to Jacob Epstein's exhibition, Edna was enthralled by
the sheer possibility of the sculptor's work. But she wrote to tell
Norman that at school some said he was too modern and decried
the exhibition. He responded:

> If you hate the tendencies of your age then either you must be prophetic
> in your inspiration or become an art critic! . . . Where work is sincere
> in its attempt to express old things in new ways or new things in old
> ways, surely the artist of all people should see the sincerity? The regard-
> ing of Art as sacrosanct, religious in its dogmatic fixity, certain that all
> that could be done is already done, that is I think the fatal spirit. Any-
> way, I see no value in art that fails to interpret the age in which it
> was produced. But I must warn you that there is no art in Jamaica.
> You would have to return to England every year to keep in touch and
> get back to the heart of things.

She had found a peaceful harmony in the rhythm of their life,
one that she was able to feel content with now because it promised their great adventure together beyond. Their letters continued
an almost daily conversation.

"Coming home to my Leopard in the evenings," she wrote to him, "I
am never alone. I turn the latch, and I open the door to what has become our
world, and it's full of flowers, chrysanthemums and flame leaves . . . a jungle for
my leopard wild!"

When she sold her Leopard for three pounds, Norman
exploded. "A piece of cheek! It represents forty hours of work a week, and no
worker is paid fourpence ha'penny an hour!"

But even with their present bliss together, and their shared plans, Norman was not spared his continuing mental anguish.

Edna dearest, I thought I was going to die last night. I started crying and fell asleep so. Then this morning I was in a lecture and suddenly felt batteries shocking me in my head . . . I swayed from side to side wondering if I was dying. I realize I have no friends. But that's probably good. Friendship curtails one's liberty.

I am capable to a fault of stripping away all personal illusions, and standing outside of a thing regarding it in purely an intellectual manner. A barren occupation except you have an abnormal power of dissection and understanding when you may do good. But for you all things are from within . . .

Everyone was at least once on the side of angels in their life . . . I am never satisfied to feel a thing unless I also find out why. For me thought only. Unless I know the why of my actions, life is perfect hell to me.

Here everyone wants to be a lawyer . . . The shadow of a wig blots out the sunshine of an otherwise golden day. I think I should really go and till a field or breed chickens.

"Externalize," she cautioned him. She knew that he had an acute innate sense of his boundaries and distances. It had served him well in the trenches but would make him lonely now. That weekend she gave him the pair of wolves to take back with him to Oxford for company. She wrote on a note accompanying them, "*Be Calm, Be Wise, Be Strong.*"

At the dead of night Norman's dreams still hawked up disagreeable pustules of war. "*I am spending a lot of time sitting quiet and just blanking my mind. One looks down the future when the present is incompletely* lived. I have been an alien first and last."

But Edna wouldn't leave it at that:

Ah Kiddo mine—we have the rough part at the beginning but sure we'll be happy some day.... We're winners—dead certs—you wait & see. I WON'T be beaten—so there now. OUR dream SHALL come true & I will ride with you over the Blue Mtns. with the happiest heart of the world knowing that we fought the good fight and ours is 'The world and everything that's in it'.

Perhaps through an alchemy of love and the flesh that made the world a safer place for her and gave her courage—as though stepping gingerly from the refuge of her mysterious connection with the animal kingdom, coming of age to join the human one that had always made her uneasy—in 1921 Edna modelled a head of Ellie. She slowly compiled what she knew of individual truth: the eminence of bone, the power of the jaw locked over its secrets, the interface of tissue; veins like punctilious civil servants, doing their work and minding their business; then the muscle and sinew and fat, the bulk—all the anatomical things with which she'd coped in leopards and wolves and horses and monkeys.

But then she came to the skin. Such a naked thing. So different from the hide of a horse or the coat of a leopard or a mouse. Layer by layer she was brought to realize how naked being human is; all those years listed in her mother's face, islands that for fear of incurable nostalgia she dared not visit, the sea she could not enter because she could not swim, the lonely sadness of her jowl because she had migrated to strangers, the squandered dream-lines round her eyes from remembering and trying to forget, from trying never to regret; the little bits of putty that made the cellulite of repetition, ten thousand nighttime baby feeds, a hundred thousand eggs fried on the stove, the quiet repose at the corners of her mouth for see-ing it all through for Harvey. And now the silver ring of steel, *Arcus senilis*, circling the darkness of her eyes, sealing away forever a legacy of love.

Edna discovered a wise face, a face seeking not power through "passing" for anything else, but the solace of being accepted as no different. In that silence lay all the mystery of family history, all the myths and magic she had intuited right there, unseen till they had passed like time through Ellie's face.

Her first human being. Her Eve. The original Epona, the Matri-arch Rhiannon, her Mother. *Ellie.*

They spent the summer of 1921 together at Milford—he to study and she to work. They booked separate quarters. They would emerge from this time together side by side, as fellow travellers on a com-mon journey. At the end of the summer they finally told Ellie they planned to marry. She expressed great fear, remembering the social price a mixed marriage had cost her sister, Margaret.

Where would they make their home? Norman said Jamaica or nowhere. *"In Jamaica one doesn't notice these things. But here I wouldn't ask your daughter to have children. They would be handicapped."* He promised Ellie they would wait two years. But Edna vetoed that and, despite her mother's displeasure, set the date for June.

Meanwhile, she continued to prowl from class to class studying animals and female nudes, modelling in clay and casting cheaply in plaster of Paris—she continued to stroll through the galleries with Norman, cogitating and discussing Picasso, Gaudier-Brzeska, and Dobson—absorbing rich platelets of knowledge and inspiration, as though gathering nuts for the long season of hibernation facing her in Jamaica. She sank her roots into the thing that was her truth, and less and less allowed the world beyond to matter. And there along her march—the replying boot—Norman interpreting, commentating, suggesting, proffering advice; these became invisible prints that only she could see embedded there in each piece of her work.

Norman received his bachelor's degree—a formality, as Oxford awarded them to whoever had returned from the war—and then he sat his bar finals in December, receiving a first. He lived on his three-hundred-pound share of his mother's property when it was sold. In May 1922 he learned that he had won Oxford's prestigious Lee Prize for an essay. And in May Edna went to Oxford for the first time to see him receive it.

Was there ever such a day since the world was first born—as yesterday? Were we ever happier! I felt so proud of you—you can't think—you looked so ripping—I felt just bubbly jock all day. Did it wipe away some of your bad memories, Norman? When you think of Oxford think of it as you saw it yesterday and forget the rest.

Norman couldn't help comparing her with every girl who passed, and she was so obviously the best girl at Oxford that he knew it wasn't even necessary to compare. "*One perfect day has made me see all sorts of good things in it and I am ashamed to say I almost love it because of you.*"

Ellie continued to worry over the question of "mixed" children. Norman bristled, but Edna soothed him. "*She, like all mothers, is a broken reed, and anyway, leave Mother alone and she gets accustomed to anything. Argue and she is driven to extremes.*"

These were her mother's final words to her daughter on the

matter: *"Then I leave you with one question which you only have to answer to yourself. Could you give the most precious thing, your inner self, to his safe-keeping?"*

Edna evidently answered in the affirmative for they married in a registry office in Kilburn on June 25, 1921. The students from Saint Martin's, knowing she loved cheese, sent them a huge Edam in its red candle-wax skin, with a bountiful bow of pink ribbons. They honeymooned in the New Forest, where Norman had walked two years earlier under the healing susurrus of solemn trees. They slept in a tent that Norman built himself, and on the third night it withstood a thunderstorm with them huddled inside. A picture of him sitting in front of it, a man and his pipe, gaunt and handsome, always stood on my grandmother's dressing table. She must have taken it, capturing the moment with him—her lean, unpredictable stallion. And then they went to France and visited Ypres, where an old map scout tracked down Norman's dugout and Edna scrambled down after him. They found the field where Roy had died. As Norman strolled by himself over the sleeping ground, Edna witnessed its desolation, the stumps of trees like refugees, their arms flailing. A decapitated landscape.

On May 30, 1922, Edna gave birth to Douglas Ralph, seven pounds, in London. It was a difficult birth. Norman gave her a little book inscribed, "EM for luck."

"Brick red—hook nose & wide nostrils—v. little hair—pointed chin—cupid's bow mouth—long upper lip—kink in jaw," she wrote in it, as though memorizing the face to sculpt.

Eleven weeks later, Norman and Edna set sail on the SS *Camito*, bound for Jamaica.

4

To Jamaica 1922–1923

*. . . we were coming home to Jamaica, coming home, it was 4 a.m. and
I crept up on deck and lay there in the dark . . . and there he was on
the rails watching the magnificence of the dawn and smelling the land
after weeks at sea. I think the challenge of the future was all there in
his face and something taut in his pose—leaning on the rail—like a
runner about to take off—a handsome spirit of a man.*

—Edna Manley: The Diaries

EDNA WATCHED THE APPROACHING ISLAND from the ship's deck in the
early dawn. She imagined the experience of birth must be like that
morning steaming into Kingston Harbour. Land had declared itself
to her not by way of a twig in the beak of some bird, but slow-
rising and indisputable, the soaring, rumpled earth both hideously
scarred and beautiful, vibrant and lazy, restless and yet resilient.
Even at that distance, she felt an immediate empathy with it. In
Cornwall, fishermen used the old saying, ". . . red sky in the morning, sailors take warning." This was a red sky, and she sensed its

prophecy—this life would be real and full of responsibility and challenge and danger. She was only twenty-two but she knew this. Morning was different here—there, it had been a tentative visitor to the northern sky modestly veiled in its clouds and mists, waiting to be admitted. Now, as she watched, this sun was rising behind the waking peaks—centuries of genesis repeating a journey upwards, the planet's daily renewal, layers of fecund green fed each by an era, bluer and bluer with distance, generations aging before her eyes—and the sky lifting and opening, a mane of intense light rising resplendent in ceremony.

Edna had no doubt that this was where the world began every single day—right here—this was where the sun rose naked and absolute, love-made and replete, bathing golden to don its robes and gather its wits to visit the rest of the globe.

Norman walked from the boat subtly less aloof and detached than he had appeared in England. It was almost imperceptible, but there was a difference. Here he was not a stranger. Edna saw him for the first time connected to his surroundings, without defences that before this she hadn't recognized as defences. The way he strode down from the ship without first pausing, his quick, resolute decisions. His certainty. His gaze took in the skyline, which held his attention for a moment, and then stopping on the dock he looked over towards the hills, renewing a landscape that perhaps had been fixed in his mind as reassurance all through a war, and through seven years of spiritual disconnection.

Although he lost none of his natural reserve, it struck Edna suddenly to what an extent he had been a stranger in England. Instinctively nestling closer to him as he proudly pushed the pram with their son, she also realized that a fine balance between them had shifted. Now it was she who needed him.

They were met at the port by a childhood friend of Norman who was a great lover of music. From childhood they had called each other Harry. Neither could remember why. Sitting in the back of the car on her first journey through Kingston, Edna felt she'd been admitted backstage. The dusty roads were teeming with people who, though dressed, moved as if they wore no clothes. Young men loitered and leered or glared, lecherous or insolent; old men pushed handcarts with arms like steel rods, heads down and eyes on the road. Women swayed along balancing their burdens, a child on a hip, a basket or kerosene can, even one carrying a sewing machine on her head, their necks held high as though the laws of nature required their defiance for symmetry. Jamaicans walked, chatted, yelled, screamed, the young played marbles at the side of the road, the old played dominoes; they rode donkeys or donkey carts, whipping the animals with a snap like revenge for a whole history, and cursed or whistled as they swatted flies, hawked and spat, drank outside rum-shops, ate with their hands while seated on the ground or straddling a wall, cotched on a bench, idling in neutral as though unconsciously waiting for someone to lead them back home.

People stared at the comfortable black sedan as they passed. Some of them waved, or burst out laughing *kyak kyak kyak*, or belched as if sending a message. Buggies, traps, and an occasional car drove cautiously by them, barefoot urchins and well-dressed schoolchildren hitching quick rides on the bumper or running-board. To Edna life seemed to be happening at a different speed, everything either too slow or too sudden, an indolence broken by a flash at her window, a child's brilliant white teeth and the challenge of eyes for a moment and then gone, jumping in and out of the picture. Each car or carriage slowed and its occupants waved or stared, their vehicles proof of membership in a small exclusivity. Some would just nod and pretend not to be staring, but as they passed a face would look back with an expression of mixed curiosity and fear.

Norman nodded now and then from the front seat, and Edna tried to keep smiling. In that one drive she felt the tearing down of a natural moat that she thought necessary to humans. Nothing was discreet or averted, and each new response to the unfamiliar demanded that she defy her comparative shyness. As she watched from the safety of her window, she felt an emotional gauntlet thrown down before her. Her need to embrace this new extrovert home would probably always struggle with a reserve that was both cultural and natural to her.

Edna had been searching for some workable system of her own to accommodate motherhood. She had noticed that Douglas was ambidextrous, which she attributed to his sign of Gemini, the twins. She sensed a personality already perplexed by indecision. She was sent a "modern" book on child-rearing by her spinster aunt, Elizabeth, which proposed a current theory that one must resist temptation to spoil a child. *See they are fed and changed, then put them to bed and leave them there. Let them cry if they want. Don't pick them up. They will learn to entertain themselves, learn that life does not revolve around them, and learn not to depend on the lap and the rocker. They will toughen. Then send them early to boarding school. They will become useful citizens.* This became her manual for bringing up Douglas. She followed the instructions to the letter, and Doug was tended, then banished to his crib unrocked and left alone to cry himself to sleep, which made the ship's crossing a nightmare as he wailed and she was mostly seasick.

But when they arrived at their host's home, Douglas's tiny figure was quickly swallowed in the bosom of a series of uniformed brown ladies for round after round of arm jiggling. There were several members of domestic staff in Harry's house, and Edna would discover that this was the Jamaican middle-class way. Although she kept up her record in the little book for another year, noting Douglas's prickly-heat rash, his teething problems, later his love of toast to work his teeth, his first wave, each loss and gain of weight—even his first kiss, which he tried to bestow on his image in a mirror—from here on he was basically brought up by nannies.

The constant presence of domestic staff was new for Edna, and though it relieved her of daily chores, the constant companionship made her claustrophobic. She was horrified by the few shillings all domestic staff were paid to work from before dawn to late at night, and to be always on call. In Harry's house they were courteously treated, but sometimes she and Norman were invited to the homes of new acquaintances and she was alarmed by the manner in which they spoke to the people they paid to do the work they didn't want to do themselves. They sounded like petty emperors and empresses. And she couldn't fail to notice in this two-tiered society that their various hosts would be mostly the fairer-skinned Jamaicans who could afford their own homes, and those who served them were always the darker and poorer, glad to be able to live rent-free in the servants' quarters at the back of the house. Once or twice Edna got up and excused herself from a home when she couldn't take the level of insult that she witnessed: the sarcasm with which they commented on some perceived mistake in the laying of the table or the shine on some piece of silver; the explosion that could erupt from tasting a spoon of soup that was too steaming or not steaming enough. The way sometimes they spoke despairingly of the staff, in starched whispers, right in front of some well-meaning butler or cook poised at the door to the kitchen, waiting to answer any command or wish, as though their employees were statues without feelings who could not hear.

Day after day in someone else's house, with the constant whispers of voices and the heat thickening, radiating like a kiln on low, and white mosquito nets tucking one in, and large rotating fans overhead that *tiki-tikied* through the day as she waited for Norman to come home and whomped above their bed through the nights, that whirred through supper and acquaintances dropping in to visit their hosts in Caribbean manner—social conversations like annoying bits of sunlight's confetti that one didn't really look at, but that hovered and danced in one's sight. Invitations to formal dinners with candlelight and grand tables set with silver that dwindled course by course, to a dullness of tedious ladies detailing the shortcomings of their maids over China tea, the men having withdrawn for proverbial port in Waterford crystal, which was usually really local rum or pimento liquor; the blessed reunion later at their temporary home, with Norman around the shiny Victrola box, his master's voice rendering its nightly concert of Harry's rare classical music records as they circled under its silver arm, and learning to play a hand of bridge once a week to keep Norman company.

And nights that were never quite still, emptiness layered with texture, with something more primal and vital than words crouched dangerously among menacing branches of moonlight, clicking of crickets and guttural rattling of frogs, footsteps on bush—a darkness whose anarchy, withdrawal from day, took every connection away—night that made Norman within her almost anonymous, their lovemaking more careless yet necessary.

But mornings began with the waking of hills somewhere in the distance, as though dawn spun itself up there before venturing down to the plains. They surrounded Edna with intimate, solid sound, pots banging, the hostess a gentle slippered creature *shliffshliffing* through corridors checking each apostrophe of her world, as the daily commencement of soft quarrelling set off irritable door slamming and pans clanking and the growling of kitchen voices that earlier could be heard singing through ablutions, the formal laying of table, while Harry—a small, astute man with a curious connectedness to her otherwise inscrutable and solitary Norman— peeled oranges for himself and his friend on the step, and offered to have coffee brought.

Norman had dreaded his first case in court, his throat closing down and his thoughts flying away. He had filled an entire child's exercise book graced with His Majesty's picture on the cover with little avenues or sublanes of questions and alternate answers, each of which took different forks depending on a witness's response, forming an elaborate maze.

That first morning, Norman took Harry to court for moral support. His mouth was dry, and he thought he must have tetanus, for his jaws felt locked, or maybe an allergy, for his tongue and his throat were swelling. He needed to calm down. He stood in a minute that grew to a universe of silence, and then something inherent and genetic empowered him, and he felt his father's litigious foible and his mother's fierce ambition for him and her love and steadiness watching over him, and he asked the first question. And he was off.

"What a strange thing," he said after rushing home early to tell Edna, "this long preparation, this near prostration, then the sudden burst of light."

She in the meantime was struggling. She had been readily adopted by well-meaning middle-class ladies and British expatriates who wanted to welcome her into their numbers. Although she knew these connections were expedient for her husband's career, she felt time foolishly wasted in their company. The small-island gossip bored her, the knowing every minute of her business and everyone else's outraged her, and she found she was uncomfortable on this side of a social divide that was the inevitable consequence of a colonial system. Away from this clique, she felt her eyes too light, her skin too frail, her Englishness an embarrassing weight of prerogative she wished to forgo. She found herself nodding and smiling at everyone till her face ached, acknowledging every passing figure for fear that by ignoring someone she would have left unappreciated some historical wrong, or slight to human dignity.

The more she tried to invoke the silent genes of her Jamaican mother, the more the genes retreated, leaving her in the power of her liberal, Fabian conscience, and at the mercy of her familiar British expressions and manners that spontaneously rose to the sur-face before she could banish them. And it all felt so false.

Having arrived at somewhere she had been connected to so strongly in her imagination, she now feared she didn't fit in. She needed her own space to get back to work, to engage her spirit to feel she belonged. Edna longed to live in the country, for she felt living in town put her out of gear. The minute inner details one had no choice but to observe when living at close quarters put things out of proportion. She wanted never to lose sight of the whole. The ego is so big in the city, and shrinks in a field when one realizes how insignificant one is, she thought.

After months of fierce heat, disillusionment and her insecu-rity, Norman, who was finding his feet as she weakened and wob-bled, decided to send her off with the baby to stay in a guest house in the lush, cool hills of Mandeville to work. At the centre of the island, the capital of the parish of Manchester, near where he had lived as a child, this small, well-organized town, with its ideal cli-mate, provided refuge for many an English painter. Now it would give Edna a break from the heat of August, which engulfed Kingston with obstinate, short-tempered persistence. Norman hoped his wife might start to work again, finding rural life more authentic. He, meanwhile, would remain in Kingston, building his legal practice and, with each case he won, making a name for him-self as "Barrister."

Journeying north to Mandeville in Harry's car was like blood return-ing through a vein of the island to its source, towards keener greens and earth that was the richest red of the heart's resilience. Winding roads pulled at Edna's waist, corners tiding life with its twists and turns to an origin far from the rim of coast, to the ancient soul of the place. Ghosts gazed out from lush shadows and history with curiosity older than either Europe or Africa— with eyes Edna imagined even older than the original Taino Indians, eyes of some mythical forest faun from the start of the world.

Norman had booked the house and arranged with the manager for Edna to hire a nanny. The old guest house was on a hill, and Douglas and the nanny stayed in one room and Edna in the other. She gave them the larger front room, with a view over the rolling hills, and took the smaller back bedroom, which was obviously expected to house the nanny, for herself.

This left Edna free to escape down the nearby back staircase and out to the market, or to walk in the gentle surrounding hills. Her arrangements caused the prim beige Jamaican ladies who ran the guest house to tut-tut and wonder if the heat in Kingston had swarmed the white lady's head, and to hope the cooler air would help, or else she might end up in Kingston's mental hospital, the fate of many a weak-minded foreigner.

The dainty managers and the quaint clientele out of curiosity would arrive at her door or on the lawn, where she sketched figures she had seen in the market or along the roads, and ask to see her work, furrowing their brows and shaking their heads. Lady artists they knew in Mandeville, mostly English, painted "lovely" landscapes, they said. She knew that behind her back they would be scathing—she heard how they talked about other people. But she couldn't get used to being treated as "other." She saw some of this expatriate work over time, and it was usually of landscapes or flowers that seemed suspiciously more reminiscent of British Somerset than Jamaican Mandeville. But what intrigued her was the staff at the guest house. They would pause to consider, leaning on a broom or clutching a duster.

"I like dat," one would say, responding in a totally natural way. Another, "Mek 'im 'ead a likka bit smaller; it too big for dat likka man." Even the gardeners would stop to admire, wiping their brows with the backs of their sleeves, smiling self-consciously, maybe not knowing what to say, maybe taken aback to find art could be about something familiar.

One day when she was modelling a figure of a cat she had watched crouched while it outwaited a mouse that had darted under the heavy, ornate mahogany bureau, the cleaning lady stopped behind her so quietly that she was startled when she suddenly heard her delighted voice: "Heh! Dat look like de puss!"

Mandeville was well ordered, with fewer people and more air than Kingston, and always an edge of rain, like the chill of breeze over a lake. Edna was immediately struck by its similarity to many a small English country town. It was neat and clean, its landscape always under control. A village green was surrounded by a courthouse, parish church, and post office, and at its centre was a market. Extending beyond, deliberately cheerful gardens around comfortable homes straddled the low hillsides.

Here a patience of green behind green surrounded Edna, deeper than summers or seasons, and seemed temporarily to steady her, giving her back a dimension more ample than linear time. Trees in England belonged within forests or within their owners' fences, or were planted along sidewalks, in parks, designated for beauty and shade. Trees in Jamaica were random and seemed to offer themselves to everyone. The ones outside her bedroom window had literally become fence posts. The children would climb up and drag down the limbs and break off the mangoes, and occasionally someone would come out from the guest house with clapping hands and shoo them without conviction, as if they were flies, and the kids would jump over the fence and Edna would hear their laughter down the road, half squealed, sounding like *meaha meaha*, country laughter so different from Kingston's *kyak kyak*, and they would be back in ten minutes. They would raid the tree only on the way home from school, the penalty for yellowing their uniforms probably more brutal facing school than leaving it.

In the early mornings Edna walked down the winding path to the main road towards the market carrying a drawing pad. She'd sit there on a low wall made of grey, neatly packed stones, much like those she remembered in Cornwall. She'd draw almost anything at all that she saw—women like monuments, some very large, some of them obelisk-thin whose heads were haughtily extended into giant baskets; goats at the side of the travel-worn road, eating grass only they could make out in the cheeky Mandeville clay, catching them lifting their heads for a moment to nibble like old ladies and contemplate grass juice (although she saw many, she drew no donkeys or mules, preferring the final magnificence in form of a horse); some men sitting outside the small rum-shop determined to be men, staring at the women, heaving their crotches and thrusting out their chests, or a labourer digging the roadside, his body a map of his toil; schoolchildren dressed immaculately with their uniforms starched, the girls with their dark hair stretched into braids and tied with bright and elaborate ribbons; the peanut vendor, a Pied Piper surrounded by children, his monotone whistle a desolate sound that any rendition of this place was nothing without, that oddly reminded her of the relentless crying of her own peevish son.

And the red of the earth, like a rare blood type all of its own. "*Can I wait for my love?*" Norman wrote to her in one of his

weekly letters. "*My love with the strange eyes—eyes that glow and shine &*
pour out the soul—that go deep in colour till they almost go black & fire is in
the heart of them—eyes too quiet with awe of reverence—I kiss them each—
goodnight."

And then more practically, in reply to some query: "*The closet*
search establishes that you forgot nothing. But the chair had a canvas bag which
on inspection reveals 2 balls of wool, 1 dress, 1 pair of shoes (middle aged) and
one pair galoshes."

She watched the market ladies day after day till she knew their
arrival by heart, as they floated across the hills like ships, their hips
like ballast as they swayed from side to side, lumbering slowly like
beautiful animals.

How to capture that serenity, that innate balance, was as much
a challenge as how to be part of this island and find a role. She felt
even more like a voyeur now than she had when, as a child, she
had imagined this place.

Her voice slowly emerged. She drew a slim figure on her
knees, replacing the archetypal market woman with a frail Cornish
girl offering her beads. She had seen the figure in the market over
and over; she drew the hands suspended as though holding a
rosary over her triangular lap, with its angles and sharpness and
reticence and unwelcome, a cubist reflection, a lap so thin that it
would offer no solace to a child, the small string of charming but
meaningless john-crow beads offered to mostly English ladies who
shopped there. In the figure was her training, bent to this season
by all she had gleaned in art galleries and art classes and books,
everything she knew brought to this moment of supplication: *Buy*
my wares, these beads no different from Eve's pendant apple in Eden,
or the trinkets brought by the Spanish explorers to distract the
Tainos before they rewarded their naïve welcome by wiping them
out with bullets and germs.

It was Edna in sunshine, small and fine like a season of some temperate place, offering her creation, the soul-spun shape of her yearning: *Island, will you have me, half-Jamaican and far from archetypal?*

Six weeks later she placed her modelled figure of *Beadseller*, originally called *The Supplicant*—which represented her credentials as an artist, a wife, a mother, and was the epitome of McCrossen's lessons on the use of planes—all wrapped up in damp cloths and soft saddle blankets on the back seat of the car, and set off beside Norman, at breakneck speed, on the mostly winding journey to Kingston.

Norman had rented a cottage in Kingston, three small bedrooms above a large octagonal all-purpose room, that you either loved or hated. Though she was happy they were on their own as a family, Edna hated it. She once compared it to a house I had lived in that was, I think, six-sided. She blamed the breakup of my marriage on it. She said a house shouldn't have too many points of view. Perhaps its endless geometry gave her a light-headed, myopic sensation of having just missed every step; this may have unbalanced her. Or maybe she felt like a toy soldier captive in a Swiss clock, doing little shifting turns to acknowledge each angle. Windows all around, each offering a different opinion. Window after window, and little wall space to hang a painting or place a shelf for Norman's various sports and academic trophies. Perhaps a back and a front, a start and a finish, the certainty of four corners, would have made her feel settled or safer.

This return was but a brief truce. It would last only ten months, ten months between snatched moments with Norman, mostly late at night, with the comfort of his exhausted weight tethering her sleep. Norman was quickly becoming a household name in Jamaica, having won several quite dramatic murder cases. He was often away from home, as he did much of his own meticulous investigation of both the facts of a case and the relevant issues in law. His cases were reviewed extensively in the newspaper's court reports, and people gathered in corner shops and rum bars to have the proceedings read to them. Sometimes men would threaten their wives with murder, muttering, "And I'll get Barrister Manley to defend me!"

But for Edna the days had become a futile search for something spiritually sustaining to hold onto that wasn't his; something her own. She was fighting to be happy, in the way that unhappy people do. Norman became more assured, seeming almost to grow beside her, while, becoming more ambivalent, she alternately fought and gave in to a myriad of small and more substantial frustrations—the need to be able to work, to have somewhere to be cool, to feel connected to her son, to find a way into her new country by some means other than her hosts or the neighbours, to be worthy of Norman and all his hopes for her and her hopes for him, to be able to get away and not have to think, not have to need to feel connected, not have to prove herself worthy, not feel she had to make a difference. Under it all, made restless by failure, just longing to call it a day and move on; wanting to go but not wanting to go.

If she could only clear these emotional decks so she could concentrate on her quest to make artistic sense of the world around her. Here was a land of such boldness! Nature was vivid and unscrupulous; the sun was a careless blessing, the trees were bosomed with fruit, and the rain came spectacularly, with the conviction of ideology. The people loved to sing and moved with natural rhythm, instinctively dramatic. They were warm and generous and funny and bright, both offhand and intent, courteous yet vulgar, always sympathetic and interested, curious and interfering as hell. Nothing she had learned as an artist gave her the range, the sheer audacity of form, nor the freedom or daring to approach the truths of this place.

One day Harry took her to a Pocomania meeting held in a small yard downtown. There she witnessed the zealous ritual, an old part of Jamaican folk culture. The women were all dressed in white with huge white bandanas, and the men in white robes. Edna watched their ceremony, a pageant of offerings and burnings and chanting and then wild dancing and singing, a protocol of joyous hullabaloo. She thought of her father's time in Jamaica and wondered if he had ever seen one of these meetings, their ecstatic dance of faith so different from the sedate ministry his Methodism would have offered.

The heat in the small yard was sweltering. Above them an attending moon, a round flag shredded by clouds, which steadied her. When the clapping started, and the beating of their drums, and the tambourine-bashing and jangling, she expected their songs to be in a language she didn't understand. But familiar black American spirituals swelled out from them, and she couldn't help thinking that the gods and ancestors of Africa reached out to this black diaspora, throwing wide-open arms around its lost children, pulling them home through song and spirit, making history and geography elastic, each member of this bright fire-lit circle defying a universe of darkness, as close to an original home as the children of imperial rule in Cornwall or London sitting round their hearths with their golden treasuries and tales of *The Mabinogion* or the brothers Grimm.

And yet nothing reflected this. Nowhere was there a black hero depicted in a monument, only Nelson and Queen Victoria. Any book of history began with Columbus. How could history start at the moment of capture? Who then was telling the story?

A small downtown institute housed the merest gesture to the island's arts, where, as though just to make sure of the distance between two worlds so tenuously connected, or to appreciate the depth of their differences, one could peruse the voyages of the Spanish galleons, *Pinta* and *Niña*, on old maps, estimate the stolen treasures of Captain Morgan lost down the throat of the Caribbean Sea after the earthquake's destruction of old Port Royal, or borrow Kipling's *Jungle Book* or Stevenson's *Treasure Island*. The measurements of history and time and significance were as English as the pound sterling, as distance in miles or weight in ounces, all obscure reckonings of another culture. She would go to art exhibitions that displayed English flowers and animals, English people, and English snow. These were the only pictures she saw in private homes.

In amongst this slavish imitation of what was considered civilized and therefore worthy of attention, she found brief moments of authenticity. The local fairy tales of Bro' Anansi had survived through the years, whispered down generations, even to her in Cornwall by her mother. They were the story of Jamaican survival. The success of the fabled spider with all its chicanery, reflected in victory after small victory, was revenge for the Middle Passage, and the rich dialect in which the tale was told had defiantly ground standard English into a smooth, melodic new sound.

Edna had no problem with the land, which lay indecipherable as language not yet interpreted. But the identity of its people—culture as it had been forged from the crucible of history—seemed always out of reach, lying like bedrock beneath a complex underbrush of mistrust and misunderstanding, from middle-class fear and repudiation to expatriate difference and indifference. By virtue of being from England, Edna stepped into a space of eminence she felt she had not yet earned in this society. The English expatriates she wished to avoid laid claim to her as one of their own. Most of the local educated Jamaicans she met, whose lot Norman and she herself must share, the people she needed for companionship and conversation, were locked in a curious self-prejudice. They were like an endangered species who feared the lower-class life they had managed to survive and avoid, and coveted the expatriate one from which they were excluded. And the ordinary Jamaicans just went on bearing the burdens, freedom and slavery both incomplete states in their psyches, the group permanently planted in a twilight world where its fate seemed inevitable.

Norman introduced her to the work of the writer Claude McKay, a Jamaican poet who had moved to America. His activist verses, some of them powerful rallying cries, were becoming a voice used by the Harlem Renaissance. He was writing things few had contemplated, things that needed another perspective. Norman was particularly struck by one on the war, which, though it had by then liberated many Europeans, had brought no liberation for black soldiers returning home. It reminded him of the fate of the British West Indies Regiment.

We, the blacks, less than the trampled dust,
Who walk the new ways with the old dim eyes,
We to the ancient gods of greed and lust
Must still be offered up as sacrifice!
Oh, we who deign to live but will not dare
The white man's burden must forever bear!

Edna preferred poems with less pointed social messages—her favourite was one about homesickness in New York, as McKay evoked the memory of red poinsettia in December. And then there was Edna the mother. She ached to be away from the baby-weight of her son, and then she ached to be with him when she was away. When she was with him, halfway through feeding him, her hand poised with the next spoonful, she'd feel suddenly infuriated by the time he took daydreaming through one of the eight vistas of their living room. She always found it strange that she could spend hours creating an armature, feeding it with clay and water, without a moment of resentment. But it wasn't the same when she had to do it for her son.

She knew work would be her only salvation, and began to sculpt a small bust of Douglas, with his square jaw and upturned nose like her mother Ellie's, and his slightly puzzled expression. That was when she wondered if maybe he was myopic and took him to the optician, who predicted an early need for spectacles. She hadn't seen this in her baby, who cried or slept or ate or pulled down his father's clanging silver cups. But then most things revealed themselves to her first in the clay.

When Douglas was a year old, Norman, in constant search of ways to entice and settle his restless wife, surprised her with a majestic six-year-old mahogany coloured mare she named House of Cards. Norman already had a small black horse called Tim, and Edna had acquired a goat to supply Douglas with fresh milk. They also had a black mongrel, a dog she had often passed tied up to a fence while walking the baby. The animal would bark in angry frustration. She couldn't bear to know that he was always tethered, and found the owner, who explained that he was a very bad dog and everyone was scared of him. So Edna offered to take him off their hands. Once liberated, the animal became a devoted pet, and Douglas was enchanted. Edna called him Tiger.

House of Cards was the first horse Edna owned. By late June, and all through July and August, the poinciana trees fanned out over Kingston in their mantillas of orange, and the mare provided her with wings of escape.

Creeping out of bed, the light in a summer sky still pale in the dawn and all rumpled over the hills, she'd walk to the landlord's stables, which they'd been given permission to use. The morning lifted its arms to release the sweet smell of the logwood trees, and the fresh guinea grass cut for the horses. There she heard the stamp of House of Card's hooves and the mare would stick her long face over the stable door and snort, and in the next stall Tim's sleek ebony face looked out for Norman, and then came the crunch and rustle as they tossed the grass to pick the best shoots she laid down for them. House of Card's existence was a short menu of the things the mare loved—eating grass and oats; meditating like a spoiled woman as she got brushed down, and slicing her eyes and tail if Edna failed to get it just right; rushing to the stable door for a lump of sugar.

On one of their rides through the foothills of St. Andrew during the hot, dry summer of 1923, Edna and Norman took an unfamiliar fork in the road. Jamaican drought skies are nothing but blue, an imperturbable, unequivocal infinity. They were searching for water for the horses and came to a driveway indicated by two gateless posts that they passed between to plunge up a short rise. Wide acres of rolling pasture land with hardy lignum vitae trees, their tiny blue blossoms unseen in the distance, surrounded a square of lawn and a house set far back from the road. The wooden two-storey building was defiantly shabby, and the beige Seymour grass lay there like long dry fur, the hide of some exotic, parched animal.

They approached the house. It reminded Edna of a loveless old widower beyond grief, just observing the world. It met them open-mouthed, apparently temporarily uninhabited—unless, of course, the cows lying still as river stones in the grass and the more resilient-looking, deeper green shameweed fern, which folded at their touch, were really lords of the manor. It was a world of its own. That was how she remembered it later.

Edna found the water trough by the milking station, and the horses drank away the white foam under their bits.

When she left, without completely forgetting the place, Edna forgot to think about it again. But Norman had noticed how she had responded. She had looked around as though with relief—as if she had at last found somewhere familiar or comforting.

"Oh, what a place," she had said.

During each ride Edna would comb through the strands of her work in her head, returning home with new resolve. Slowly she started to work again. *Listener*—originally *The Call*—came as though in response to *Beadseller*. She built him up from the stand like a stem, or the fine trunk of a tree. He was a seller walking away with a tray on his head, paused to turn round; he didn't actually look back, but provided a profile with Norman's features. One elbow was raised to steady the tray, and the sweep of his other side was curved like a sail sucked in by wind. He waited and inclined his head, something having caught his attention.

But October came and her plaster moulds lurked by the studio door in a state of hiatus, waiting for bronzing. There was no foundry in Jamaica.

"These children are stillborn," she sighed disheartened, and in that sigh Norman recognized all her turmoil and restlessness.

"Only gestating," he soothed.

The room littered with drawings was a reproach to Edna, who knew that these were only preliminary drafts. A nude reclining on a landscape, and then one waking from a deep sleep as a wave would rise from the sea, other figures grown from the land, the land absorbing their roots.

The wind was dry and kept blowing. And on one of its high gusts arrived their cousin Alexander Clarke, who'd been away for years, he said in Spain, appearing finely dressed like one of that country's grandees. He had changed his surname to Bustamante. It was a short and cheerful meeting, and after a couple of drinks the flamboyant figure was gone. His presence seemed to make Norman somewhat uneasy, for Bustamante was a great extrovert, and had been a careless, sometimes reckless cousin, both physically and verbally, in their youth.

Then another small but unsettling thing happened; thieves broke into their house one night and stole all Norman's silver trophies. These by now battered mugs and shields stood like a testament to her husband's youth before it was cut short by his mother's death, the ravages of typhoid and then the war. Norman brushed the incident off as unimportant, but to Edna these symbols should be inviolable. She was profoundly troubled.

And following some inner drum roll that had been building since she arrived, whose crescendo came at a moment of evolving truths that only a soothsayer could have recognized, Edna decided. She declared everything a damned mess, and packed up herself and Douglas and his plaster bust, and the two models waiting for casting and the small volume of poems by Claude McKay.

"*Mother, I am coming back,*" she wrote in a letter that would probably travel on the ship with her. Leaving Norman sad but, inexplicably, not hopeless—he had the good sense to make no fuss of her going; "It will do you good to get back into things . . . see some good shows, go to galleries and plays, hear fine music again . . . live it for both of us, Edna . . ." She promised him she'd use "the break" to think things over.

She boarded the *SS Bayano* for Southampton.

5

English Interlude 1923–1924

SHE HADN'T MEANT TO RETURN, but here she was back in the bosom of the Swithenbank family in tears, declaring that Jamaica had been in all ways a terrible experience. Finding herself in Neasden in her mother's house, with all her sisters doting over the sole nephew in the family, instead of feeling relieved or safe again she felt she hadn't moved forward an inch. She was at a standstill, and her life had gone back to square one. The only one who was truly happy was Douglas.

She had no choice but to sit quietly at the heart of her turmoil, and gradually accept the fact that square one was now an important crossroads. Already she missed Norman, and ached to be with him again. With Douglas happy and off her hands she had time and peace to think. It was true the island was small and full of colonial prejudice, but hadn't she shown such high-handed intolerance with it all—such disdain for their nosiness and narrowness, for their imitative culture? Was it really that bad? Couldn't she work with Norman to be a small force for change? Hadn't she been unfair resenting the time Norman took away from the family to make his practice grow? Hadn't she taken this out on Douglas, refusing to give him more of her time, more of her attention?

The only thing she knew for certain was that she couldn't ask Norman to return to England. She believed that Jamaica was his destiny, that he belonged there as surely as one of its mountains. She already believed that his fate and the island's were interrelated. But if she returned, she had to be certain she wouldn't promptly run away again. She might be able to sort out the practicalities of her work, but did she have the will and the spirit to meet all the challenges she'd face to make Jamaica her home? She fought back feelings of failure and shame, and tried to think things through, tracing each possibility in her mind as though in pencil that could be erased if she took a wrong turn. She was realizing that loving Norman was not enough. She had to love his country, and his love of country too. She had to be prepared to face its realities head-on and have the energy to help build a future that would be worthy not just of Douglas but of every other Jamaican child. That was the kind of life it would have to be, because of who her husband was; maybe because of who she was, too.

She made use of her time and visited the galleries, absorbing their messages. The English remained unchanged, locked in their social places, their manners unfailingly reiterated, even their speech never faltering from its practised drill. Yet in the galleries the artists said what they needed and wanted to say, socially and personally. That was it. There was the passion, the outrage, the worship.

The impressionists had slanted their messages in at an angle that delighted the unconventional who shared their vision, and caught the righteous and the precious off guard, but Edna felt that a generation of moderns speaking in a world that had seen mankind create such a war, witnessed savagery and death repeated over and over till their horror was trivial, had to resort to a starker simplicity. Simple spaces and shapes, to be outlined again and brought forward as proof of the certainty of certainties. The modern painters whose circles and squares, areas of light and shade, some audiences railed at: *We are older and bigger and wiser and more complex than this*, they insisted, when what they really meant was, *We do not deserve innocence. There is blood on our hands.* Sculpture like Moore's or Dobson's, whose masses spoke of the resilience of earth, spoke of form as more enduring and tireless, timeless; less vulnerable to the tragic whims of human fate.

Edna contacted her sculpture teacher. McCrossen had worried when his young student left for Jamaica, uncertain if she was experienced enough to manage sculpture there on her own. In England there were professional casters. There was also help if you needed to erect a complicated armature for a figure like a dancer. Edna had had elementary training as a caster at St. Martin's, but not nearly enough experience to manage anything complex. She shared with him her upset that the cast of *Listener* had developed cracks during the journey. She explained to him that none of these services were available in Jamaica, and anyway the bags of plaster were seldom ever fresh when she opened them. Two weeks on a ship and then a month on the wharf caused the quickness in the plaster to subside. She had lost so many pieces of work this way.

McCrossen proved to be a saviour. He agreed to arrange for the casts to be bronzed in London, and introduced her to Italian Plastelina, which he said was virtually indestructible and would survive almost any conditions. He recommended Edna to the Society of Women Artists in London, who exhibited *Beadseller*.

"Lassie, go out and get some tools," he advised her one day. "There is all that wood around you in the tropics, so it's the ideal medium to use. Learn to carve wood—I will show you." She got some tools, and when she brought them to McCrossen he laughed. "Dear, if I know you and your work," he said, "these are not tools—these are toothpicks."

"What do you mean?" she asked.

"When you get knocking a mallet on a piece of wood, they would break with the first wallop. These are for somebody doing pretty little things."

So he accompanied her to the shop to buy the correct tools, and proceeded to teach her in three months everything she needed to know—most important, how to respect the grain and not cut against it.

That was when the thought first occurred to her. Trust life. Let it open its roads and see what it has to offer. And a calm descended over her situation, and she waited for a sign and for certainty.

Edna was already yearning like an animal pulling at a leash— missing Norman, dying to get home to find suitable logs of wood— when Norman wrote the letter that finally called her back home.

I know you won't want to come back to the old house. I have found a larger place, a place without . . . memories. I am thinking of buying us a car . . . a second hand Durban, a two-seater, so we can fly wherever we go! Business continues to tumble in. The horses both miss you, the dog is pining, just kicks at his fleas all day and looks morose. I must bathe him. And the goat is amazing . . . just eats and eats and never gets fat . . . it must be all that energy to keep chewing makes her slim! I wish arguing my cases would do me the same favour! I miss Douglas under my heels and calling all day long for his Mummy. Now it's me calling out for her too.

You say you are getting homesick. I am homesick too. You are not here, therefore I am not home.

PS For your Xmas present I am going to give up smoking for a week. No greater love.

And then one day she was looking through the little collection of Claude McKay's poetry that Norman had given her, and she found the familiar poem "Flame Heart."

I have forgotten so much, but still remember
Poinsettias red, blood red, in warm December.

So in the brittle March wind, with England as certain as always that its bleakness had settled in forever and that winter would stay this time, Edna gave the plaster head, *Douglas*, to her mother to fill the space left by her only grandchild. She got the shippers to pack *Bead-seller* and *Listener*, which, bronzed, looked like a dark tree swaying on the horizon, and booked their passages to return home on the SS *Montagua*. She had decided to own whatever lay ahead as her problem.

Norman picked them up at the dock in the Durban, and when they drove to what he called home, Edna was looking at a square house in twenty-five ungroomed acres of land—the place she had forgotten but not forgotten, like a planet with its surrounding rings, and land that listened through time. He had bought the property and made rudimentary efforts to start fixing it up, circling the front of the house with a driveway that changed the lawn from a formal square to a friendlier circle.

"Oh, Norman, look . . . the cows! The cows are still here."

The dairy came with the place.

The dog, Tiger, nearly knocked her over. By the side steps Douglas found his black goat tethered, and raced to hug her. The horses were there in the stables with their heads over the stable doors. There were plums on the tree and an old swing hanging from a bough.

Drumblair. This would be home.

Nine months later Michael arrived, weighing eight pounds and four ounces. It was a quick and easy birth.

"*Very red—plenty of black straight hair. Small pretty mouth. Strong chin—nose flat,*" she wrote. "*Eyes very wide set & a little inclined to be sore, bathing with Boracic—showing signs of a contented happy nature—watched people from 14th day—a more slender child than Doug.*"

Born on December 10, 1924, he was a Sagittarian with a thousand arrows for his bow, and for Edna's romantic imagination.

Part Two

6

A Green Time

I feel sometimes that life is just a struggle to free oneself from oneself.
—Edna Manley, in an interview with Easton Lee

IT IS DIFFICULT FOR ME to separate what I actually know of their life after my father was born, what I simply ingested through family lore, and what I later interpreted as I retraced Michael's steps behind his parents, being in many ways more his sibling than his daughter. Maybe with my father's birth I was, though unborn, already invisibly part of their world, absorbing my history, the strands of my DNA weaving in him. Harder still to separate what I actually knew of my grandmother, whom I met when she was fifty, as distinct from what I intuit from my vantage point as the grandmother I am today.

I think whenever writers recreate someone they know, the picture is always partly their subject and partly their own. People we love or care about, even those we don't like, take on a shade of our essence. They are who they are plus who we think they are, and

who we are in thinking we know them. So my view of Mardi—
for she was always Mardi to me—becomes more certain and maybe
less pristine in its truth as my story approaches the years when I
was there with her. Unavoidably, the story becomes both hers and
mine.

I need no research to conjure up the world in which Edna's
sons were raised, though that life had little to do with the predictable domestic day-to-dayness of most families. What I imbibed
was the gestation of islands, the humanness of needing to freeze-
frame time, to clothe something as nebulous as yearning or thought,
or the birth of gods, or a nation—not just thought as learning,
academically bound up, nor as building blocks of philosophy; not
just the joy of thoughts in the books that we read. But thought like
the tracing of a map, fingers pressed down against the outline of a
shape, then released again to lift a corner and glimpse the reference
point and sigh at the elusive river, blue upon the page but so pale
it proves untraceable, memorable only as a shade, a colour or a
mood. Thoughts that other families called daydreams when they
told you to stop.

More down to earth were the dogs that were part of each generation. After Tiger there was Biggums in my father's time, a huge
mastiff, the breed Mardi said ate so much meat they almost died
out during the war, when there was rationing, or later Skittles—I
don't know the breed, but some sort of terrier small and fast—
whom my father used to sit with on the floor, racing against him
to finish his supper first. When I arrived there was an old, white,
hopelessly good-natured mongrel called Wrath of God, and after he
died and broke the household heart, a silly pair of dachshunds,
Rusty and Goldie, who would get excited and dribble pee on the
wooden floors.

And through this landscape wander the characters of my family,
intent on their tasks, Edna relying to a certain extent on others' care

and the hope that fortune would smile on the noble-minded, whose purposes she felt the gods respected, their well-being safeguarded in the meantime by an efficient household staff.

Those years before I came, I have reconstructed from this second-hand knowing of mine.

Each Drumblair morning Edna became inextricably one with the dawn, a small particle of cosmic process rising and moving out over land and water and sky like a farmer or fisherman, a bird or the very sun. And whether she visited the horses before she worked or after depended on the grain of wood and how palely its underflesh had glowed overnight through the mind's dark. She would flee from their bed on a quiet tightrope of uninterrupted movement—leaving Norman, who often knew but pretended sleep, past the children's rooms, Michael's and behind it Douglas's, across the whispering straw mat in the hall, and down the stairs between their memorized creaks. Sweeping through the descending steps, she attempted to join one to the other, each sound emptying as it morphed into the next, opening the side door to a world outside awaiting her in freshly yawned clarity.

Michael would wake much later and throw himself into the day, pleased to see whomever he found in the home around him. For Edna, Michael's energy arrived as randomly as the uncomplicated pleasure of primary-yellow alamanda blooms. It needed neither inspiration nor answer, tending or grooming. It just blossomed all by itself and left its happiness strewn in her.

But Douglas would be startled awake by the dreaded Morse of the mallet tap-tapping out his mother's indecipherable longings, and there would be no pause to his pining between sleep and waking as he sat on his bed, defiant of loving household caregivers, his morning already defeated by the natural charm of his younger brother and the prospect of having to face school without seeing his mother.

Armed with her new sculpting tools, Edna had returned to the island to speak an indigenous language. Yamaye is the earliest recorded mention of Jamaica's Taino name, in 1493. It is the Arawakan word from which the name "Jamaica" derives, though it is mistakenly thought to come from an apocryphal word of various spellings such as Xayamaca. As close as we can translate, Yamaye's meaning is "land of wood and water." She had always connected with water, but now in her carving she would move from the cold flint and unforgiving permanence of stone, which she always associated with Cornwall—its skeletal coast and smooth grave-mounds, the invincible grey shapes of omens and magic that littered the treeless moors—to the creak and bend, the warmth and resinous bleed of once-living wood.

Edna had to create a world against the jagged edges of her own disharmony. She could never entirely suspend the domestic concept of "home" from her mind—home with all its unspoken admonishments, none of which came from her husband; they just drifted in from habit and worry, from memories of her mother's patient, dutiful sacrifice, from the reproachful sadness she sometimes thought she saw in Douglas's eyes. Her family was always with her in a deeper way, as though she were an earth mother, or one of the animals she loved to watch in the zoo, lying there dreaming while the cubs fed at her teats; suddenly having a change of heart and lifting up like a mountain, with no worry, to push them away; as though love were a mighty river or land mass, a surety for ever and ever that didn't have to be stated or explained, and its permanence made their world a safe place. Her children, all children, were small creations one could only prepare for the fiery furnace. One could make them safe as much as was possible, and provide them with the tools and a sense of values and a taste for the ecstasies of life, but after that it was really a question of their mettle, of the give-and-take of their material, of their own willingness and determination to survive. This was, she reasoned, all she had taken from her own mother, a framework of home and safe haven, and from her father nagging questions about his certainty of faith, and a sense of the wonder of things. After that one was on one's own.

The presence of her sons provided a sheet of carbon beneath her life that made her accountable, each imprint a bearing of responsibility. But she failed to connect these feelings with customary domestic rituals, probably because she was able to delegate these to others.

And yet she loved her sons. Loved them with all her good wishes and faith. Would have encouraged them in anything, believed in their possibilities, lived at a brink of terror over their health; she observed obeisance to every omen, such as not walking under ladders, placing no peacock feathers in the house, knocking on wood, pinching spilled salt to throw over her shoulder—all this to ensure their good fortune.

So she was usually startled to discover the world watching her when she heard someone pass an opinion.

"Michael has a bad stutter," remarked Muriel.

"Douglas is a very nervous child," surmised Vera.

Aunt Vera thought Douglas should be separated from his mother and his ebullient brother for a while so that he could "steady down." Mardi took all these remarks very personally, interpreting each observation as an indictment of her as a mother; but it was finally agreed that from time to time Douglas should be sent to stay with Vera and her daughter, his cousin Pamela.

The studio, a rough ark, was tucked away among the hollowing *ha-has* of the giant whispering trees at the edge of the grasspiece, in sight of Drumblair. Edna's wooden embryos grew in the damp of this rustic womb between branches of oaks and guango trees, lignum vitae and woman's tongue, and the smaller interruptions of ebony, all of which she sensed fold in protectively behind her whenever she entered. The walls snapped their joints; bats flew out like stale belches from the shingles overhead on the exhalation of overnight breath as she opened the windows, pushing them out against the drooping wrists of the long dewy grass. Each morning she felt it was she who woke her forest kingdom, fresh from yesterday's guilt or discomfort, herself one of its rare plants.

And here a menagerie of Edna's caged thoughts began to take on form. From her first block of wood emerged *Wisdom*, a sphinx-like mahogany head settled deep in thought whose emptied eyes had that inward quality of a mask. Her first try with cedar was *Ape*, a squat figure with precise square-shouldered symmetry that seemed to combine animal and human kingdoms. I would get to know it well, as it was always crouched by the door as I entered my Aunt Muriel's cottage. After modelling several heads that she plastered, she returned to mahogany to sculpt Harry. Finally, as though all this had been in preparation, she modelled a bust of Norman that she would later bronze, the head slightly tilting back as he regarded life with a wry, quizzical look.

And then in 1925, with no preconceived idea of what stood before her, she gazed at a block of wood balanced on the stand, and as she turned it round the wood showed itself to her. On the pivot she could see its vast shoulders, each mother and granny, each fostering, the heft of a lioness, the embrace of Drumblair, the mountains of Jamaica, the comfort to orphans, to sons—sons left orphaned.

With this mad world of voices in her head and lives demanding to be born of her time and her patience and hands, she tried to imagine orphans her breasts had never fed, her arms would tire holding, her lap ache to release; to conjure up the mother she herself could never be, a being whose every physical trait manifested a fullness of giving. Her tools sought that indulgence so elusive to her from the mothering memory of mahogany, the bulge of stomach, the generosity of breasts, the strength of shoulders, the watchful regard; meanwhile, her own face was that of a shrew, withdrawn, antennae poised, her eyes torches she shone down a tunnel of birth.

Earth mother. Her *Demeter*. She felt this was a state of being, a form she'd been unconsciously searching for since childhood. In the torso was the hefty ballast, a dark brooding whose movement was liquid as the sea's yet enduring as the land's, with memory its rhythm—a rhythm Edna's own nervy personality could never master.

Leaning this way then that, as she did whenever she needed to sharpen perspective, Edna was now balancing masses. She modelled two archetypal mothers with flesh like udders, pillowing a kneeling boy between them, *Adolescence*, a smothered figure hemmed in by the softness of their voluptuous concern.

As she created each, Edna was happy. She was on the outside looking in, carving them for a morning and stepping back to appraise them. Their emergence was thrilling to see, and emotionally uncomplicated. These wooden orphans needed no mothering. She liked to think of her own sons as beings independent and getting on with their lives, guarded and guided by nannies, eating well, going to school, anchored to a yearly-kept family promise of summer together spent with the boys and their friends—George, Mike, maybe Dossie—in a rented cottage on the north coast by the sea.

Mike Smith and George Campbell had grown up with Douglas and Michael. George was the nephew of Miss Boyd, a tiny, devout woman who worked at Drumblair running the house and deputizing as mother to the boys and later to me. Douglas as the "troubled child" had sometimes been sent to the country with Miss Boyd for what was described as "a break," though whether the break was for Mardi or for him, and who or what the break was *from*, was never made quite clear. Michael and George and Mike went to Kingston schools. At Jamaica College Michael was a weekly boarder, ensured home pampering on weekends.

Mike and Douglas were the same age, but Douglas was sent to first a junior boarding school on the other side of the island, then a senior one known for toughening soft Kingston boys, which was viewed in curious British tradition as a form of healthy, necessary banishment. I guess this was either Aunt Vera's decision, or maybe just part of Mardi's original child-rearing plan for Douglas, which she abandoned when it came to Michael. The two brothers were so very different in personality, Douglas more introvert, Michael a charming, extravagantly buoyant enthusiast. Michael was always intrigued by his mother's art. As soon as he got home, he'd run into the studio to check on her progress, and she'd ask his advice. He'd pat the wood as he left. Douglas was proud of her work but more quietly mystified. He would look at it thoughtfully for a while and then leave without a word. Mardi would think he wasn't that interested, and then days later he'd suggest that a hand was too large or that she should drop a figure. Once at school a boy teased him about his mother having nude models posing for her in her studio. Douglas, who had taken up boxing as a school sport, doubled his fists and punched him unconscious.

For Edna each holiday was a hiatus from the continuum of her work. She'd sigh with satisfaction as Norman and the boys set off in the small canoe made for them by a local boat-builder, which they took turns to row along the coast of coves, diving over its side to swim, sometimes capsizing it to climb back in. They'd all gather for card games in the evening, or Norman would take the boys nighttime fishing, dropping anchor somewhere out there in the dark with their flashlights—"Ah," she'd think to herself, "every-thing is working out all right. Trust life."

She'd return to Kingston with her contradictions fallen into place harmoniously within her and carve something gentle—*Boy with a Reed*—a turning figure of a boy softly playing an instrument as though drawn by some deeply personal, comfortable inspiration.

And then in 1929 came *Eve*. She was the earth virgin, like a figure emerging from water, a wetness still shivering, a nakedness. Seven feet high, also turning, proud and determined, curious, shrewd, unknowable, and Edna wondered if she was looking back, or reconnoitring as she prepared to change the world, to make mortality infinite by repeating the finite over and over, creating life to relinquish one's own; setting a precedent that would endure from Eden till the here-and-now. By this time several carpenters and foresters were on the lookout for logs for Edna. She had found an enormous tree that had to be cut down on the city's Half Way Tree main road, and she bought it whole for twenty-five pounds. She used it for *Eve*, and was able to do another five carvings after-wards out of what was left.

Edna, who by now had learned to cut wood and handle its hollows, had been searching her technique for a formula to carve the Jamaican figure. She knew that though her subject matter had become local in the sense that it reflected the life she found there, the figures she modelled, even the market vendors, were still, like her, strangers in the landscape. And now the form suddenly came to her in the high scalp, strong, long back of the neck, highly arched spine, thrust-out buttocks, high calves, and big heels, the exact opposite of the Spanish figures familiar to her Guatemalan friend Gherke—scalp way back on the head, with the long calves practi-cally right down to the heels, "flamenco legs," she had called them. If you looked in the market, Jamaican mountain women were not lean and wiry, they were massive; strong and sculpturesque.

Edna had found her way to *Eve* by instinct. The mahogany
had opened its heart and let her in. Her work was developing like
a baby that suddenly finds its balance, no longer falling with the
effort of trying. She felt all her lessons coming together, the practical power of learned craft, the universal mind of the metropolis,
the rhythm of islands. The figure of a woman planted in her pre-
occupation as she looked back to her creator, fists clenched in a
moment of uncertainly, a child to a parent, seeking reassurance
before setting off on the unknown road.

It was a turning point for *Eve* and a turning point for Edna.
She was twenty-nine and she had made it to Eden, and innocence
was not a thing one calculated in terms of Norman or passion or
one's children, but as a state of grace and fortune to be born at a
time that gave one the chance to determine the shape of a culture.
In any country there might be a single generation ever blessed to
be able to do that. If until this point she had felt invisible con-
straints, with *Eve* came release. This was her land, and she could
be part of making it whatever it was capable of being.

She was learning how to work towards meaning through mass
and the round, through curves and movement instead of planes
and angles. Planes and angles now seemed to be the intellectual
joining of dots, the simplification of metaphor into formula, geo-
metric shorthand for the versed. She was moving into the language
of this landscape; she could feel it in the forms of these beings as
she coaxed them from the wood. She felt it as she swayed in front
of them, celebrating new gods with the slow saunter of their muscle, the insolence of their indifference to earthly time.

Were these the spirits her father had once come to convert?
Now they danced for her, not to entertain, but illustrating music
she had always heard faintly within. And that was when it began
to occur to her that when she had first arrived, she had come as
her father had, a stranger bringing her own culture and ideas,

whether she meant to or not. She hadn't come to be part of this island. Everything about it had been uncomfortable for her. She, like her father, had wanted the place to change, people to become different from what they were in their own reality. What was the difference between her imposing her ideas as to how people should think or behave and her father, in all his goodness, arriving as a missionary to win these spirits over to a Methodist way of believing?

Now she felt she returned to Jamaica not just as Edna the wife of Norman, but as Edna the daughter of Ellie, come to lay claim to what was hers through her mother's birthright. Without any disloyalty to her father, she had to face the fact that Harvey was an alternative she would have to forsake. As she worked through the giant piece of local wood, she felt she was working her way back through the rings of time to her own Genesis—back to the world of her mother; *Eve* had become a starting point for Edna in this new land.

The more Edna came to terms with her work, the more she discovered Jamaica, the more her resentment grew towards the flamboyant side of social life around her and all that it represented; ". . . *most of the time the world goes by unnoticed by people who in their vanity are busy powdering their noses and sitting in their deep chairs wondering what the neighbour is having for supper, or the guest at the next restaurant table, while planet Earth is doing the big, the brave, the daring things for this little crowd of pygmies to gape at!*" she noted in a letter to Norman.

But the truth was, they too were counted among the privileged few, content to go to the racetrack on a Saturday and lead in their Derby-winning four-year-old roan gelding Roysterer— descended from Giddy Girl and Callonby who were from Gay

Polly and Sicyon, Enbarr and Hurry On, who were from Gay Bird and Polymelus, Polkerris and Sunder on one side and Abrazia and The Tetrarch, Tout Suite and Marcovil on the other, and the list could go on painstakingly back to Louis XIII and Freia through Samedi, Isonomy and Moorhen through Gallinule, Hampton and Quiver through Maid Marian, Bona Vista and Arcadia through Cyllene, Galopin and Assegai through Knobkerri, Cyllene and Maid Marian through Polymelus, Common or Hawkswick and Schism through Divorce Court, Amphion and Sierra through Sunridge on one side and St. Simon and Miss Middlewick through Butterwick, Isonomy and Deadlock through Isinglass, Bona Vista and Castania through Vahren, Le Samaritain and Roxelane through Roi Herode, Thurio and Meteor through Star, Springfield and Sanda through Sainfoin, Hagioscope and Dinah through Lady Villikins and Barcaldine and Novitiate through Marco on the other; names going back to the previous century, an island's who's who in which horses, not people, had been conscientiously enumerated.

Norman and Edna were content to escort each other to the Glass Bucket Club, where Edna puffed at cigarettes she couldn't inhale and danced the nights away with her strange little rushes of movement, incongruous steps, as though she were escaping. Their pictures were featured in the social pages, Norman drinking and small-talking with those who preferred not to ask real questions, feeling besieged by island socialites revealing the stories of the day as they simpered around him, posing their ridiculous questions about whether he asked clients if they were guilty, did he ever attend an autopsy? did he think so-and-so's jockey had used a battery in his whip? would the boxer Kid Bangarang knock out Flinty? would he write a constitution for a cat club, oh do, please? Content to mutter a courteous thank you and avert his eyes from the waiters who said *yes sah, no sah* obsequiously as though he were their colonial master.

Driving home thumping over the tram lines, the road wet with rain that unexpectedly spits in the tropical night out of nowhere, with the moon bounding along beside the car, lifting her skirt skittishly across the puddles, a lantern of light, Edna must have thought how easy it would have been to simply immerse herself into this mix—the parties and dinners and bridge games, the steward's box at races (where she went to see the horses, not the people) with mutterings of cheating and fixing of races, the ringside seats at boxing (where she loved to watch the fighters as models, since it was almost impossible to get anyone to sit for an artist in those days), ladies competing harder with Flossie's or Joyce's fashion designs than the welterweights, performing a minimum or even a maximum of charitable deeds at the St. Andrew Women's Club, saying the right things, and basically going along thinking cautious, correct thoughts, whilst keeping a clean, efficiently run house with well-trained, reliable staff.

But all alone in the quiet of early morning, she had to account for herself.

She had started teaching free art classes at the Institute of Jamaica in Kingston, hoping to find young artistic talent and to share experience and technique. But even there she was horrified by the head of the board, a tart, fair-skinned Jamaican who was intent on keeping things as British as could be. Edna had grown weary of being invited to school exhibitions, sometimes to judge, and finding the work filled either with yellow-haired children or with snow and reindeer, or alternately some stereotype of a Negro with a plaid bandana or braces, as though fit to be featured only in a minstrel show. If only she could get them before they were trained to imitate their traditional masters of subject and thought, and encourage them instead to follow her on a road to self-discovery.

When the classes began, an unexpected crowd of forty turned up on the very first day. The institute had secured the use of an elegant private home that had been left by a wealthy citizen, Altamont DaCosta, for the use of the government as long as it wasn't changed from its Victorian glory. The trustees had been persuaded to empty all but one room, to give space and let in light, and the students and teachers were often aware of the ghost of its benefactor stomping disapprovingly around.

Edna would later describe those days as the most enchanting and glorious of her life. I think she found something almost as satisfying in teaching as she did in creating her own work. When she witnessed the pittance that a road worker or a domestic servant earned, she could only reflect helplessly on their plight. But nothing gave her such a sense of achievement as the sight of young students arriving each week at the institute, and sometimes on a weekend at her studio at home, with a hunger she recognized in their eyes, to unwrap their crude tools and return to the wood or the clay.

Edna had learned to sublimate life to art, and sometimes she would find herself sitting at a dinner party—each one was set like a stage for the night's captive audience—and would escape to her thoughts, remembering a student with whom she felt special kinship as he hammered away not noticing the time, and how hard it was for her to finally disturb him when she had to make him go home.

Norman had done an odd thing. In 1929 he had sold Drumblair and taken the family to live nearby, at Bedford Park, in a large, rambling two-storey wooden house not unlike their old home. They stayed for four years, until 1933. I have never known why— only heard the sale and the new home referred to without rancour—and wish now I had thought to ask. But they would later do the same with Nomdmi, sell it for a year and later buy it back. Wayne Brown, who knew them well in that burrowing, intense way biographers have, said that Edna explained they sold homes or land when they ran short of money, but he suggested it also reflected a restlessness they shared. Maybe Wayne was right. Maybe they had just reached a point where too many people had their address.

Who knows why, but as soon as they settled into Bedford Park, Edna and Norman took in another son, Frankie Fox, a fair, tall English boy whose parents, if they were alive, were not on the island. He had been adopted by a family in Jamaica called Heron, and had become friendly with the Manley sons and asked to stay at Bedford Park when the Herons went for an extended stay in England. The young Frankie was absorbed into family life and seems to have added a note of great harmony to the home. Norman knew that Frankie was another of Edna's birds with broken wings, and perhaps never contradicted her when she spun her myth that he was now officially their adopted son.

Just before she left Drumblair, Edna had abandoned a carving of a woman towering over the sleeping figure of a man. She was never satisfied with it, uncertain whether it was Delilah hovering over a sleeping Samson, or really an idea for Eve and Adam. It had sat on the studio floor for years, and served as a leaning post and rag-rack.

"It reminds me of yourself and Norman," some acquaintance had said shortly before they moved. The visitor simply wanted to offer an opinion, needed to feel she knew them well enough to make some sort of personal connection. Island people were like that. They wanted intimacy, they loved secrets. They liked to think that they knew you well, that they could touch what you touched. They liked to relate art to the artist because everything they produced in their own lives was related in an immediate way to them. In any case, Edna's art was still just an exotic rumour to most people, as only a few had seen her work at home, or a few pieces privately owned. The local *Daily Gleaner* reported with pride her recent successes abroad, and those who read this tried to imagine the work of this woman they knew as an ardent fan they saw at boxing or cricket or races, sitting with her husband, always elegantly well dressed and knowledgeable about each sport. She now stirred more than the usual island curiosity.

Edna noticed little else about this inauspicious visit, but after the lady left, she attacked the carving, kicked it and hurt her toe, pushed it over on its side, shaking the whole studio, rolled it down the steps and down the slope beyond till it bumped into a tree, where it was left for dead in the high grass. She never knew who righted it, but standing there the male rotted in the damp ground. The female higher up survived and was rescued when, on their return to Drumblair four years later, Norman sawed the work in half, leaving the male figure where it lay in the grass.

During their time at Bedford Park, Edna sculpted prolifically. In addition to completing her mahogany *Eve*, she carved several torsos in both stone and wood. If she discovered herself through the women in her carvings, she seemed to discover Jamaica through her studies of men.

She created her first *Dawn*, a theme she would return to again and again in the sun-flooded island. Seated in sandstone, a young sun waiting his turn, restless but not apprehensive, his leg folded up like an erect phallus, his male power inevitable though as yet unrealized. Then she joined male and female in a quiet bas-relief, a seated *Adam and Eve* poignantly connected, mutually sensed presences in common conundrum facing the price of their humanity, she reaching out for him yet looking wistfully away, he reassuring, his hand on hers.

Then she staked out her world in another bas-relief—a family tableau. A sprawled island of a man, his back to the rest of the world, emotionally detached yet the base of all things, looking up towards a crouched ancient ancestor. One small child reaches out to his mother, and an older lurks shyly. The mother's head is bowed as she reaches to the smaller child but crooks her other elbow under the raised arm of a performing flautist standing beside her. It is the muse to whom she listens.

Out of Portland stone and mahogany came *Seventeen* and *Sixteen*, brooding self-conscious adolescence, perhaps while preparing for her own sons—or a young, evolving Jamaica. Then a man emerged tenderly holding a wounded bird, again in mahogany; Edna knew that the wounded bird was the vulnerability of Norman. When she offered a female sun to cradle the male earth, she carved this reassurance in stone.

Before she left Bedford Park she had found her blessed Biblical *Beulah*, no longer forsaken. "Married to the land and he who rebuilds you," she jotted down in a note to herself. *Beulah*, like the land of promise, she created as a gift for Norman. Extending the theme of the phallus as life force, again using Portland stone, she carved a massive woman embracing her bent leg as though the smooth dome of protruding knee rises from a womb of arms.

The summer of 1929 bloomed for Edna. *Eve* and *Ape* would be two of four wooden carvings she took to London to exhibit in the summer Goupil collection. The telegram received by Norman from his wife in England on his thirty-sixth birthday read, "Eve *gets headline!*"

As her carvings were shown, her name came to the notice of magazines and newspapers in London and on the continent—*Apollo*, *The Morning Post*, *Les Artistes D'Aujourd'Hui*, *La Revue Moderne*. Her work was variously described as "primeval abundance," as "drawing emotionally rather than scientifically," and as "ideal work for the expression of form." Edna had the unbalancing sense that she was being taken seriously. She came to the attention of Kineton Parkes, the reviewer for *Apollo*, whose cover she graced and which would often feature her work at length. If Europe had been her destination, she could be said to have "arrived."

Norman received the telegram the day after his birthday. So *Eve* was a smash. Smoothly gazing back at London with her darkly glowing composure, solidity amassed from how many thousand hours of pain and surprise, ecstatic discovery, and disappointed dullness that he had witnessed, how many of his wife's renewals and how many missteps, all the guilt and fury and forbearance, the asking how many times for one glimpse of godhead, one moment's sight from the eyes of the muse? And now here she was, complete and serene, ignorant of the agony of her birth. Was it *Eve* or was it Edna who flamed towards the skies eating up the world, making dense substance light as carbon, infinite and permanent as air? Norman wondered at times if he was just a heavy paperweight holding her down, pinning the wings of a spirit made to fly.

After this tour, Edna was admitted into the London Group, the same year as Henry Moore and Barbara Hepworth. At times she felt high on the glory of this achievement, and then she would snatch the feeling away from herself, considering it either unlucky to gloat, or treachery both to her new faraway homeland and to her gift as an artist. She was always uneasy with success.

Through the work of Hepworth and Moore that summer she was introduced to modernity in carving stone.

I am going to carve wood. Wood is warm and it lives and moves and dances!

I am going to carve stone, wood is too fickle.

These two mediums vied for her interest on her return to

Jamaica, as she'd succumb to the temptation of one and then to the other. Norman lived with repeated moments of panic when he felt he'd taken Edna away from the mainstream, from the centre of the cultural world. He feared she would become peripheralized and ethnic, an oddity in a cultural backwater.

But like her *Beulah* she was now ready to rebuild, and despite Norman's doubts, she returned to a new surge of creativity. Jamaica was becoming a love affair so powerful that it provided the natural energy of passion; and for all its adjustments, Norman's hold on her heart and imagination remained firm. Whatever helped to inspire her, that voice had grown strong and would sing come what might.

A new mood of optimism about the future may have been inspired also by the presence of a lively Armenian painter, Khoren der Harootian, who had recently arrived in Jamaica and came to stay with the family at Bedford Park. His enthusiasm as they worked separately towards a joint exhibition in 1932 gave Edna a great sense of hope; not just hope of establishing her own art on the Jamaican scene, but of creating a surge of enthusiasm for the island's fledgling art movement.

The exhibition brought Edna's work onto the public stage in Jamaica. If, as one reviewer suggested, she had been a prophet not accepted in her own country, it was probably not the fault of the general public. Up till then there had been almost no tradition of Jamaican imagery in art. The well-meaning writer of the *Daily Gleaner* review wondered why Mrs. Manley would sculpt a powerful Eve instead of an English cricketer like Milford at the wicket, or an "ebony" boxer like Pitt "*delivering his soporific right hook.*" "What," he pondered, "*mean these swelling curves? These limbs in positions in which no respectable limb should find itself?*" But after flailing at what the meaning of her "*inchoate symbolism*" could possibly be, he described Dawn as "*a fine example of her technique—the significantly exaggerated curve and pose of the left leg, the massed muscle of the arm and torso; contrasting with a quite exact realism in the modelling of the muscles of the neck, the line of the cheek and eyes. Of such is the work of Mrs. Manley."*

The *Sportsman* writer didn't tackle a review but commended Edna Manley, somewhat gushingly, for the ". . . *joy we all feel in her achievement.... To Jamaica, cobbling so long and so hopelessly in the arts, Edna Manley is giving such talent as possesses her . . . we are all very proud of her, and so sincerely hope that she will go marching down to posterity with divine honours."*

It seems to me fitting that when she carved her Biblical *Rachel*, my grandmother was safely back in Drumblair, where, as its namesake, I would live one day.

Rachel, she who goes to the well, where she finds the biblical Michael—one arm flamenco-raised, balancing her gourd. As Edna worked on the maquette's birth with brusque strokes, words tapped aloud in her head in time to the mallet, to the steps of women she'd seen saunter over the hill on Mandeville mornings, or stride bravely down Kingston's paved roads with loads on their heads, or at the city market as they hoisted things up onto a shoulder, their backs strengthening like aging tree trunks. I believe these words ran through her mind as she carved: *Pass the jar, woman of the mountains, Mankind needs a refill, pass the jar . . .* words instructing the tools as they shaped the mahogany figure with its eyes sleeping through time, lost in its own balance, its inner communion. Another mountain girl smoothed out of the wood with the jar moved from her head to her shoulder . . . *the seeds have spilled. Passing by mankind moves, the fire has died, the seeds grow cold. Pass the jar, man comes by . . .*

I found this half-made verse nearly fifty years later, in poems she had written over the years that she left me as part of her legacy, the part she large-heartedly would not daunt me with by sharing in her lifetime.

Creatures she offered to the gods, dances she could not perform, only choreograph; in exchange she hoped for things going well despite herself—the staff in the house, Norman in the world, the children busy and safe, eating and learning and growing. These were the members of her magic kingdom, safe in their wood from an arbitrary cosmos, safe from time in their stone. Island beings, the surrounding sea a moat to keep history out—or to keep history in?

"Islands and their people are separate and elemental," she decided.

Soon she'd be docked in her studio at Drumblair again, building a library of souls for this world, a phalanx of soldiers to send ahead, to hide behind.

When the workers struck for better wages in Frome in 1938, it heightened a drum roll that Edna had been aware of, ominously, enigmatically, before, but that only now, beyond herself, could she clearly point to and identify. When the canefields were set afire, and men injured and killed in battles with the police, labour unrest spread to Kingston. There was little doubt that something epic was happening on the island.

Norman had felt it coming as something detached from himself; it was a logical progression of events prompted by the Great Depression. The prices of all raw products fell, and European beet sugar had recovered sufficiently after the war to become competitive: hard blows for the West Indian sugar trade at a time when Jamaica's banana industry was already flagging. Conditions in the British West Indian islands were deplorable. Low wages, low exports, unemployment, and the doors to migration were closing. In 1935, sugar workers in St. Kitts struck for better wages. Unorganized strikes with bloodshed followed in Barbados, Trinidad, St. Lucia, and St. Vincent. The huge wheel of poverty continued self-defeatingly around, to return where it had begun. Norman felt its inevitability intellectually, but as a member of the professional middle-class he was still a participant in the governing system.

But Edna had sensed it coming through the lines of life at unexpected moments. It had no name. Just the two-shillings-and-sixpence wages offered to workers, and the poverty all around her. She sensed it in the shock she got when, on a panel to judge the first exhibition in which all the schools on the island were invited to participate, she saw the picture the other judges had chosen. There were these market women walking down a hill in their head ties and local plaid skirts, and they had white faces, yellow hair, and blue eyes. She decided to offer her own prize for a self-portrait or a portrait of the child at the next desk. She realized the children were being inspired by the calendars and illustrated English books and paintings of saints in the churches—even their Christmas cards and the stained-glass windows in church. The struggle for identity would be as difficult as the struggles about politics and economics and class.

Visiting the trainer's stables near the racetrack, she would see a young stableboy who had paused in his sweeping to watch her commune with her horse. He would mechanically return to his chore, and she would wonder if his own probably overworked and ill-treated mother had ever had time to connect with him in any meaningful, personal way. When the trainer arrived, she would hear the car door slam and his authoritative voice shouting something like "You damn fool, you don't finish yet!"

Perhaps she saw the youngster in the beam of light shining in from the opening at the end of the long row of stables, and he leant both hands on his broom as he paused and looked up with such innocent resilience, his head thrown back for a moment and his throat stretched wide over the deep backward arch of his neck, a gullet ready to open itself up for whatever quenching it needed, the light mysteriously surrounding his head—and she knew that soon it would be a new day. The vision touched a chord, reminding her of the workhouses that haunted William Blake in his youth. She remembered the drawing of *Death's Door*, and the figure of resurrection looking up as though drawn to the light by some innate instinct of optimism.

When Norman saw the mahogany half-figure of a man yearning towards light, his strong back braced with one arm akimbo forming a gateway, his head flipped back in awoken curiosity, it struck a deep note within him too, and he wondered whence she had plucked that powerful moment: *Negro Aroused*. It was 1935— three years before Frome rioted or the Kingston workers struck— when the Kittitians went on a labour strike, and he found it odd, as he hadn't mentioned this to Edna, but that was what came to his mind.

Workers became alarmed at the lack of jobs and the closing gates of migration as word came that the Depression was having an effect on Cuba and Panama. These were problems Norman had not thought to discuss with Edna, the full implications of which were not yet clear to him. Soon after that, she completed a wide-awake figure standing with his arms raised up like crossed rifles over his head, his body so strong and the face so powerfully focused.

He was her *Prophet*, she decided.

Then she returned to stone to entomb the memory of *Pocomania* before she forgot, before what was ritualistic expounding, prayerful complaining, or rejoicing, was overtaken by the emergence of something more conscious and temporal. Head bowed in observance as one arm curves against the chest, forming a nest for the face, which hides from the world of surrounding reality, the other arm shooting up with the soul most high in joyful recognition of its imagination beyond—a dismissal of this world. And then, as though she was transferred from trance to cognizance, in sudden reversal she carved a man upon his knees, his back arched the opposite way, his head thrown back facing heaven, his hands like flat tablets before him as though to be read. *Prayer.*

She saw the strike coming when she passed the roadwork gangs as they sat on the embankments glaring at those who passed, how they sucked their teeth or just stared at her, intimating a dangerous "soon." But her smile often appeared to disarm them, and she wondered why most people passed them by without greeting. There was nothing sporadic or desultory in her *Diggers*: three stylized figures, symmetry in the hardness of their faces and their muscles, their physiognomy as revealing of their history as an emaciated beggar's. It was carved on an accommodating length of mahogany Harry had located, grain that offered little opinion of its own, three diggers lifting their pickaxes in a united action as though where one ended the next took over, and the next, until they were a single continuous movement. A chorus of intention. Another dance. And Norman said, Oh that the Kingston parish roadworks could be so efficiently served, as he watched the rising bas-relief.

She saw it coming around her, and she had the uncanny sense that change was taking place within her too. Through the last few months she had had a sensation of unease, no more than that, when she walked, when she rode, when she got too hot and thirsty, when she tried to carry anything heavy. One day, lifting her arm to get a sense of a movement, she felt a sudden excruciating pain rip through her stomach and side, through her back, and when it eased she knew with certainty that it would come again. In the next couple of weeks the pain became a half-sleeping inner presence that would stir only occasionally but which she now knew had been there a long time. Daily journeys to the studio were made gingerly, her hand tenderly steadying her side. Visits to doctors and more doctors, to labs and X-ray departments, needles and samples and the clang of loud doors, the efficient certainty of white-shoe steps on spotless floors, the cutting smell of medicinal alcohol, breathe in, hold your breath, breathe again. Was it kidneys or uterus or ovaries or a rumbling appendix? Norman worried.

Another exhibition was on the horizon. The French Gallery in London. When they requested mounting a one-man exhibition of Edna's latest work, along with a rush of pride, Norman felt the familiar concern. What had he done by bringing her here?

But she insisted that she had always felt straitjacketed in England, even in art school. Maybe more in art school, for her work tended to be instinctive. Here she felt released. Perhaps she would always be a prisoner in her armature of solid physical Englishness, but in Jamaica her thoughts found voice, her longings escape. He could look around, from *Demeter* to *Boy with Reed* to *Rachel*, as though following the unnerving proof of the hands of time, wondering if anything else about Edna was solid save these. This was her dance, who she was meant to be; perhaps the sum of these.

But in many ways she had already chosen to reject being part of the contemporary European art scene. Perhaps she repudiated what she saw as its premise that art was something one could sublimate as separate from life and movement—that one could simply intellectualize it all, adopt a persona as an artist. In Jamaica she seemed to find the raw source of life and movement. The brashness of a landscape and its people inspired her. In England, Norman had tried to persuade her to sculpt people instead of animals, but from the moment they arrived and she saw Jamaicans sauntering along on that first drive through the streets of Kingston, she knew in her heart that she had found her landscape: sea and mountains, bodies dancing like joyous trees, hips see-sawing like drawers opening and closing. She had at last come home, spirit and flesh at one, combined in a medium. She had found a world that had not separated itself from the earth, or people from each other; worship that was con-versation—back and forth—spirit with gods. She had felt like origi-nal man in his cave, recording history on the walls.

"What would it mean if all of Europe recognized my art but I could not?" she asked him.

Another show was planned in London, by the Suffolk Gal-leries, Pall Mall. Norman felt there were still too many unanswered questions about Edna's health, and they decided she'd see a spe-cialist in London while the exhibition was on. The Atlantic cross-ing was mercifully uneventful, and back at Neasden with Ellie for three weeks, Edna kept appointments with a clinic while the gallery mounted her latest pieces.

"I'll be just fine," she reassured Norman. Ellie reassured Norman. More and more telegrams. Norman fretted.

Without conferring with him, Edna agreed to an operation described as a "look-see." She liked the swiftness of the decision, the certainty of action, and the unspecified exploratory nature of it. She left the glare of those white lights over her head suspended on a flight of chloroform, a slingshot that sent her soaring through a life's incar-nations with the conviction that this look-see was somehow the sort-ing out and correct placement of all the pieces of the very complicated puzzle that had been her life, and that when she woke everything would have been organized and simplified. Like a well-run office, she would now have a system and everything would make sense. Norman would be cheerful, Douglas would be at peace, Michael would be Michael, they would have located and activated her wifing and mothering genes, and the exhibition would be a success.

Coming out of the anaesthetic, she had the feeling she had journeyed back to the very start of herself, where she glimpsed the reason for who she was, the answer to her entire personality for better or worse, some untouchable kernel. She suddenly knew who she was and who she was not.

I am not sure what was wrong with her. I remember she told me she had massive adhesions from an appendix scar, but I have no idea if the appendix came out then or if it came out earlier, or whether it was really a hysterectomy, as Wayne Brown asked me the other day. But after three weeks in bed she learned to walk again, slowly and at first painfully, easing loose the pinching stitch in her side, a knot that had formed from the ropes of scar tissue extending like a gnarled vine round her trunk. It was a rough road travelling this tender, now controversial part of her, but as she straightened a little more every day, she felt growing relief. As the disfiguring scar healed across her tummy and side, she remarked triumphantly to all who would listen that these keloids (which she had heard somewhere were characteristic of scarring in black skin) were the final proof of her coloured ancestry.

Meanwhile, a debate began in the English papers on the ques-tion of female sculptors and, more specifically, Edna's *Eve*.

A reviewer in the *East Anglian Times* described Edna's *Eve* as

> . . . *primitive woman—broad, sturdy, enormously powerful. . . . Would such an Eve as Edna Manley's listen to temptation or make experi-ments with forbidden fruit? Would she not without hesitating innocence have knocked the serpent on the head with a stone, or caught it in a strong branch while she dismembered it, telling Adam to get on with job in the meantime and to quit his poetry? Mrs. Manley clearly puts the onus of the fall on Adam.*

A review in the *Daily Express* was brutal: "*Eve in brown wood through the modernists' eye looks like the zoo's prize baboon. Office girls strolling by hooted with laughter.*"

Despite Hugh Walpole (whom she had met first in Jamaica, where he had bought two carvings, and who was sufficiently impressed by her to base his character Romney Carlisle, in his novel *Captain Nicholas*, on the Jamaican sculptor) and Jacob Epstein expressing admiration for her work, this would be the last show she held in England. She would return home by the end of summer 1933—"home" was now unequivocal.

Unable for a while to mount a horse, she went for gentle walks. Left, left, with still a little limp, then a stronger left, left of the forward march, the forward dance, the purpose, the unison of things as they approached. Left right, left right, into the future, lighter and brighter, and it wasn't any more to do with roads than her father's mission had been about how to get to the chapel in St. Ives, or her journey back to health, or how many extra pennies the workers of Jamaica would press for or receive. It was the knitting together after purging oneself of the pain of one's personal story and a people's history; it was what was left of what was worthwhile. It was something to do with coming of age and intent and clarity. Though hers was only a single, sensitive lens, she knew that the truth comes to those who look long enough.

And then Frome happened, and Kingston erupted, and a labour movement began. And there on the back of a truck where she sat gallantly but uncomfortably waiting for her husband—who was negotiating for better wages for the workers, for a better deal, for peace, and with the governor for the release from jail of their cousin Bustamante, now emerging as a major activist for the workers—there as she helped hand out Drumblair soup to the hungry dockworkers—Edna saw the young black journalist staring from the back of the truck, leaning on the siding, his chin resting in his hands, absorbing what he saw, taking his notes, sorting out issues in his mind. There it was. She had arrived at the crossroads—out of the clay rose a bust of a thoughtful man, chin resting on the open hand of a bent arm in hiatus: *Strike*.

Norman saw that even if she wasn't asking questions, the wood

was answering her, history using her as its mouthpiece, its inter-
pretations providing moments of clarity that he, despite much phi-
losophizing, had not been able to reach on his own. She must have
seemed a world away from him. He had tired of the law, and more
and more young nationalists, influenced by the writings of Claude
McKay and the movement of Marcus Garvey for black advance-
ment, were urging him to enter politics and lead them on a road
of self-determination. They were drawn to Norman in need of a
leader. Perhaps they considered Norman, with his quiet wisdom
and ease with the law, less threatening as an instrument of radical
change. In many ways they were asking him, without realizing it,
to bring the themes of his wife's prophetic works to life. He felt he
was slowly being tugged by some inevitable movement that he had
not planned to be part of, but for which at times he felt fated.

Edna liked the flow of young patriots and nationalists and
thinkers through the home. She encouraged Norman, who was
instinctively shy and reclusive, the way a parent does a child,
believing unselfishly in something that one day must separate them.
That is the thing about the myth of both of them that often puzzles
me: the assumption that they were creating as a team, he building
a political philosophy of independence and she nearby, working
on a blueprint for its attending culture.

I think for my grandmother it would have been the hardest
thing to see that sensitive, war-torn man engage in another battle
less easily defined, one she knew would ask of him thankless,
unending service like that asked of her late father. I know she
always worried about his health; I know she distrusted movements,
and as their home filled with the early intellectual warriors of this
struggle, she knew this was a movement no different from the
banding together of those Cornwall women whom her sister had
joined in fighting for votes, no different from the throng of voices
and posters that, bent on war, had shattered her generation's youth.

7

Forty

The first time I saw the phrase that life begins at forty, I thought it nonsense . . . I thought that life began every time I found a new experience, every time that I learnt to look at life from another angle, I thought it was always beginning . . .
—Edna Manley: *The Diaries*, December 12, 1939

THE YEAR 1940 WAS A COLLECTION POINT into which many gullies rushed their end waters.

The century was back at war. Europe had spilled into its habitual fault lines. Most of the time the Manleys rode horses instead of driving a car as, due to the war, gas was going to be limited. Norman was the first public figure to purchase a two-wheeler, built like an English dogcart but with motor car-wheels, so it was high off the ground and harnessed to horses. Although Edna was the horsewoman and rode every day, she didn't like driving it, fearing slipping on the tar or breaking the long, slender reins; she hated running on the bit that driving required, and Norman was good at this.

By 1940 Drumblair had brought up a generation, and two of Edna's three birds had already flown their own way. Frankie Fox, four years older than Douglas, returned to England to join up for the war. Maybe he felt the call of his faraway mother country in need. Douglas, an amateur sprinter and boxer as his father had been, had represented Munro College in both sports, and equalled his father's ten-flat schoolboy record in the 100-yards at the all-island interschools championship. Michael, a strong swimmer like his mother, captain of the Jamaica College swimming team and a Sagittarian idealist, had spent hours in the gym to develop his muscles, as much to fight the local thugs as to win his races. Both sons had taken a stand in school against bullying. Douglas, the purposeful Taurean who, to be aroused, needed to see a red flag, was seldom rash. Despite the war, by 1940 he had left for Columbia University in New York to study sociology. "For me, struggle has to be personally relevant," he explained. Though many demobilized soldiers subsequently enrolled there, and beat up some students as pacifists and cowards, Douglas never felt a moment of regret.

Michael, still in school, was preparing to sit exams, then leave to study journalism, determined as soon as he became eighteen to enlist and fight against Hitler. "Don Quixote was a Sagittarian," mused Edna. Two years later he would briefly enroll in McGill, but he never settled into school life there, joining the Royal Air Force in Winnipeg as soon as he was able to train to be an air gunner. When he got leave, he took a train to New York to visit Douglas for two weeks, and there they would sit in Jack Dempsey's bar, Michael in his air force uniform with a twinkle, Doug with his glasses and academic look, drinking their rum and gingers and forever rehashing the comparative strengths and weaknesses of Joe Louis and Max Schmeling and the legend of Jesse Owens.

Douglas moved to England to do his postgraduate work; the

Second World War ended a year before Michael could graduate to go to battle, so he decided to apply to the London School of Economics, where, months later, he would marry my mother.

By 1940 all the ardour of progressive thought and feeling and the imperative of change that had grown with the past decade seemed to flood Drumblair. With the boys gone the house had become in some ways an empty chrysalis, but politically it was a burgeoning one. Mardi sensed an island evolving rather than changing, moving with restless intuition towards its destiny. The educated, well travelled, and sophisticated were interpreting this as a sign of political intention, pinning it to known formulas, engraving spirit as intention. As though ribboning drifts should be tied down in place, the inevitable somehow captured and validated by a recognizable name—Lena's suffragettes, Hitler's nationalists, Britain's imperialists—the armies that fought in something's name.

Edna had come to realize that, noisy and vociferous as the island was, the noise was mostly voiceless and never got seriously heard. In the past, Jamaica's victims of history had had no voice of their own. Their problems had been articulated by the conscientious privileged, then incompletely solved by the Colonial Office, the plantocrats or the church, liberal British citizens or local business houses, well-meaning club wives absolving their well-trained, unobtrusive consciences.

Now something indigenous was emerging—a growing trend being tied firmly into knots of intent. It was like a convergence of colour and sound, the gathering of ants on a crumb—new things were happening, new voices were being heard. After years of powerlessness, the workers in Frome had made themselves heard in 1938 with a voice that reverberated over the island—and then again in September of that very same year, with the birth of the People's National Party, with a constitution and philosophy, launched at the gracious colonial Ward Theatre in Kingston with

Norman as its first president, its inauguration graced by Sir Stafford
Cripps from the British Labour party.

It was felt that the *Daily Gleaner*, the only daily newspaper, was
a mouthpiece for colonial rule and the status quo. Spearheaded by
O.T. Fairclough, who was influenced by Garveyism and inspired by
the example of Haiti's early independence from France, talk had
begun of starting a second national newspaper. Fairclough, a
Jamaican, had lived and worked in Haiti as a bank manager, and
when he returned to Jamaica had applied to Barclays Bank. On seeing the black applicant, the manager had responded that they had
no vacancy for a messenger at that time. This was apparently all
an educated, trained, and experienced black person could hope for
professionally in the Jamaica of those days. The incident had had
a profound effect on Fairclough.

Public Opinion, a controversial new national weekly paper, was
founded by Fairclough, whom the Manleys always called Fair-C. He
became a regular visitor at Drumblair. He was a most dignified
man. He had a large, beguilingly tranquil face, and he always wore
white linen suits and sat with his legs elegantly crossed at the
ankles. His face held a regal composure, as though he was already
certain of the political outcomes for which they all agitated—it was
a certainty born of uncompromising determination. He seemed to
coordinate much of a network of radical nationalism and socialist
thought and action that led to the creation of both the party and
the newspaper. He had connections not just with the British
Labour party, but also with key people in Harlem like W.A.
Domingo, Adolphe Roberts, and the Reverend Ethelred Brown,
Jamaicans who had founded the Jamaica Progressive League and
the West Indies National Emergency Committee, both fighting for
independence from colonial rule, and who would add inspiration
and some financial aid to the struggle for Jamaican nationalism, to
which Norman was now deeply committed.

Only Jamaican landowners could vote in those days. Already the fight was on for adult suffrage and, incrementally, more local political autonomy in government. Norman and his band of PNP candidates had already started campaigning across the island with their ideas.

Edna was proud of all this but, and mostly by choice, she felt excluded. A culture may speak, but the voice of each artist is solitary. How to provide a mouthpiece for its voice without violating its language? How do you express the quality of freedom without imposing a format? How to give the horse its head, loosen the reigns; how to understand the horse as part of its landscape, altering neither but encouraging each to accommodate the other? Freedom had its own unique alphabet.

Everywhere, Edna had been struck by the natural creativity of the island. Whether it was boys whittling pieces of wood, Pocomania worshippers dancing, limbo dancers or calypsonians, Sugar Belly at the Glass Bucket with his bamboo saxophone, women weaving baskets and mats, her friend the boat-builder with his fisherman's hands singing his sweet and low songs. It seemed to Edna that only the formal mediums, taught skills like painting and writing—mostly middle-class pursuits—were driven by education to imitation. She had grave doubts about her own contribution. She was in this category, middle-class and educated, a hybrid who had in fact lived her impressionable youth in the country that in this context should not be imitated. What credentials! A recent review of her work had raised even more self-doubt when it was described as sentimental.

For years she had taught art in Kingston, either at the institute or at home in her studio, and kept in touch with a circle of artists and writers with a common cause. They sensed the energy of Drumblair, and felt drawn to its mood of optimism, along with the political nationalists. Among these were those young men who had been in school with her sons—Mike Smith, George Campbell, and Dossie Carberry. They had spent summer holidays with the family for years, sitting at the table in Drumblair or at a seaside retreat, listening to Norman and Edna speak of Jamaica with such original, respectful ideas, as though not describing some small upstart backwash of empire, but celebrating some just-discovered gem of the future; watching Edna drawing and carving a lowly Jamaican animal, or creating a face that was familiar and that they therefore would have thought not important enough to carve.

That the future lay in their hands was the challenge Norman and Edna had left them thinking about.

Joining them, as though drawn by osmosis, were young prose writers like Vic Reid and John Hearne, two brother poets, Clare and Basil McFarlane, and a maverick genius, the young writer and painter Roger Mais, five years younger than Edna, who would always arrive quietly watchful, becoming more outlandish as the drinks went down. Roger, a bearded Hemingwayesque figure with thick, unruly hair who drank a lot and drooled a smoking cigarette out of his mouth, was the most fiery of the group, always arguing, outrageous and quarrelsome, funny and keenly perceptive. Roger had been part of another established group of older, well-meaning, very traditional, and in some cases quite talented writers who valued what became known as "Wordsworth, daffodils and snow," and held tenaciously onto rhyme.

When Roger first met Edna, he told her he had written 254 poems. She was surprised he was old enough to have written that many, and asked to see them. She read them and realized that they were worthy poems, well written and feeling, but that the feeling was about the unfamiliar—daffodils and snow, winter with bare trees. She knew he had never been to England, had never seen snow or daffodils, but was being inspired by English literature. Everyone who was educated was.

"Roger, you know you are being inspired by what you read, not what you see," she told him. "Art must be born of reality, even if reality is a fantasy." She suggested he write about Jamaican ram goat roses, the season of drought, and hurricanes. And she would caution with fervour as he was on his way out the door, "Remember it's goats, not lions!"

He brought back a poem to read one evening: "*The wind is a great maestro.*"

"Darling, that is the wind all right," Edna said to him, and hugged him, delighted.

Roger was gradually drawn into Drumblair, and Edna watched him over the years move steadily into the heart of his own land-scape, first experimenting with his poems, plays, and short stories, studying the plight of the common man in ghetto and mountain, and how each unique response to the colonial equation that had created Jamaica was shaping a people.

These younger writers wandered in and out of Drumblair for a drink and a sandwich and a conversation with like minds, but they were never an official group with a day or a plan or an agenda. They would often bump into the parallel ideas of the more political heads who visited Norman. Norman's groups tended to meet rather than gather. The political nationalists would sit more formally inside the house around the dining table, or on the back verandah, where there were always enough chairs for their various meetings. But Edna's artistic bunch—call them accidental cultural nationalists—sat on the verandah with papers they had brought along, their own work or extracts from the work of others, over-seas papers' clippings, letters or reviews balanced on the arms of the deep wooden slatted chairs or on their laps, some sitting on the front steps or on the verandah rails. Sometimes they would drag their chairs out onto the lawn on a moonlit night, or when the scented frangipani blossomed or the pink-and-white annual night blooming cereus was opening its brief, spectacular hush of flowers. Drumblair was their watering hole. It was never a book club, never the Drumblair Literary Group, as it would later be called.

Drumblair had become a focal point for this yearning that the politicians called nationalism, and for which the artists had no name. This urge defined itself at first simply by what it did *not* wish to reflect; their themes would not be determined by England. This was an embryonic process. Slowly, drawing by painting, carving by model, poem by essay by story, their themes began to express a Jamaicanness, not audacious at first, but like the probing of a stick down an overgrown, unknown path, with the crackle of underbrush and the breaking or straining of branches, and with each moment of self-discovery and insight it progressed.

Edna rose like the prow of the group. She'd always preferred the company of men, though there were women, too, there—Cecily Howland, an English playwright, and Vera Bell, a Jamaican poet and playwright. These women would become her friends, but for the men she always occupied the spotlight, shone for them and charmed and flirted. She loved them sitting there drinking rum and talking literature and history and ideas; their arguments and petty competitions; the way they all performed in turn for her. They were her warriors, young pioneers of a green time, a time when every word was new and counted for something. To hell with what anybody thought; amongst them they were determined to produce the first collection of literature that was Jamaican.

George Campbell was a thin, nervy man with a narrow, bony face that looked alternately haunted and surprised. He had become gradually shriller with age, and as petulant as a spoiled child. He always demanded Mardi's attention.

Mike Smith also was thin, but had a large face with a very wide, high forehead, and his eyes gave him an appearance of intelligent, alert twinkling. He never looked tired and was never in neutral. He was a curious mixture of no-nonsense impatience yet painstaking thoughtfulness, of jovial mischief yet a most judgmental humour-lessness. He was, like most things in Edna's world, pluses and minuses, bewildering side-by-side opposites.

Mike and George had not always got along, and I suspect this was all to do with Edna. They would vie for her attention. With her ferocious loves and interest, she was known to inspire great rivalries. Though appearing exasperated by their feud, she enjoyed the intrigue, which continued over the years. She felt the rivalry made them write better.

"They are all in love with you," Norman told Edna.

"And with you," she'd reply, and it was probably true, for at first their poems were about leadership and history makers and the dawn of a new day, all themes generated by his political idealism.

It was a time when her husband's life had become all the things about which she was habitually skeptical. What had begun as a dreaming, the way men hold out hope for change or justice or nationalism, had now coalesced into a group of ardent ideologues who were making these things concrete and real. The creative minds that flowed into Drumblair were almost like an echo to his thought. Writers and artists surrounded her; she with her imagi-nation and the sense of how nebulous a thing "being" is, how it expresses itself in movement and shape, colour and texture and sound, all of which imitate its truth. If his group was like the rays round the sun, hers was the haze that surrounds moonlight.

What was it about writers? Did they make her feel in love? Did they appeal to the romantic in her? With artists—painters, sculptors, potters—she was wise and helpful and concerned and supportive, generous to a fault, but never seemed to indulge their foibles. They often visited Edna, men like the poised Albert Huie and the excitable Ralph Campbell, or Ceceil Baugh the beloved potter with a face like a mask of fired clay, talking quietly on the verandah and sometimes accompanying her to her studio to discuss some logistical problem or to share her work. And when they were not there in the flesh, they were always there in spirit—in Baugh's serene ceramic pots and in the paintings on the walls, Huies and Campbells and Dunkleys and Pottingers; they were like birthmarks on the skin of Drumblair. But with writers Edna admired the way they loved and hated, how they exaggerated as if to find the essence of things, as a sculptor would exaggerate perspective.

Week after week for years to come they would sit in the long, book-filled living room, drinking and smoking and sharing their work and discussing the work of others. One week someone brought Eliot's *Four Quartets*, and some in the group wept. Everyone thought Yeats worthy. Someone liked Edmund Spenser, others dismissed him as "balls." They discussed Joyce and the Irish writers, often comparing the ambiguities they must have felt about the English language with their own Jamaican response. At other times, out on the lawn, they would argue passionately about even the most trivial things, the indenting of a line, the placement of a comma, the laziness of using a semicolon; the use of dialect in local writing, should it be taught in schools? Was the prose of Dylan Thomas superior to his poetry?

"When is a poet a poet?" asked Edna.

They didn't know that for sure either.

"What is an amateur poet? When is one *not* amateur?"

"I think when one could publish a book. Say fifty poems."

"So if you had fifty poems and they were not published you would not be a poet? Or if you had fifty bits of foolishness and paid someone to print them you'd then be a poet?"

"Poetry isn't description," she told them after reading a black American anthology someone had sent her, in which she said a few good things were drowned in a sea of bathos. "It isn't argument, it isn't meaning well—it isn't respectable platitudes. Poetry is fire and air and water and earth . . ."

And so the evenings wore on as they discussed art, or politics and art, whether one served the other—was art a catalyst? Could art reflect politics without becoming doctrinal and strident? Could political thought reach into the hearts of people if not upon the blood-beat of art? How long would the opportunity to effect change last, and when would that window close? How long was the poet's green time?

And war and art made their way into their words. From Mike was heard:

The trees are peaceful here
The trees are still. Birds without bombs in the air
Curve as they will.

Who knows at what point the collection began? But like all things that came to pass through the influence of Drumblair's cosmos, a series of Jamaica's first national literary journals was germinating.

If Edna was also in transition, it was more in the way of something intangible, like smoke curling away, seeming less dense only because it is less present. As usual the unknown was lurking in her work, which was forever changing.

Late in the decade her studio had begun to spawn new beings more sinewy and lithe, their brown limbs smoothed. Tall trees with dancing branches, quickened with a flurry of chips, the bark of a tender tree, like the skin of water, a thing Edna had not known before—that under brighter light, water sweats and skin ripples.

Symmetrical faces without eyes, inscrutable as African masks, faces like flowers opening between the hands of leaves. *Youth* with high breasts and one swaggered hip; *Idyll*, two fine-stemmed figures choreographed in the dance of life, eyes locked in recognition of the promise of a relevant Eden, a challenge: "Two trees planted far apart," wrote George, a writer of more spirit than substance. *The Sawyers*, two men working the instrument back and forth, as though in continuing, older and sterner with each stroke, they were constantly exchanging the roles of duty and accomplishment.

Sometimes she modelled first in clay, which was the only medium fast enough to catch the suddenness of movement, the breathing changes of mind. With each throb of mother's worry at the back of her mind came a surge of relief and love and pride when she thought of Douglas and Michael out in the world and getting on, their letters radiant with youth and dreams. Norman's distraction of late—and his distance, as in his mind the dream of nationhood replaced the tedium of law—she sensed in each press of her thumb.

She modelled a new figure, his nearly emaciated frame making human form radical—it gave bones a language. It had the wiry energy of her young poets, who had become like extensions of her absent sons—ebullient defences, a sometimes sulking, puerile bewilderment. She loved this new figure's youth. She would look at him half-modelled on the stool, leaning forward on his elbows, his head thrown back as he exaggerated or gossiped—for this one just couldn't keep quiet—his large hands opened as though he were waiting to catch the sun's fiery ball.

When she was finished, it was too awkward to fire, and so she had to carve it all over again. It was Norman's favourite piece, and when he'd polished it and she saw the small lit face staring out unrelentingly above the powerful hands that opened as though in amazement or delight, she shrugged and thought, Okay, I can't do much about it now, and maybe we all have bumps in the road and crosses to bear, so we just punch someone in the nose and get on with life. So she called it *Tomorrow*.

By forty she knew that gods rise and gods fall; that they fade for a while and re-emerge. At forty, though Edna's legs were still firm as they clung to the sides of a mount, her inner thighs no longer completely rallied. Her breasts, not yet totally listless, pended less alert than before, and a small lip of wobble blurred the outline of her arms following each rap on her mallet.

And now, at forty, tomorrow had arrived with middle age, walked in with the casual certainty of someone keeping an appointment; years had been lived, full of their agonies and uncertainties, their mysteries. Edna's hair was now totally grey, the texture of its natural wave calmer, making her face seem softer, perhaps wiser. Her eyes, which had seemed aloof, sometimes glacial, now under grey hair seemed more participatory—more friendly—their substance mottled, a collection of moods and concessions. But with two resilient boughs on either side of her natural centre part, her defiance appeared resolute as that of a coconut tree against a high wind. And the same confidence was evident in the gouges of her sculpting tools, as though the bark of herself and her beings was all coming of age. At forty, a new rawness began to flounce straight out of the wood.

The texture of her work became looser as she became more certain about what she wanted to say. Though she would always be overly sensitive, shaken by even the mildest criticism of her work or people's opinions of her, when she went to work, she always let the chips have their way.

And though she made no move towards formal faith, and proclaimed herself agnostic to all who cared to listen (never daring to go so far as describing herself as an atheist, which would have been a declaration of war against omniscience, an admission that she wasn't ready to concede), she was returning to the themes of her father, needing at this halfway mark to rehitch her life to Harvey's universe, if not to his worldly home, her gait to the comfort and continuity of his stride. She spent her fortieth year finding Caribbean faces for his Biblical heroes.

She pulled her models from the landscape. If they were from Port Royal, she extracted them from their fishing nets or their boats, from the sea or the proximity of coconut trees. She saw them as timeless symbols of man's struggle with the world in which he lived, their frowns as old as Biblical men parting oceans or climbing mountains. The human condition as fluid as the sea, as connected as the hills.

Samson and the Boy, a sightless man sitting holding in his lap the child who would lead him to the temple. She captured them with charcoal from two figures gazing out to sea facing the blinding afternoon sun exploding from the water. I wondered why her Samson never brought the temple down, but tragedy always interested her more than triumph. She retrieved *The Dispossessed*, a man she watched strolling raggedly dressed and barefoot with his "baby-mother" and two children; he turned round to see a hunched old lady assisted with great difficulty by a cane, and he seemed to look from one fruitless alternative to another.

From her writer's group she stole the conflict and the passion, the sacrifice of creating, the endless human conundrum of the agony of *Cain* and the uncomplicated joy of *Abel*, and gave them Jamaican life, outlines so rough they were left more wood than feature, their forms as basic and arresting as charcoal on paper. And *In the Fiery Furnace* displayed the three figures of Shadrach, Meshach, and Abednego burning fiercely, unquenchably, and they were not consumed, perhaps just three old fishermen who sat by the side of the road with their catch in front of a small fire with a tall kerosene pan of boiling water—their spirits undefeated, their defiance representing yet another expression of freedom.

Father Forgive Them she may have seen late one afternoon in a young man standing with his hands shielding his eyes against a flaming twilight, as if to see farther and, not liking what he saw, staring in resignation at the day's reflection.

And at forty, Edna had a change of Piscean heart. She decided that the sea was only for the young and foolish. It came to her spontaneously on one of her escapes to the remnant coastal town of Port Royal, where sometimes she'd swim or just sit by her old friend the sea. One could not tell that across the harbour Kingston, diminished by towering mountains, seethed at the past and shouted ever louder about its future. Its spirit appeared to be no more than small trails of dissipating smoke from there.

Edna found it easy to forget she lived on an island when trapped in the lap of Kingston. But here in Port Royal was the familiar smell, brisk salt of the waking thought, of the energetic endeavour, morning salt of fishermen rising, salt so pure it corroded the damp, chewed away the feeble-hearted, dispelled the dankly insidious, ate things down to their root and preserved what was good.

Over the years the legend of Port Royal, like a decoy light, continued to attract the curious. In the twentieth century it was difficult to imagine that this small port had once held the fate of two mighty empires in its insubstantial grasp. It was once known as the wickedest city on earth, despite the active presence there of Anglicans, Roman Catholics, Presbyterians, Baptists, Quakers, and Jews. In an echo of Sodom's rebuke by the hand of God, the town was almost totally destroyed by the earthquake of 1692. Sand and water combined to create quicksand. Heavy vibration caused the ground of loosely packed sand to open, swallowing citizens whole and vomiting some of them back out again. As the earth gobbled down the main wharf and two entire streets complete with brick houses, the waves spat out ships from the harbour onto the rubble.

Over four thousand lives were lost, half of them immediately, half in the aftermath of injury and disease, though the figure may have included corpses hurled from the cemetery's earlier graves, washed out to sea on the retreating tidal wave, where others were later seen floating.

Two-thirds of Port Royal was reclaimed by the sea. A magnificent ruin, it had lain in state under the water until recently. A clock had stopped at seventeen minutes before noon. The locals claimed that when the waves were high, their movement caused the bell on the submerged clock tower to rock, and that if you listened carefully the bell could be heard pealing softly under the water.

History had punctuated the quiet town like noble features on an old face. By 1940 only a lonely grandeur remained of its ancient defence, Fort Charles, called Fort Cromwell when it was built in 1655 and renamed six years later. Horatio Nelson had arrived here in 1777, when he was only nineteen. The Royal Engineers' Archway, restored in 1853, marked the line where an earlier wall had enclosed the military headquarters. The solid jail and naval hospital appeared to have outlived their usefulness. Shaped like a cross, St. Peter's Church with its cut-stone walls and shingled roof stood in frozen, cautionary reproach, its churchyard laid out like a parable with the tombs of both the earthquake's victims and, with later dates, its survivors.

Its commercial power long since stolen by Kingston, the surviving twenty-five acres of Port Royal land, with its unassuming citizenry—like children of famous parents who alternately avoid or cash in on the notoriety of that fame—remained comforting reminders to Jamaica of the fragility of empire. Despite its infamous forebears, Port Royal was now the island's barefoot, dispossessed child.

From the tales of her youth, Edna had half expected to see the ancient city, its face a complex formation amidst the coral, in a clear mirror of water. But the water was dark and kept its secrets. Meanwhile the little town survived, as did other small Jamaican communities that eked out a living by soil or sea, patching a life together with thatch and scraps, odd bricks and stone, ragments and fragments, tin cans and advertisement plaques, sea grapes and coconut husks, in spaces either dusty or sandy, where animals were hungry but children always appeared sufficiently nourished and, to Edna's constant astonishment, emerged spotless from the rust and insufficiency of poverty, shining—cleanly polished with who knew what source of water—and tidied for school or church.

St. Ives or Port Royal—along the shore, the carcasses of canoes, cottonwood or guango, were hoisted high enough to bare proud hulls.

My grandmother once told me she knew a local boat-builder there who said that the first boat he ever built was just a toy for an old lady to give her grandchild. He got fifteen shillings, which he told Edna he needed so badly that he gave the boat to the lady before the paint dried. Edna shared with him how she too worked with wood, and cherished the memory of the story. Whenever she saw a fisherman's boat, she'd pat the small ribcage of hull as though it were the flank of a horse, and I have seen fishermen do that— maybe for luck.

Across the harbour, Edna knew, Kingston was teeming with its commerce and politicians. Above, the mountains dreamed on, their umbilical connection from this small town extending precariously upwards like a green wing of a butterfly, their thin mountain spines hunched like old dinosaurs marching towards oblivion.

Time, she decided, to make her way from the frivolous water's edge to the land's sterner, truer core—the years demanded, one state inevitably led to the next. Perhaps this was disingenuous, the truth a lot simpler. This liquid body knew her own so well, knew it stripped down to her modest swimsuit, which perhaps she doubted she should still wear; knew each intimate change from the hard muscle of youth whose powerful strokes cut through its core to each tendering wrinkle. Perhaps as a Piscean she saw her reflection more accurately through the passing years in this, her element. Instead of ebullient dives, nowadays she let herself in more quietly.

She realized that though she had lost the clench necessary for a gallop full tilt, she had the patience now—and the tenacity—to climb the slower, steeper hills. She would find a place in the mountains. And so the idea of Nomdmi was born.

Islands are self-sustaining worlds, microcosms of extremes found elsewhere stretched across the planet. Mountains are visionary places, and islanders are often multifaceted, complicated and surprisingly resourceful. Edna found her acre of land four thousand feet above sea level, beyond a small village called Guava Ridge, an hour's ride from the nearest mountain ranger's house but yet only a sweep of the hand from the sea beneath.

The hilltop land in the Blue Mountains was a rim perched over a south-facing valley, the view revealing the distant harbour in Port Royal's lap, though from there looking back at the Blue Mountains as a backdrop, the range would loom as haunting as memory. She moved from the sea to the mountains, and settled there as naturally and unobtrusively as an undiscovered spider's web.

From the westerly view Edna could see the sun reflecting on the harbour. Roads wound round mountains in gradual slopes, disorienting distance and truth. From this vantage point all things appeared related and close. It helped her to see more clearly the things that mattered. Yet with its distance the vision kept life mystical and supple.

Norman took on her project, and he designed a little two-room upstairs-downstairs house that he and a local carpenter constructed on weekends. As usual, Edna intuited and imagined what he then made real.

As the effects of the Second World War gathered momentum in Europe, its impact had created inevitable ripples that were felt in Jamaica with even more hardship. In Edna and all her generation it evoked memories of all those they had lost in the First. The year 1940 had been tough for the party, and for Norman, who came out with a socialist manifesto, opening himself up to scathing attack and further straining a relationship with his cousin Bustamante that would eventually break. Edna felt so many familiar pangs, the sadness, the worry, and out of these she found herself ending the year with *The Dead*, a sleeping youth with his head thrown back on one side, leaning away from a shrug of sleep on a sharply raised shoulder, his hand resting on his heart. He basked like the shipwrecked, undreaming but alive, unalive but dreaming, cavernous circles of bone beneath his closed eyes, the complacence of his mouth powerful without speech. The head lolled sideways in an exhausted rapture. She described it as a longing for peace. This work returned to the care and containment of the finer chips, and the passion of the full circle seemed to have ended a chapter in her life.

Meanwhile, Norman made furniture at Nomdmi on weekends—simple things—a shelf, a table. He loved to build. Sometimes he'd think he'd finished, but like Penelope waiting for Ulysses, undoing each day's work, he'd find yet more to be done. He brought up his wife's stands one by one from Drumblair, and a set of tools—chisels and her battered mallet. Edna's drawings started to reflect this place, at first no more than would a consciousness of shapes below the surface of water. But Norman knew that given time and tools and mass she would build her own universe here.

He was setting her on her path as she had set him free on his.

8

Garden of the Gods

Over the years a voice calls
Through the scent of flowers
Shrilling crickets
The hoot of an owl
And aching moonlight
The path to the house
Is black and silver
Shadows and moonlight
Over a thousand years . . .
A voice calls . . .
Through a veil of tears . . .
Is anyone there?
                    —Edna Manley

I HAVE DISCOVERED that not all stories begin at the beginning. Chronology can be confusing. Time is chronological but living seldom is. Fact is not always a way to truth.

For in that magic kingdom, I am sure it was my grandmother who roused those gods. Maybe they had been there, dreaming on through the mist of mountain forests, for centuries, but I cannot imagine them without her. *She* was their congregation. As though hers was that spark of faith whose connection started their creation—the firmament of Yahweh's six days or the moment of the Big Bang, that excruciating orgasm from which nothingness lurches to form matter. She the receiving eye, the moment of recognition that stirs the comatose to consciousness in a tiny island of Caribbean peaks.

Nomdmi was Edna's resistance; her refuge from the possibility that dreams took on flesh. A place too far away for visitors or people dropping in; a place withdrawn, what it always was, too locked in its nature to ever comprehend change. Even its name was derived from Mike Smith's misspelling on a no-admittance sign, consequently abandoned. The mountain people she met were darkly medieval, the mountains too steep, the earth that clung to its basic but tentative shale too undernourished, its creatures and foliage settled into enduring metaphors of an ancient kingdom. Here, she thought, she would always be imagining.

Edna sensed the base of her world shift as Norman moved into a leading role in the national movement. He became its world more than hers. Despite bursts of gregarious enthusiasm, she remained the loner she was, suspicious of movements: the party he founded; its executive, which plotted and planned; people streaming in for various meetings all day long and late into the night; the endless demands on time and resources and courage and commitment; the wide-openness of their life—even the car, their joyful means of escape, had a flag and a loudspeaker as, when there was enough gas available, he travelled around campaigning. Drumblair had become a movement. It was the headquarters, the beating heart to which warriors came to report and complain and reconcile and

decide, from which each left with a message and promise and itin-
erary and rescue and solution, the war room where the strategy for
each political battle was designed.

But then she would remember 1938, the massive meeting on
the last night of the National Strike, as people listened to Bustamante speak after his release from jail. No one remembered her
husband's efforts to secure that release or settle the strike—when it
was over, Norman left unnoticed by anyone in that fickle crowd.
But though she had her misgivings, how do you fight an island or
a birthright? And anyway, when it came to the national movement,
she knew you can't fight something whose truth, no matter how
personally inconvenient, you ultimately agree with.

It was Mardi's nature to live in the firmament that creates
rather than in what Mike Smith once called its "realisis," a term
coined by A.N. Whitehead which, in the sense Mike had used it,
probably meant the extending of the effects of an event's or person's influence as it ramifies outwards, but which I think she took
to mean the turning of ideas and imagination into something concrete and therefore finite. For a while, I believe she was content to
be just beside the process of national change, an unspecific figure
of inspiration, escaping to the mountains as soon as the cottage
was completed in 1940. I think these writers—friends of her sons,
who now surrounded her with their talent and fervour—had
become extensions of her grown and absent children, filling an
empty space and maybe providing proof that the seeds she and
Norman had scattered as parents had taken root.

In that ecstatic time, who knows what their truth was?

It still seems to me that all the things I found there, in those
withdrawn and dreaming hills, had come to pass inspired by her
passion. By the time I came into her life a decade later, Mardi had
already given this far place its own history. Nomdmi had become
a myth, a world of allegory. A perfect poem. Edna had spun her

cosmos before I came, to cast her spell on sun and moon, on dawn and sunfall; she had named the mountains as they rose and fell, evolved and weakened, the land as it woke and slept, so that they stood for eras or epic events, whether of glory or defeat, each a moment of truth, sculpted in her imagination, iconic as godhead. I grew up living that allegory and absorbing the magic she bestowed on every facet of that place, a magic that became its element. I knew its secret trails on all my walks, its plaintiff voice of solitaires and pines, its mist breathed in, its curtain of fog that locks us in and the world out. And so her lyrical carvings became for me a confirmation, like pictures for a child who searches for meaning in a favourite story.

Young as I was, I could not help but know something profound had happened here.

Edna's gods were born in 1941, and for eight years that sky with its furniture of mountains and its weather of moods would preoccupy her. She reigned over that verge like its high priestess. Here were the forests of fauns, naked and primal; arms open in unanswerable questions, the sky assembling its formations, a living creation.

Down the path from the house the carpenter built her a small, perfectly square studio out of the leftover shingles from Nomdmi, walls and a peaked roof, with shutters that opened out west and east propped up by a stick to let in the dusk and the dawn, and a double door latched in the middle at the front—Edna's need for symmetry. The floor was just a slab of roughest concrete in which the mason drew lines to suggest tiles. A hard surface just outside, where they had mixed the cement, provided a base on which to balance a large, square iron water drum with a tap. By the door she placed a flat iron shoe-scraper in the looped shape of a fish—which

Ivan, a local farmer, thought appropriate as the sign of the early
Christians, but which Mardi probably regarded as Piscean—with
which to remove the claylike mountain mud before entering. She
called the studio Minimus, which became known as Mini.

There atop her mountain, far away from all the nationalist talk
about the birth of Jamaica, Edna knew that this land had been born
long ago, before anyone had come, before the island had got its
Aztec or Spanish name, before the wild frangipani had got its
French one. Up here was land-self, not defiantly, just uninterrupt-
edly. Nothing in these hills had been invented or procured. Nothing had been won or lost. From this distance, consciously creating
nationhood must have seemed futile. Things would evolve by
themselves. After an initial joyous surge, surely everything would
just be politics? To which her husband would probably give his
practical reply: You can't give birth and stop. Someone's got to bring
up the baby.

Looking up from mountains you see only sky, so Edna with
her relentless curiosity began to consider the heavens. What are
the themes that draw all men to myths and gods; the Celts to
Epona; the Jamaicans to Pocomania, obeah, Jesus, or Jah; the
Haitians to voodoo; the Muslims to Muhammad; the Jews to
Yahweh; the Chinese to Buddha; the Hindus to recognition of self
as part of atman? Is the personality of a god that of the people who
worship? What is it that we all begin by knowing enough to
believe?

Mardi would come for weeks on end. She would ride up the
steep path that threaded the mountain, seated firmly on Doris the
mule, whose belly was almost as wide as the path, the valleys and
an occasional breakaway plummeting down. She brought the provisions that Len, the unflinching giant said to have water in—or
was it on?—his brain, packed onto a tightly wrapped cloth cotta on
his head and in the hampers on a donkey. He held onto the donkey's

tail as it fought the incline to trot gallantly, following the mule carrying Edna. Her only conversation with Norman was the exchange of telegrams carried down by Len—"Yes'm" as he received a carving or an envelope in his massive hands for transport with equally uncomprehending stoicism—to the postmistress for trans- mittal, the reply carried back up by some postal porter, or the let- ters they posted to each other that, because they involved the same mountain route, took nearly a fortnight to arrive.

"*I walked through the pine wood at daybreak—there is nothing in the world as timeless and still as a pine forest—even a whisper seems to shatter the silence*," she wrote to him as, more and more, she withdrew to the magic of this world. "*At a certain level the mind knows everything—we erect block- ades because mankind cannot bear too much reality—*

"*Me and my alter ego moved thro' the trees to a wider reality—*"

"*They say neurotic women have* something. *I only hope so!*"

She was safe from the opinion of others here, and could play mischievously with her own. Mountains don't give a damn. Charg- ing across the skyline were the arched necks of unharnessed peaks on the first day of the world. Here she was given a glimpse of the raw power of creation, rising vertebra by vertebra—a new morn- ing, a new world, a new faith. So she picked up charcoal and started to draw; she was breaking them in the way only she could.

Her company during the day was Janie, a *joyous* mountain woman who laughed at anything Mardi said, and wore bright scarves, never wore shoes, and cooked for her; and Len and Clin- ton or Ivan, mountain farmers whose plots of land she would never see but who would bring offerings of their produce, or tether a cow or a goat to graze, and walk down to the village to fetch condensed milk or slabs of cheese and butter or several-day-old Jamaican Hard-Dough bread for her.

Some came to cut the grass or tend the coffee trees or the gar- den. They would take long breaks sitting under a tree to light up a small chillum pipe stuffed with ganja, staring far away, sightlessly inhaling—*tuf-tuf-tuft*—the seeds spitting and snapping as if summoned to life, and exhaling again—*pfwooo-o-o*—tongue and lips all tensed to sense and caress the body of holy smoke as it left; the distance in their eyes somehow within. Edna smelled the sweet yet acrid smoke, which seemed to come soaked in clothes and sweat, a sort of funny humanness it had taken on through the geography of their hearts and minds and finally their lungs. Their sacred weed kept them outside the present and, watching them so peaceful, Edna was left wondering what they cared of notions of nationhood—was it really tomorrow that enticed them with its hope, or was theirs a longing for their history?

She knew she with her small mortal hungers was only an interruption.

"What do you think, Miss Janie?" she would muse.

And Janie would just hold her hips and bend over with laughing.

As though man's only way to the gods is through the human image, her first drawing was a young male nude. He is a frail, nervy figure standing against a horizon of stacked hills and clouds, two rays of light beaming down from his head, his unusually long hands open expectantly at his sides. It was the beginning of her cosmos. She called the drawing *Before Thought*. Then *The Dark Horse*, night like a stylized black Chinese ceramic stallion, one eye ferociously intent, forelegs outstretched over the globe, and the nude figure now sideways as though trying to hold up the last of the sky, knowing he would be left with his yawning, empty arms.

Edna drew and she carved, stopping to shake her head in agreement and disagreement with herself, all the time listening to an inner meter peculiar to her that made sense of what she saw. She was a mote of busyness in this wildness of majestic indifference. She kept marking this record to keep herself real.

She combined her two themes together in mahogany, the unmistakable head of the original figures now gazing up between the familiar hands cradling the faces of two horses looking away from each other, to either side, as though each moment in universe-time is a balancing act between decisions. She called it *The Forerunner*.

The sun rose and flew through the sky and drowned in the distant harbour beyond the Watsonia lilies, night after night. Conducting the symphony, Edna was perched on her long thin feet at the edge of the mountains, facing this grand celestial orchestra, whatever audience there was an unseen darkness behind her. She became its metronome keeping time.

Jamaicans must have their universe, she decided, so Edna began to define it. We can know only what we recognize. The land must be made human. The dying sun is a god with the gold-drenched face of an old man reflecting his day of life; she carved a mahogany orb of his sinking face in *The Sun Goes Down*.

The theme of fathers and sons began with *New World, Old World*, two faces with marked resemblance to each other and the same expression, one older and settled, with his dimmed globes and a dreaminess of reflection, the younger one brighter, leaner, a new world jauntily risen and balanced, an impertinence of hope upon his father's tired shoulders.

There is always a moment when they touch, the new and the old, at dawn and twilight, in memories of light or night; she created that moment on a horizon of waves out of mahogany, *The Generations*, a face weary but fulfilled, glowing and weighted down towards the water by time, his son staunchly resolute in his wake behind him, completing a visual circle.

And standing back to look at her children in the evenings, these new static lives that would never outgrow her, moments engraved—the light of the full moon arriving through the windows blindingly exotic, vivid and intangible as mercury, the night making

Nomdmi a place that you couldn't capture in colour, a world of black and white where what is must be, and cannot be taken back—she supposed this was the world of gods.

So came the woman of her universe. A serene, benignly ecstatic, implacable *Moon* with her hair drifting like a wisp of mahogany cloud.

Some nights Edna would sleep in the studio to wake with the light peeping in through the shingles like children who wished to be let in. She would rise and scrape open the wooden door of slanting planks, and decibels of light would lift, curl, and spread from the mane of morning. *That* was when she saw him. The golden horse of dawn. He was so pale that at first it was opaque, a pristine hymen one dared not penetrate. Though on unsteady new legs, he shone with inevitability. It was the forerunner, a leaner, wilder horse than Epona, a tight, wilful animal who had hidden here in the mountains from the dawn of time; a cunning, elusive fugitive who offered no allegiance to Arawaks or Tainos, Spanish or British, Africans or Indians. A creature with no ethnicity, no one's legend. And here was Edna to catch and tame it, break it and claim it for her cosmos.

In mountains the eternal cycle is always on view; while the smaller, ancient hills reminisce, the younger ones conference higher up. So she painted the horse of the morning, and also the horse of the night.

Then Edna received the gift of a huge log of Guatemalan redwood from her art school friend, Gherke, in which she placed Epona on record, a Jamaican horse of the mind's imagining, *Horse of the Morning*, a young country's claim to name and place, a tropical Rhiannon lunging up the sky, raging light of birth, tumult of dawning. An island's hope.

In 1943—the same year she said she found the horse of the world's first dawn, the horse whose plinth I climbed throughout childhood to bestride and embrace it—in Kingston the first issue of Jamaica's literary journal, *Focus*, was printed. Edited by Edna, it was the inevitable conclusion of years of work and thought and meeting by the new writers at Drumblair.

Through Edna's own wonderment, she had in many ways inspired the connection between the landscape and these ardent young Jamaicans. Already compiling a second issue of *Focus*, the writers looked at their work in print and thought of themselves in a new way.

The first collection's foreword was written by Edna: "*Great and irrevocable changes have swept this land of ours in the last few years and out of these changes a new art is springing . . . Historically art gives a picture of contemporary life, philosophically it contains within it the germ of the future.*"

Her work wasn't simply to inspire the writers to write. The production of the book was in itself an uphill task. In order to produce the weekly *Public Opinion*, Fair-C had installed a printing press in Kingston at Edelweiss Park. There was no money for publication abroad, and until now there had been few facilities at home. A liberal voice, *Public Opinion*—owned and managed by Fair-C—not only played an invaluable role in the gradual emergence of a nation, but exposed poems and stories to the reading public, helping to make *Focus* possible. No other printer in Jamaica would have taken this job on trust, knowing sales might not yield enough to cover the costs. The production became like a family affair. The writers did their own proofreading and laid out their own design, to keep down costs. The paper was the most inexpensive available, and the binding quite crude. Not many issues were sold of this physically modest effort, but its profit could not be calculated in pounds.

Focus was a single spark, its words the beginning of a tradition of Jamaican literature, and it joined the sparks of the fine arts movement and local drama groups, and the publications of the Eastern Caribbean—Bim, an earlier journal in Barbados, and even earlier, Trinidad's The Beacon, and the later Kyk-Over-Al in Guyana. Edna realized that she was witnessing change that would be as telling as anything politically motivated. In another generation schoolchildren would be able to draw their own images, knowing that those images were their truth, as were their words and one day their music, and that this was worth putting down on paper whether by words, pictures, or musical notes.

When the reviews came in, many were negative and reflected the view that these would-be writers were upstarts to believe they could branch off, taking English with them and doing as they wished with it. But some were filled with pride and optimism, recognizing the worth of both the venture and much of the work.

Despite her mountain studio, Edna had remained devoted to her task as editor, which often required travelling up and down between Drumblair and Nomdmi as though between husband and lover. Sometimes she allowed the writers to hold meetings at Nomdmi, and they would come sweating up the hill, unused to such walking, and she would feed them and give them stiff gins; then in the afternoon mountain cool she would offer them hot toddies and ponchos to warm them up again. They were always getting excitable or drunk or morose, which Edna put down to the high altitude, and once one of them arrived with an illicit lover, with whom he fell into the hydrangeas below as the verandah rail collapsed. Mardi decided that this was a sign; he lost the lover, but Mardi thought it more to the point that, in her opinion, he never wrote a good line again.

Perhaps, as Pardi said, they were all in love with her—with her obvious yet charming coquettishness when she was happy or inspired, tossing her wayward bob of grey waves and spinning her wide cotton skirts or wrinkling her long, thin, sensitive nose at them, saying things they had never heard before in her soft-spoken, breathy voice—"I saw the horse of the morning today"—as casually as if what she said was normal or even possible; inventing gods and playing with concepts till one believed it was she who had invented freedom; or just believing in each of them so. Their passions all mixed in with hers, of course they were in love with her.

Over time, many of Mike's and George's poems came to be viewed as ardent love letters for Edna, as mentor or mistress or goddess. Maybe they were. Maybe love was the more poignant and evocative for expressing an unrealizable yearning. It is difficult to understand, in the jaded heart of these days, the spirit and passion that fuelled that time, how near to the flame they flew. Islanders tend to make facile and often fierce judgments, as though there is not space enough for margins and nuance and areas of grey. But she had such ardour. It was infectious. She flirted with plants to entice them to grow, with dogs to train them, with horses—not cows or cats. She flirted with nurses in hospitals. She flirted with her sons. She flirted even with me. It was her joy of living and knowing. She was capable of enthusiasms so frantic that those of us less capable of raw, jugular emotion could relate to them only in the equivalence of romance.

Once it was time to leave, Edna would send them off down the hill with flashlights or small storm lanterns, and watch them weaving round the precarious bends, small suns unable to dispel the wider dark or compete with a universe of stars and blinking peeny wallies, their voices receding gradually till once again she could hear only the tree frogs with their shrill, uninterrupted, whistling chatter.

When she was alone again, perhaps the memory of her visitors remained standing in front of her and arguing, each with the other, George reading one of his poems and stopping all the time, his hands gaping open like jaws in astonishment, in question after question: Do you like this, Do you like that? And smoke from Mike's pipe seething heavily into the cautious mist, Roger arguing till nature called him away and later George found him sound asleep, slumped on the lavatory seat in the outhouse, and the sky in turmoil behind them throwing up its hands in twilight.

Nomdmi is in the passion of these early literary pages.

"*I hold the splendid daylight in my hands*," wrote George.

"*None but the brave shall see the horses of the morning*," wrote Marjorie Foster-Davis, an Englishwoman who'd married a Jamaican and thrown her lot in with this island and this group after Marjorie had seen Mardi's mysterious horse and been inspired by it to write a poem with this unforgettable line.

"*The wind breathes a mellow oboe in my ear*," from Mike, (pen name now M.G. Smith), the motherless child whose wound still evoked its sad enchantment for Edna. "*I have come away with a deep longing for peace in the green hills . . .*"

"*It takes a mighty fire / To create a great people*," from Dossie Carberry.

Today those voices that once rallied like echoes through Nomdmi's world of valleys and hills are still being heard from the extravagant spiritual hedonism of that time. They had been set free and, like Mike's birds, could "*curve as they will.*"

Free of the past, free even of her—just free.

Maybe, from the moment their words hardened in print with their stories and poems, she knew that an essential truth was safe. Like her children, they would move on from there, down their own imaginations.

In 1944, as the Second World War raged in Europe, Edna joined
Norman for widespread campaigning for his first election. Night
after night they set off, either in the car with Vivian the driver, a
five-foot retired boxer known as St. Andrew Pup, or in their larger
buggy, when rationed gas supplies ran out. Once, Norman rode so
hard on the way home that he turned up at Drumblair with only
the front seat and the front two wheels. Sometimes late at night,
after the meetings, they'd get back to Drumblair and saddle the
horses, including Norman's old horse Tim—now used as a pack
horse, but still holding the record to Blue Mountain Peak. They'd
send him on ahead with the provisions to set the pace, and ride
on up to Nomdmi. If the road was too dark, Norman would tie a
white handkerchief on his horse's tail for Edna to follow. What
did they care if they were tired? For Edna and Norman the nights,
especially the clear ones, held such romance and magic:

> . . . the fireflies, millions of them—peeny wallies—and in a wave
> all their lights would go on together and light up the track . . . and
> in a wave all would go out and it would be jet black darkness
> again. No one who hasn't seen this phenomenon could conceiv-
> ably imagine—it would start from somewhere and follow like a
> wind across the hillside—a golden glory

Life went on, war or no war. The campaign continued, and
they felt that what they were trying to do was of great value to
their small world. But Norman lost the election; he lost it to someone Edna considered no more than an unworthy charlatan.

Neither Douglas nor Michael was fighting in this war. Despite
that, Norman and Edna did not escape personally unscathed. On
October 7, 1944, the Daily Gleaner reported:

Corporal Frank Fox Killed in Action

News has been received that Corporal Frank Fox, son of Mr and Mrs James Fox of England, only brother of Mr Wilfred Fox of Kingston, and adopted son of Mr and Mrs NW Manley, was killed in action in Italy on July 22. Mr Fox joined the RAF before the war but was unable to qualify for flying owing to defective health. He went to France with the first overseas campaign and escaped when the British withdrew from a port a little below Dunkirk. Later he was sent to Africa with the Eighth Army and went through the whole African campaign. When this was over he went to Italy, where he met his death. Frank Fox was a brave and modest man, and his death is terribly felt by those who loved him.

All I ever knew of him was a soft sigh that Mardi breathed years later whenever his name was mentioned.

She wrote to her sons, "We are moments in time," and again left this world behind. She returned to her universe, to a mythical woman who reigned over the heavens at night.

She'd sleep under the pines and watch the moon seducing the tired old world into dancing with her. Maybe that was just how one coped, living with gods on their mountains. Busy hills taking their little journeys, and suns rising till they became fathers, and fathers setting till they drowned, sons again rising to be suns. And in between the father and the son the moon puts on her slippers, the world now all to herself, picks up the night-lamp, and goes to the library for a book—". . . she will read one book every night till the end of the world, like my brother Leslie," she once told me. There is music where the men have gone, wild music lifting its notes, floating through air and winding round corners, stars that bark at the dark. She delivered an ethereal *New Moon*, the full-length figure of a young woman, darkly juniper-cedar shining like rippled

water—a film of skin engrossed over boiling milk—her hands
extended straight down at her sides, flipped up backwards at the
wrists in contradiction, her hair rising and steaming behind her
like a shadow tiptoeing across the sky.

I can imagine nights that lie in the lap of pines on the bedding
of brown needles, somewhere George's poem *"The night is naked and
wears no clothes,"* and Mike and her holding onto the remnants of a
conversation in numerous letters that wind in and out of literature
and beauty and heartbreak:

> *And now, Moon, soundless swear to me*
> *Hope is no phantom.*

And deeper than all these, like the mind's backdrop, Norman,
the heart's rhythm Norman, physically often far away now, somehow taken from her by a world of boltlike institutional bits of
buildable things; but still her Norman.

In 1947 the second *Focus* was published. Edna's voice as editor seems
almost startled, slightly stilted, as she blinks at reality:

> *Five years ago when the first Focus was published, we had hoped to
> make it a yearly event. But the war and the difficulty of getting paper,
> coupled with the fact that so many of our writers had gone away,
> made it impossible . . . There are signs people are becoming more con-
> scious that it is essential that we should produce books of our own . . .
> There is a move to have history taught in our Jamaican schools, along-
> side of it there should also be a move to have Jamaican literature . . .
> The theatre movement is urgently calling for Jamaican plays . . .*

RIGHT: Edna

BELOW: Norman and
Edna at Drumblair

Ellie and Harvey Swithenbank, Edna's parents

Douglas and Michael, Edna's sons

ABOVE: Rose and Mardi with oil painter Albert Huie in the background

LEFT: Roy Manley, Norman's younger brother

BOTTOM LEFT: Mike Smith

BOTTOM RIGHT: Mardi and me

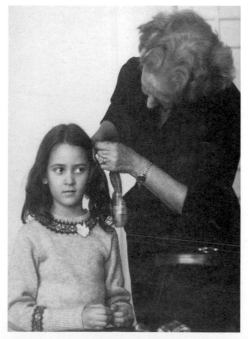

LEFT: Nomdmi

RIGHT: Mardi on horseback at Drumblair

Mini—Mardi's studio

ABOVE: *Norman* (plaster), 1924

LEFT: *Eve* (wood), 1929

ABOVE: *Negro Aroused*, 1935

RIGHT: *Pocomania* (stone), 1936

RIGHT: *Horse of the Morning*
(wood), 1943

BELOW: *Strike* (bronze cast),
1938

RIGHT: *Growth* (wood), 1958

BELOW: *Crucifix* (wood), 1951

ABOVE: *Bogle* (back), 1965
PHOTO BY GLEANER COMPANY

LEFT: *Bogle* (front), 1965
PHOTO BY GLEANER COMPANY

ABOVE: *Grief of Mary* (wood), 1968

LEFT: *Angel* (wood), 1970
PHOTO BY MARIA LA YACONA

LEFT: *The Voice* (ciment fondue), 1980

BELOW: *Rainbow Serpent* (fiberglass), 1975
PHOTO BY GLEANER COMPANY

ABOVE: *Journey* (wood), 1974
PHOTO BY AMADOR PACKER

RIGHT: *Ancestor* (bronze casts), 1978
PHOTO BY GARTH MORGAN, JIS

RIGHT: *Jacob and the Angel* (clay model for bronze cast), 1982
PHOTO BY EASTON LEE

BELOW: *Ghetto Mother* (ciment fondue), 1981

ABOVE: Edna with *Goat*
(painted plaster), 1984

RIGHT: Edna at a party, with
Birth (acrylic on canvas) in
the background, 1986

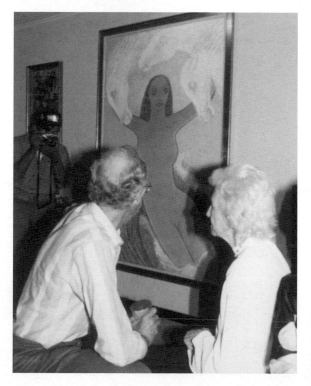

Edna, circa 1980

By the time this was written, Edna considered the project well on its way and, even without her, inevitable. That same year came more carvings—*The Announcer*, a young male face with his palms outstretched like enormous ears on either side. His lips are sealed and yet he comes to announce, the voice of tomorrow, the voice of all years to come, a face between hands balanced as if gymnastically. And the face and wavy hair and the huge ears are, to me, unmistakably my father, Michael.

She carved *The Land*, strong and enduring, gleaming, wrought of the finest of chips, a woman leaning over the smaller, shrinking hills, the plains and the coast, the harbour, perusing the horizon with a hand between her breasts counting her heartbeats, aging by sorrows. The morning and the night, stallions and men, Edna created male, but the moon and the land, reflected and nurturing, she always created female.

Last to be created from this fecund exuberance were *Night* and then a final morning, *The Rising Sun*. *Night*, serene torso of a man whom the moon cannot dispel or affright. *The Rising Sun*, now strong and dominant, a man, her Norman raising his hands to the heavens, basking in light; it echoed an older figure, as if *Before Thought*—a figure that reaches like a child to be lifted up, or for the sleeves of a garment through which to thread its arms—now returned with muscle and elegance, self-reliance and courage.

Her cosmos was coming to a close. She had drawn and carved every aspect of it, from morning till night, in all lights and at all times and through all meanings, drained it of living for herself. It seemed fitting that, before she left, she should carve a final sun rising. She lifted him from her soul and mind and put him back at a distance to guard the mountain ridge, a figure standing tall, his hands held high as though they were conductors of light, left there balanced aloft as a final statement, the possibility of an illumined world.

As though in a ritual washing of hands, Mardi then sold the house to Cecily Howland, one of the *Focus* writers. It is said they needed the money, for Pardi was always financing the PNP and he was broke again. That was probably true. But like Drumblair, after a couple of years, as though the time away had exorcised its ghosts, Nomdmi was repurchased and returned to us.

Her time or mine, the night still lies in the lap of those pines on the bedding of their own brown needles. We are intoxicated by the wafting smell from the bodies of the trees, and the powerful, capable smell of the kerosene in Pardi's lamp. Pardi is a footpath farther away, behind the house among the apple trees, building something; I hear the ringing of his hammer. I hear the tap tap-tapping of her mallet and Mardi is still a spirit, like a sky of stars that can't be counted. She could arrange them any way she liked and it would be another universe tomorrow. And the point seems to me that she invented a universe because she believed she could, and because she thought every person had a right to their own. But try to explain that and it's like explaining a sky full of questions without having any answers. But Pardi is inside my head providing answers, hammering in those nails, making something certain for tomorrow, when Mardi's moon has replaced her lover or her bookmark and gone back to bed.

That was the point of them—he needed nails and she didn't.

The great cycle of sunrise and sunset remains the cycle of generations in the universal comedy of gods and man; a father looks down and his son turns away, fingers touching for a moment longer where the light flashes green before night, or blushes pink before dawn, and then one or the other is gone again. It's in the wood, *Generations*, the faces of Norman and Michael departing or Douglas returning, older and lined and defined, someone stronger than his youth, the theme of renewal, a thousand suns rising, a thousand suns setting over ten thousand years, three hundred and sixty-five thousand times, and every one different.

Sons were born, sons grew, sons went away, but she would remain pale and used, with the wide spacious face and the chips as smooth as the skin of the fragile moon-echo woman who borrows light from the sun, each night a new story.

"Oh blue silver dusk of lovers / How strangely my old heart grieves," wrote Mike from England in 1944.

"Let my dreams hang intact around my tree . . . / Spread thus my dreams . . ." wrote George from New York.

Our diaspora had begun.

And Mardi made peace with her spirit at home in her own words:

I wake from a strange
Enigmatic glance
Steel like and piercing
Through the haze of centuries
And a wild improbable return . . .

Facing a world of destruction
The endless phoenix
Rises on sinewy wings
From ash and fire . . .

Time was a river that, having flowed through her, would continue beyond. This world was certain, the one she had created out of wood. The need for a sterner approach.

At the end of this bedlam I arrived. Is it any wonder, then, that I am hopelessly sentimental?

9

Crucifix

Oh, isn't the whole problem of growth a perpetual struggle between realization and responsibility? How much of you is your own to reserve to yourself, how much must you control and discipline and how much leave free, and finally how much must you yield to the demand of something whose demands must perforce be inexhaustible?
—Edna Manley: The Diaries

I ARRIVED IN JAMAICA during the carving of Mardi's *Crucifix*. I hope this was merely coincidence.

The parallel roads of my grandparents seemed merged to me, fused into what I would always know as landmass. Though at fifty-seven and fifty they still pursued their own purposes, their marriage had settled into a lower gear of love and truce, and the inclusion of grandchildren was probably an exhausted gesture from two restless people reconciled, with some degree of contentment but also moments of uncertainty, to the fact that the remainder of the journey, however long, would be spent together.

Flown over the unknowable Atlantic, I came to safe haven but was separated from a previous world; from my father for two years, and from my mother for the rest of my childhood. As a child I sometimes had a sense of my emotional life as a drowning; I knew instinctively that in order to survive, I had to have the skill and the strength to swim.

It was early in 1950 and I landed at the old Palisados Airport. Now Norman Manley Airport, a well-meant but insufficient and confusing modern building that, in a strange reflection of the Middle Passage, separates families before the opportunity for traditional moments of emotional greeting or departure, it was then a simple grey wooden building rather like a barracks. Families huddled together to say their farewells, and children lined the fences around the tarmac to wave at the planes and sometimes their families as they departed or returned home.

I am told I wouldn't stop crying, probably overtired after two days' travelling. I was reminded only recently of what I had long forgot, that I was accompanied by my older half-sister, Anita; little girls of seven and two. She would stay only a brief time in Jamaica, returning alone to our mother, probably the reason I didn't remember. The BOAC propeller plane had been delayed with engine trouble for twenty-four hours in Iceland, where the local newspaper had done a feature on us, one my family never read because no one we knew spoke Icelandic. But then, the newspaper clipping was no stranger to us than was this new place, and suddenly being surrounded by extrovert Jamaican noise instead of clipped British humdrum, and the pillowing heat as I tumbled through an entirely new birth passage to be met by this unfamiliar welcoming grandparental presence.

I can and cannot remember my arrival, and my grandmother's story of me in the car on the way from the airport, pulling away from her grasp to sit on my grandfather's lap, below the steering wheel. Mardi said I was looking at goats that she pointed out at the side of the road, where they stopped the car to distract me. "Saved by the goats!" she'd say. I don't remember the goats, but I would become part of a uniquely exciting and often stormy life I embraced with beloved grandparents, whom I christened Pardi and Mardi, mixing that experience in with many subsequent visits when I was taken to play at the edge of the harbour. They would park the car in one of several square concrete inlets with low walls and short white pillars, like children's stools set intermittently at the side of the road, or take me to swim on the rough side of the long Palisados peninsula. It is a road that has special significance for Jamaica, leading both to our history in the old town of Port Royal, and to the harbour and airport, which signal the terms of our future of trade, tourism, and modern re-diaspora.

Crucifix was my grandmother's first publicly commissioned work, ordered by the Anglican All Saints' Church in Kingston. This expression of confidence from the Anglicans was a challenge she could not fail. Despite the news of Edna's success in England, at times her work had been ridiculed at home by most of the British expatriate elite and their Jamaican middle-class imitators, who resented its reflection of the Negro form; the final affront to Jamaica's middle-classes and their sensibilities came from *Focus*. It now appeared written in the King's English, but spoke about Jamaica not in the fashion of a travelogue but audaciously, with a uniquely Jamaican viewpoint.

It's not strange, therefore, that an animal, not a human figure, had finally persuaded Edna's doubters. Along with many of her Dying God series of drawings and sculptures she created at Nomdmi, she had exhibited *Horse of the Morning*. The most hardened critics of her work had been wooed by this majestic carving. Men, women, children, the young, the old, had paused to circle it shyly, and had invariably ended up rubbing the forelock or mane, patting the wood with unexpected familiarity, staring at the far-away eyes and pondering the long, enigmatic face. The critics had hailed it as a masterpiece. I think it was with this horse that she conquered the Jamaican heart.

The commission signalled that she had "arrived" locally, but only at one level. Few working-class Jamaicans had ever seen her work, and when they did they stared at it and stared at her in wonder. They had never seen Jamaican themes in landmarks of art anywhere. Edna hoped that when her Christ was placed in the church, Jamaicans of every walk of life in this large congregation would have access to it.

The demands of public life had been taking a toll on her work, and Edna by now had fled her wooden studio at the edge of the grass-piece at Drumblair to set one up in an immense room at the new University of the West Indies Mona campus, which lay in the lap of Kingston's foothills, the reassuring Blue Mountains rising behind.

She needed this place to work; to dream and to be alone. For a couple of hours a day she escaped Drumblair and what had become a life of interruptions.

All things converge in islands—history, opinions, politics, faiths, bits of fragmented family. Drumblair, my new home, had become a watershed for many things flowing down from the past, taking redirection for the future. The house was besieged from dawn till late at night—people planning election campaigns, striking union-ists coming for meetings, the stream of the needy from Pardi's con-stituency and the nearby town of Four Roads, whose daily visits crowded our circular driveway; a daily queue snaking up from the front gate, despite the prescribed day set aside by Mardi for that purpose, looking for jobs or food or a doctor for a sick child or sick mother or whatever they needed, and they all needed something so desperately that she could never turn them away—the official and political meetings at home, the social visitors to be entertained, and now a grandchild.

Mardi christened the new studio with its view of the mountains by doing a serene carving—*Hills of Papine*—a mother and sleeping child, describing them as the mother of all men and the child of all women. Leaving me safely behind in the mornings with my appointed guardian, the treasured housekeeper Miss Boyd, she was grappling with the concept of Christ, one that must have seemed like her nemesis all these years since her father had abandoned this world for what he considered Christ's service.

Mardi at fifty must have been nearing where I was in life when I started this book, light moving westwards, beginning to be able to see outcome and meaning, the strands of many years collecting and combining, flowing into denouement for better or worse. Now able to count the last bends in the road, the journey no longer seeming endless nor the outcome completely mysterious. And with this creeps in a weary sentimentality which embraces the opportunity of playing life more softly, more vulnerably. I was her motherhood's second chance.

Norman had faced his initial defeat at the polls in 1944 with characteristic silence, an unapproachable introversion that he reserved for life's disappointments, but his political work moved steadily on. Edna had expressed her hurt with habitual defensiveness, a flinching sensitivity more obvious in her than in him. Although Norman would win his seat in 1949, Edna—who was always given to what my uncle called "high drama," and who to some extent enjoyed orchestrating the form and shape of the relationships around her—gave voice to her resentment over the initial result in such a personal, compelling, and continuing way that despite her letters to her sons, which speak optimistically of his constituency victory, to this day I feel her disappointment as my own. I remember this as my earliest impression of family—my

noble, wounded grandfather, and Mardi and me charged with the
job of protecting him, bringing him back from some lurking abyss,
keeping his spirits up and making life worthwhile for him.

Mardi's altruism, rooted partly I suspect in guilt for what she
knew to be her own wayward spirit, was in full swing. My arrival
as a casualty of my parents' marriage gave her another opportunity
to administer to a victim—this one far more willing than my grandfather—lavishing on me her inexhaustible reserves of sympathy and
goodwill. Maybe as she replayed the role of nurturer and mother,
she started looking back, the way we do when we are no longer
as greedy as when we can look only forward, being reminded of
her own childhood, her need for attention and recognition. Or perhaps someone as superstitious and omen-oriented as she was
would feel compelled by the coincidence of my birth, like hers, in
Cornwall (she had long forgotten that hers was actually in Dorset,
since facts, as I have said, were bothersome things, often inter-
changeable for her).

By now my grandmother's life was fully invested in Jamaica
and her family; she had gradually made a name as a sculptor, finding a voice unique to a landscape that had difficulty defining its
own. Though no longer teaching, she became an inspiration to
many young artists and helped them find their materials and their
way. She was a constant presence at art shows, which became more
frequent, and her name was readily associated with the kindling
world of Jamaican literature and art. Norman was deeply involved
in national politics, held a seat in the colonial legislative council,
though his party had still not yet won a national election. Both
sons were living in England, so I think my presence was a welcome
distraction in their lives, to reawaken the dormant back bedrooms
of Drumblair.

Edna had come of age under the influence of Sigmund Freud; she
laid all things emotional and spiritual at the feet of early experience

and, like the Jesuits, believed that by seven we were basically who we would be—I often heard her joke that in any case children weren't human till then. Childhood trauma was high on her list of personality shapers, but character could overcome any of this. Unlike physical characteristics (she always checked for a telltale "cubbyhole" at the back of the neck of anyone bearing the Shearer gene common to herself and Pardi), she appeared to feel that one's behaviour had no basis in genetics, and that parental "understanding" (which demanded that she come up with excuses and explanations for every misdeed) worked far better than parental discipline.

In other words, although not indulged materially, the young in her care were spoiled rotten. After what she considered her mistakes with Douglas, she reverted to type, becoming as defiantly original and creative at parenting as she had always been with everything else but food, which remained simple and bland and British in our house.

The result of this was that everything I did as a brat was blamed on the loss of my mother. Yet I have no recollection of losing her at all. I am fairly certain that despite my initial shock and subsequent inner processing of my disruption, no sadness motivated my demands, my rants, or self-will. I suspect that my grandmother's sympathetic explanations only facilitated this behaviour.

I was totally secure of my place in my new home, where I more or less reigned supreme. Mardi assured me that Pardi and she had adopted me, a detail my father disputed angrily whenever I brought it up. Whether it was true or not, I believed in the sentiment behind it.

As a child of two and a half waking up in Jamaica that first morning sometime early in 1950, I had lost life as I knew it—a country, a mother and father and walks with them in a big black pram in Hyde Park, my uncle, Douglas, and my aunt, Carmen, a French Grandmother Kamellard who smoked a pipe, and, in a short while, Anita, who would return to England; and West Indian students who with my father spent Sundays planning their return home to end British colonialism and establish Caribbean federation, while spin-bowling me in my parents' garden as Valentine or Ramadhin would during test match season, when the West Indies played at Lord's, as I shrieked delightedly from one to the other, my mother shrieking as well but in terror lest I fall.

By the same journey I gained a whole new life, passing from colonizer to colony—Jamaica, my grandparents and great-aunts, cricket piped over the big Rediffusion network box, and a world that I would learn to view in rare and sometimes wonderful ways, not always historically and politically, as Pardi did, but more often emotionally and artistically, as did my grandmother.

My first memories of Mardi are sporadic. Not that she comes and goes, but like all childhood memories they seem to emerge in patches, like clumps of grass around a tree, or the feet of animals in a child's picture. She was always moving fast in beelines between meetings, visits, duties, and her studio, dropping crumbs of poetry, which she tended to mumble, especially when she heard music.

I am flying along in her car, a restless grey Humber Super Snipe she always drove very fast and very boldly, and I am leaning out of the car window, and it's in the day even though I see the moon, but it's gauzy, the way it can be in the Caribbean sky, like a verandah light someone forgot to turn off in the morning, and it's literally tearing along the sky following us. Long drives with me were always a challenge for my grandmother, who had to distract me from carsickness; other than the trek to Nomdmi, these were usually beside the connecting cartilage of Mountain View Road, beneath Long Mountain, south to the sea, or north to the university at Mona. I guess we are coming up Mountain View Road after a swim at Palisados, for Mardi is reciting a breathy, rather choppy rendition of a favourite Sherlock poem:

Long Mountain, rise,
Lift you' shoulder, blot the moon,
Black the stars, hide the skies . . .

I am already used to this grandmother who does everything fast, mutters poetry, visits her huge blocks of wooden people, and has an intimate relationship with the moon. And I say to Mardi, Is this the same moon at Nomdmi and how many moons are there in the world, for the moon is running along beside the car? And she says it's the same moon that came to Kingston to see me—yes, the moon does that; and when she was a child it used to follow her and her father on their walks wherever they went, but it didn't have to move so quickly then for they didn't have motor cars. She says it wasn't till years later that she got on a train and discovered that it could run faster than a horse if it had to. Now with all these cars—she does her mouth in that funny O, a puffed-up purse where her lips disappear like a cat's, and shrugs her eye-brows—she feels sorry for the poor old moon. What a lot of running it has to do now.

I remember being amazed that the moon travelled everywhere, and then Pardi told me one day that it was not the moon that moved but us, and that Mardi was a little bit mistaken but not to mention it to her since she liked it better like that.

And in the evenings, like a ritual, being led into the dining room to listen to their classical music—Bach or Rostropovich, Chopin or Shostakovich—my aunts now ancient as rock face, Vera having started the Jamaica School of Music, and Muriel the pedia-trician at Kingston's public crèche, my grandfather disciplining him-self to relax as my grandmother peeped across to make sure he was doing so, and that I was truly listening, whispering her favourite verses, in this case George's, as if translating the music to me as she lifted her hands between records in devoted absorption:

Music pure and fine
Two thin cacti leaves green and clean
Bend in the air . . .

Within a couple of years the family grew, and in addition to Wrath of God, who'd been old when I arrived, there were two more dogs—boxers—Dizzy and Tunday, always wagging their non-existent tails. Douglas had arrived after his doctorate on race relations at Liverpool University, much to Mardi's relief, because she had become convinced that all the statistics he was gathering there would drive him mad. He now worked at our university as a lecturer in sociology, and had brought with him his exotic and creative wife, Carmen. Accompanying them was their son, Little Norman, so at last there was another child in the family to keep me company. He was often at Drumblair, and in the afternoons, if it wasn't raining, we'd be allowed to ride, I on my grandmother's tall golden mare, Gay Lady, and he, being younger and therefore shorter, on a smaller old grey mare called Harriet.

Little Norman was our grandfather's warm brown colour, and with his Roman nose and thin lips he resembled him. He was fast, well-coordinated and athletic, which I was not. I was not as pale as our blue-eyed, Caucasian-haired grandmother, and had the con-solation of brown eyes and dark, wavy hair. As a child I used to think that when we grew up we'd replace our grandparents. I don't think Norman ever thought about things like this, and he had a far less idealistic and sentimental view of our world.

I would always see Drumblair as Pardi's world—solid and stable, adventurous and brave; the main course of life's meal; the practical heart of my family's somewhat missionary life. It was the place from which I would one day watch him building his nation of islands; and the people who passed through for inspiration and guidance went out, I presumed, to build hospitals and schools, institutions and rules, protests and ideals, to write songs and stories of a new day. It was a hub of ideas and activism.

Nomdmi was dessert, the ceremonial closing in which you placed the meal in context and etched its memory. And although my grandparents were approaching an aging smouldering by the time I arrived, that is the impression those years left on me.

"Let the blessed sunshine in" is what I remember about waking in mountains at Nomdmi, and this was not hyperbole but in fact a life uniquely blessed, as time with Mardi would make evident. I cannot remember the pattern of the curtains in the dormer window, and if I remember the ritual it is because of that phrase of hers, which has stayed with me, so much so that I still cannot open my northern blinds without muttering it. But then, my computer screen saver scrawls *Trust Life*, her familiar saying, and I still stare at digital clocks that display numbers like 5:55 or 4:44 until they change, because long before the advent of such clocks, matching numbers attracted her attention as they conjured up good luck—a house number 44 or a hotel room 22, a licence number on a truck ahead that mesmerized her with 888 and scared the dickens out of me as she followed it up a mountain road whose bends curved like the promise of weekends, and the anticipation as we waited years for May 5, 1955. I still advert my eyes from 11:11 because these are snake eyes, and I think of a zero between them to avert bad luck, typing 101 if I am on the computer, and often finding these 101's on my manuscript weeks later when I go back to edit.

Then, as she'd turn from the opened dormer window of the rough-planed attic, the cool air rushing through like an animal let inside, she'd continue brightly, clapping her hands, "Now, let's plan the day. . . ," and that's how she started all things—days, places, people, rapprochements, denouements, enlightenments, romantic chance introductions, beguilements, and connivances—with a plan. A study, rough drawing, maquette. And a small meeting would take place at the long Pardi-made mahoe-wood dining table (his pride and joy), a drawer at either end for placemats, napkin rings, and silver—and a walk to the spring, then breakfast at eight, mountain breakfast cooked by Janie of fried breadfruit and plantain, fare of which Mardi didn't entirely approve, preferring bacon and eggs, but she made this concession to the mountains. Then she would go to her studio to carve, leaving me with Little Norman for a morning of cowboys and Indians. I was always the Indian being shot by my cousin's loud but painless bullets (girls never got guns and a holster and cowboy hat and boots for Christmas presents in those days—mark you, I didn't get dolls, either—I got books and board games), the acrid smoke lingering in the pines, and fortunately my Pardi-sharpened green pliable arrows of bracken shot from my bamboo-and-string bow would usually miss their mark.

Our childhood battles raged over the hills, the locations usually named for whatever landmarks or fruit trees were there—ambush in apple grove, attack at tree tomatoes, chase through ortanique trees, refuge at pines, slippery retreat down Watsonia valley, charge from the unknown grave (only three foot long, its cracking cement probably enshrined a child), gunfire at eucalyptus (we never descended into the coffee valleys, afraid of disturbing Pardi's temperamental crop or the rats in the underbrush)—places that seemed somehow compromised by us, safely contained and indulged with their past glories discreetly turned from this silliness. And all this was under Mardi's personally christened peaks, Dillmoon and Kablan and Hooman, Lady Peak, the Edna-honoured wife of Blue Mountain Peak, their gaze indifferent.

Then at six on a Friday afternoon Pardi would arrive for the weekend, in time for his gin and tonic, his rumpled exhaustion shrugging from side to side on the mule's back, to the movement above the animal's careful clops. Sometimes he'd bring two friends of mine for the weekend, Jeannie and Lindy, trailing behind like two little bumps together on the back of a mule, and we'd search the horizon as they grew closer and closer round each bend till I was sure they had come.

When it was the four of us, three girls against Little Norman, the games changed. We didn't like cowboys and Indians, but preferred playing doctor or school. I think Little Norman liked to play doctor, perhaps using this as a guise to examine our formless young female bodies. School was my favourite game, as I always got to be the teacher. I'd sit my often protesting students down at the dining table to draw or write poems, their only subject land-of-our-birth-Jamaica, and heaven help anyone suggesting that Mardi, Little Norman, or I was not born there. I also insisted on prayer, assuring them that our school was of my great-grandfather's Methodist faith.

"Well me and my sister are Anglican," said Jeannie, who resented being bossed.

I stood on the chair and, pointing at the stubborn faces looking up at me, roared, "I am a Methodist. And my cousin is a Methodist. And if you're not Methodists, *get out!*"

Little Norman took the opportunity of confusion to escape, *pi-pying* his gun as he left, Lindy sobbed, and Jeannie had to be stopped some way down the hill as she marched determinedly towards Kingston. I was punished for the weekend.

There was a glowing wooden Victrola box, and after soup and macaroni cheese, with Little Norman like a choral phrase repeating its entrance and exit as he tore in and out of the house to and from his forays through the pines, I would be given the difficult job of winding up the machine with its stiff metal arm, clutching the smooth wooden handle, so Pardi could balance the needle onto his precious spinning 78 records, and we'd listen as Pardi and Mardi argued gently over the virtues and shortcomings of various sopranos and tenors, or sat enraptured by Marian Anderson and Paul Robeson.

But during the week Edna was back in Kingston, wrestling with the figure on the crucifix, quoting George Campbell: "*Death is no end of faith*," as she drew various heads in preparation, the first one of resurrection, whose radiance she decided against, then another she called a "stark and tragic little corpse."

Pardi had left for a lecture tour in the United States and was detained in Ellis Island in February 1951, an experience I was only vaguely aware of and viewed positively because he got such a grand welcome at Victoria Pier from an outraged island when he arrived back home. But Mardi ached for him. Pardi used to travel to America a lot in those years, staying in the homes of strangers, with non-stop schedules speaking and travelling to promote Jamaica's fight for nationalism, and he hated being away from home but he was raising funds from Jamaicans living there, and from sympathetic black groups and organizations like the People's Progressive League. The detention was only for a night, and I suspect it had a more profound effect on her back home than on him there.

All Edna's old fears for Norman returned, and her sense of what she described almost with awe as "his strange loneliness." She kept thinking back to how solitary and racked he had been during the First World War, stuck in the ghastly trenches, and to the reality of colour prejudice all over Europe, even if he was fighting their war. And she knew from personal experience that America was even worse—once when she was there with him, he was refused entry to a restaurant. And so she took to fretting over him whenever he was abroad, calming down only when he'd returned safely home.

"After that things went awry," she wrote in her diary of the carving, and later, "Everything has crashed again."

But turning to the wood, she searched it for the figure that I suspect she sometimes saw as Pardi—"a man of authority and vision"—and then, as she described it, "a mystic in union with

God." She saw Christ as the son of God and the son of man, and as God himself. Despite her nagging sense that she was not able to give the work all she had and all it deserved, finally, as she'd later describe in her own words, she resolved the conundrum of the Christ: ". . . *a quiet, floating spirit—eternally rising, eternally hanging over this world of men and women . . . A figure floating before a cross and yet nailed to it?*"

If Mardi hadn't been so driven a spirit, so restless under the some-times becalmed control she imposed on herself, her life could have seemed in many ways a time of aftermath—her sons married, the nascent art and literary movements launched, her husband's party pursuing its cause of nationhood; the high point of her work locked in Jamaica's mind as *Horse of the Morning*, which remained everyone's favourite piece, except for Pardi's.

"I might as well stop carving," she'd say belligerently. And for a while she almost did. Her work became sporadic, the decade pro-ducing only a few sculptures up to 1953, and then a five-year drought ending in 1958 and 1959 with two more, most of them commissions when they urgently needed money.

In 1952 she entered a British competition for a monument *To the Unknown Political Prisoner*. If she wanted to return to her studio at Drumblair, she couldn't, for it had been used as a relief centre for victims of the recent hurricane, Charlie, which had devastated much of Jamaica the year before. She seems to have had great dif-ficulty concentrating on this work, ending up with what she con-sidered a half-hearted piece being sent late for the deadline. Maybe the fact that it was being created for England had something to do with this. Perhaps this is why it was never photographed. A mod-ern British sculptor, Reg Butler, won the contest. Her entry sat in the Tate exhibition for a while, and after this closed, no one was ever able to locate it. Without a picture, no record remains, and perhaps it became Mardi's ghost of conscience for that fallow period. But the subsequent years sucked any sustained creativity out of the air around her. There wasn't enough time for dreaming out themes or weaving threads into legend, as she had done in the thirties and forties. In six years she produced little more than a few minor terracottas, and as her life went into the forward march of public life with his, she sometimes had the feeling that as a sculptor she was over the hill, just the washed-up mother of *Horse of the Morning*.

I arrived shortly after Pardi's first success at the polls in his own constituency but his party's second national defeat since the advent of adult suffrage in 1944. He was sworn in as the member for East Rural St. Andrew in early January 1950, and though his duties as head of his party would mimic those of a leader of His Majesty's Loyal Opposition, he was still just a member of the legislative council, as they continued to fight for constitutional change to wrest political power from colonial King's House. The next few years would be a long campaign for internal self-government, and the PNP quest for victory in 1955.

Mardi was held hostage to Pardi's fortunes and to mine. She was taking care of a child in the home again, and taking care of the house, which now had to cope with all of its new duties and was badly in need of repairs. And she had to play more of a public role. Her old dairy ledger books were pressed into service again to keep track of her activities on its fresh sheets. Miss Boyd became her coordinator, laying out everything from her appointments to her dresses, gloves, and hats for the day. The mornings were usually kept free except for the official day she held once a week when she looked after Norman's constituents. As soon as I was off to school, she would jump into her Humber and drive up to the university to work, sneaking out before too many people arrived for help, because if they caught her there she could never say no.

On weekends if we stayed in town she'd take me with her and put me to sit in the studio, and encourage me to draw or model with Plasticine while she carved. I was always aware of the great change in her when she entered her studio. As soon as she was near her work she got very quiet and become a little like some-one else. It didn't seem to matter how intermittent these times were, she could withdraw from the world. In these hushed moments her studio reminded me of a church, hallowed and full of consequence. She would become so absorbed, I sometimes feared that she would one day leave us all behind and forget to come back. I suppose it was her fierce concentration, but I could feel the world recede, and some profound change was made in her. All her laughter and participation in the world would stop, and she'd become this pair of burrowing eyes and this quiet breathing as she circled the thing she was willing to life, and settled it.

By midday she'd return to the house to face some lunch of ladies from a local charity club, or a wife of some visiting digni-tary from England or the States. If her guests stayed too long, she was very clever at standing up and escorting them with confidence towards the door with a lusty "Well, hasn't this just been lovely!" but on occasion was driven to signalling Iris by a look to resort to an old Jamaican custom, turning the broom upside down and sprinkling salt on the bristles—it always worked, probably because Iris, the cook, was seldom tactful and usually did it in plain sight. She always claimed an hour from two o'clock to get her rest, which I also was obliged to observe in my bed, whether I was tired or not. Then she'd bathe and dress to give out prizes at a school or cut the ribbon at a clinic or a library, judge an art competition, watch a bal-let recital at a dance school, open a fair, or meet with one of many groups.

Evenings became a series of official or social dinners, hosted or attended with Norman, or declaring open some show at the crafts market or the institute, making speeches and more speeches. Weekends had their fair share of agricultural shows and fairs, of beauty pageants, dances, and fundraisers. And squashed in amidst all this were the things they still loved—their boxing and horse racing, their bridge and their music, the aunts, the trips to Nomdmi, the stolen week now and then by the sea.

An event created around this time became a source of great pleasure to Edna, and would be established as a yearly institution. It was a Christmas charity dance to provide treats for children, held at home and called the Drumblair Dance. Planning for this gala would begin as early as June or July, and the Drumblair living room would be pressed into service for weekly planning meetings. The committee was a talented and loyal group of comrades and some experts—caterers, a lighting technician, decorators, and choreographers—who decided on the artistic theme, the food and the bar for drinks, and the band for that year. This was a whole new experience for Drumblair. I can still see them all in a wide circle of dining-room chairs that the gardener, Batiste, would arrange around the living-room mat. They would sit there for ages with a joyous hubbub, the older women members getting sleepy as the night wore on, Mrs. T with her stockings slowly rolling down her legs till by midnight they had shrunk to tired pools around her ankles as she snoozed in her chair. One of the members always brought a stiff punch that was laced with what Mardi didn't realize was white overproof rum; ignited by this potion, many flirtations would develop. On each of my visits downstairs to check on some eruption of laughter or shouting, I would find the seating had been rearranged to reflect these building liaisons.

Since they were less edgy and cerebral than the politicians and the writers, and not only allowed me to sit in for limited periods on their meetings, eating the delicious snacks they often brought with them, but also made a huge fuss of me, probably to placate Mardi, they became my favourite group. There I met Rose McFarlane, a young red-haired journalist of whom Mardi was very fond. They had become close over the years as they worked on various committees and promotions. Mardi was always encouraging Rose to marry one of her sons, but Rose wisely adopted them as brothers so they would remain her friends forever.

By now the political process had produced a consciousness that, in the ambitious middle-class, had paradoxically backfired, expressing itself in a third great wave of migration (the first two had been labour opportunities digging the Panama Canal and harvesting in the Cuban canefields). It must have seemed strange to Mardi how many of her poets, flushed with the ardour of nationalism, nonetheless left hoping for greater opportunities in London and New York. Mike and George had gone, and sent her homesick, sometimes heartbroken poems. Their verses suggest that she had made it possible for them to go and yet remain who they were.

Mike in London, having turned to anthropology, still heard music:

> Once the wind was a flute in the lime trees . . .
> Till it comes again . . .
> Deep silent river
> Roll Forever Over Time.

And George in New York:

> And the sun has followed me:
> Even in winter silence . . .

Into this nostalgia and partial void, and despite their plans and hopes and ambitions and fullnesses, Mardi seems to have welcomed me as her project with single-minded devotion. Perhaps I arrived as a novelty or a diversion—an echo of her youth, another piece of unworked matter to sculpt.

The decade of the fifties falls into two acts for the family: a tough upward climb to a plateau and then, with Greek predictability, a steady downward decline towards inevitable tragedy. For the first five years Drumblair was gearing up for the 1955 election. The house was busy, always full of campaign paraphernalia, boxes of pamphlets and microphones. Thermoses of coffee and bags of bland Drumblair sandwiches and spicy bakery patties and flasks of brandy, the air full of hope and dreams of Caribbean federation and volleys of fighting words. Looking back now, I realize that I was unaware of the death of England's king, or the subsequent crowning of its queen, or in the wider world of such news as the death of Stalin. My child's imagination filled with the struggles and triumphs of my Jamaican tribe, such as our unparalleled joy at hearing Jamaica win the 100, 200, and 4-by-100-yard gold medals at the Helsinki Olympics in 1952, or, shortly after, Mardi's silent, accepting pain, when she heard that her mother Ellie had died.

She sat at her metal dressing table, staring at her brush and comb and trays of odd things, looking lost.

"Don't leave me," I begged, suddenly insecure.

She rallied at once, slinging a cheerful arm round me.

"I *can't* leave you, scallywag," she scolded. And she told me that daughters become their mothers, as sons become their fathers. Now her mother was living in her, and one day *very* far away she'd be living in me, and that was how people became eternal.

We were focused on an election still years away, which with each of my birthdays—one day from my grandfather's, and always celebrated in a joint party where we cut the cake together—came closer and closer. And as it did, the meetings became a blur of intriguing place names, some familiar but many names I hadn't heard before, as Pardi and Mardi set off in the evenings with first Vivian, then Graham, the drivers, and Davidson, the campaign singer, to Cross Roads and Half Way Tree, Jonestown and Rollington Town, Waltham Park, Hagley Park, and Kenkot, Matilda's Corner and Coronation Market, Four Roads and August Town, Belfield Square and Islington in St. Mary, Gilchrest Street and Jackson Road, Langston Road, Bercombe Road and Deanery Avenue, Thompson and Asquith Streets. These meetings were announced by Vivian, driving around in the car with a bullhorn all day long, with fierce words like "Invasion of Bull Bay tomorrow," and each evening the many meetings would open and close with Davidson singing the PNP anthem, "Land of My Birth," as tens or hundreds or thousands of comrades clenched their fists in solidarity.

Pardi's face would stare at us from the daily newspaper with headlines like "Manley clashes in House rumpus," "Manley expresses concern over election dates. . . ," "Manley and Mrs. Rose Leon clash in House," "Manley protests irresponsibility of government. . . ," "Manley makes proposal for longer sitting of house. . . ," "Manley: I will expose all the frauds and rascalities . . ."

"Here we go again," Mardi would say with each headline, as though exasperated, but her face full of mischief, so one knew she thrived on the drama of it. And I no longer saw Pardi as a wounded, defeated grandfather.

Despite the excitement, I dreaded them leaving me at night, preferring the Kingston schedules, which meant they came home soon after midnight. After they had gone there was such a quiet in the rambling old house, as the night seemed to arrive and darken outside the large windows the minute they left, and the floorboards would suddenly start creaking and the dogs and the cats desert me to find their spots to sleep. Miss Boyd or beloved Edith, the guava jelly lady, would try to settle me down, promising when I woke in the morning I'd find my grandparents safely back in their beds.

I have always woken with some anonymous sadness that could start the day in tears. Mardi named it my "trauma," which she always said sadly, and I thought it very grand when she referred to my fear of abandonment.

"She's missing her mother," she'd say, and find ways to divert me.

So Drumblair, which had in recent years become filled with high-minded projects, got pressed into more lowly service. I would wake in my father's old bedroom with some pending thread of interest from yesterday, whether it was my chemistry set prompting Pardi's installation of a rough laboratory in Douglas's old bedroom, a shaky tooth whose extraction we planned with Pardi's ritual door-slamming, or the letter I was working on with Pardi in which I was reprimanding the editor of a children's book, *One Thousand Beautiful Things*, in which a line of Blake's "The Tyger" had been artfully changed. Mardi would cluck approvingly.

Drumblair had its own cast who ably assisted in these projects. I was blessed with Miss Boyd, who had virtually brought up my uncle and my father. She was a tiny grey-haired lady with a bun who always wore socks, and shoes with sensibly stacked thick, black heels; Mardi and Pardi seemed to have known her forever. Pardi called her Miss B., Mardi called her Beesie, and every child I knew called her Aunta. She often brought her nephew and niece, Milton and Juanita, to keep me company. I think Mardi, liking to equate one thing with another, considered this a good match as they too had lost their mother. My frequent tantrums caused Aunta and Mardi to resort to prayer while Juanita and Milton watched in amazement, knowing such behaviour would bring them severe reprimand. Then there was Batiste, who drank beer and smoked unfiltered cigarettes that stuck to his lips, Edith who sang spirituals, and Iris the brilliant but bad-tempered cook.

Theatre was always Mardi's contribution. On weekends she'd choreograph our plays to be performed for the aunts on Sunday evening, before musical recitals. In many ways these productions represent the youth Mardi created for me, and reflect my relationships in Drumblair. So a play would see my grandmother assisting with scripting and acting—"So what would *you* say to the world if you were a tree establishing your freedom and the wind was there to carry along your messages? You don't *want* to be a tree? Okay, now *who* wants to be a glorious lignum vitae tree?"—and Batiste, an imperturbable spirit like one of the Drumblair oaks, handling the larger questions of set production, which usually required upending and moving the mahogany living-room furniture as, hands full, he left a trail of cigarette ashes, muttering, "De furniture go get scratch." Miss Boyd as wardrobe mistress was in charge of Mardi's cupboard and all cupboards, and she'd lament the misuse of their contents. Milton and Juanita, or Jeannie and Lindy (who had also temporarily lost their mother, through divorce), and Little Norman and I were the actors, which meant the play always had to have a cowboy part or my cousin wouldn't join in, but as the eldest only Juanita—who disliked playing any part that was non-human, calling it foolishness—could ever remember her lines, though Mardi said it was fine to ad lib.

Pardi would join Edith, Miss Boyd, and the aunts as audience, would bravo and clap for encores, but invariably he'd leave the critiquing to my aunts, knowing that any suggestion to improve my performance would incur Mardi's displeasure at the notion that I was less than perfect.

Iris stoutly refused to be involved in either my traumas or my dramas, in fact anything beyond the domain of her kitchen, and could not be prevailed on to stop the racket of her pot-slamming during performances.

But the most memorable of these projects was my first book of doggerel. In the wake of Mardi reading to me Blake's *Songs of Innocence*, I started writing rhyming couplets . . . *little frog, on a log; the sun shall arise, make happy the skies* . . . etc., etc. All who entered Drumblair, from poets to priests to politicians, were encouraged to hear my painful couplets, and Batiste in his garden provided me with a captive audience while he watered; he would say, "Oh my," as he jiggled his hose encouragingly at the flower beds.

When I had written a dozen of these travesties, Mardi announced with triumph that I'd have my first book when I got to twenty-four poems. On my reaching the magic number, she decided that I should type them out. This is where I first remember my father joining the cast of my life.

Michael had returned to Jamaica and was living in my grandfather's study downstairs. And it seems that this project opened up some fault line in the relationship between my father and Mardi which involved me and the fact that, absorbed as I was into Drumblair life, Edna and Norman had become my de facto parents. This became the start of a tug-of-war over how to bring me up.

My father was working as a journalist with *Public Opinion*, writing a column called "Root of the Matter," and he had an ancient Olivetti that had served as hostage in many a pawnshop when he was broke in England. Mardi suggested he help me get the poems typed, and at this point was happy to see us busy together. But as time wore on—my father teaching me how to match the carbon between two sheets so I would have a copy, scroll in the paper, and set the left margin; how to capitalize, how to make spaces, indent lines, and create paragraphs, how to shift the long handle in to move onto a new line—I would sigh with frustration over having to get everything right, my father would become irritable, and

Mardi would fly to my rescue. She thought the great fuss over lin-ing up the letters was unnecessary, as was the copy. When Pardi suggested that the poems needed editing, Mardi threw her hands up in the air and said they were all getting in the way of my cre-ativity. But my father stuck to his guns; he objected to Mardi being overprotective and spoiling me, and said the job should be done properly or not done at all.

In 1956 the third edition of *Focus* was published. In its fore-word, Mardi wrote of its greater variety and depth of experience, "*the emergence of Jamaica itself from behind the geographical, cultural and polit-ical barriers of the past, and secondly the emergence of an increasing number of Jamaican writers into the international literary scene.*"

"*All women I have loved were tigered in a rose,*" wrote George from New York.

And Mike from England, like Port Royal's underwater clock stirring in memory:

Only the river remembers under all
Unseen unheard remembers the lost dream.

In the last three years Roger Mais had produced his three novels, *The Hills Were Joyful Together*, *Brother Man*, and *Black Lightning*, telling stories of Jamaican mountains and ghettos in a way probably no other Jamaican prose writer had done as truly. He shone the light of the Jamaican spirit on the page, each character brightly unique, some rising in triumph above their plight, others succumbing to its statistic. His play *The First Sacrifice*, his last contribution to *Focus*, would appear a year after his death in 1955, its closing words rem-iniscent of him, chorused by all the characters:

Where the light falls . . .
O, life is wide, and the giving of it

O, life is good, and the living of it
Let us make salute to life.

And in that very same year my small anthology was completed, and presented at the Drumblair dining table in its orange
linen jacket which Aunta had helped me make, with the title
embroidered in black: *"Poems by Rachel Manley."*

"You are a poet," my grandmother declared, with a sigh of resignation that made it all seem rather grand. It appeared to bring
almost more fanfare from her than the national anthology she'd
edited, though its typing was somewhat uneven, its embroidery
somewhat untidy, its poems somewhat unedited. Along with the
papers she left me, it lies in a trunk in my basement in Toronto to
this day.

I clearly remember, but never understood at the time, a phenomenon that began in those years. Talk in the house was of a probe
and a purge and a post-probe, terms incomprehensible to me. It all
had to do with a wing of the party being communist as opposed
to socialist, a distinction my family always made very clear, falling
themselves into the latter category. So in 1952 Pardi purged the
party of the left wing, and according to Mardi, who always iden-
tified traumas, this was another big one in our lives because these
were good people, and in my child's perception what was remarkable was the fact that all four men bore a surname that started with
H, thus being called the Four H's. The tag of leftism stuck to the
party after that, and everyone worried that this latest debacle
might cause another electoral defeat, but despite Bustamante's
final, desperate appeal in the *Daily Gleaner* to save the country
from socialism, in early January 1955 Pardi won. And though many

were ecstatic, and Mardi for a few days became peaceful—almost wafting, as though some awful wrong had been set right, some deep wound healed—she soon fell back into her habit of worry over Pardi.

His law practice, which I had been only vaguely aware of till then, he closed, and with a promise of fair play and a determination to lead "a now or never drive for federation" Pardi became Jamaica's second chief minister, leaving each morning for his office with a good breakfast provided by Iris, a red rosebud that I'd pick from the garden for his buttonhole, and admonishments from Mardi not to work too hard, not to lose his temper, to be sure to take intermittent catnaps at his desk, and not to worry.

This was the plateau.

Their lives appeared glorious. A look at the old newspapers shows an array of dazzling events, Mardi's dresses often a feature of Sam Watson's fashion column—"powder blue embroidered with white. . . ," "dramatic black and gold print . . ." There were royal visits, premieres, more and more art exhibition openings and concerts to attend, lunch with Winston Churchill—who grumbled about the weather being too miserable for him to be able to paint, to which my grandmother replied defensively: No wonder . . . Jamaica wasn't accustomed to all these dignitaries; tea with Adlai Stevenson, visits of Magloire from Haiti and Muñoz Marin from Puerto Rico, visits of various English-speaking Caribbean leaders. Pardi is often reported as travelling to England and the States having to do with the banana industry, the citrus industry, internal self-government, the unrest of unfairly treated immigrants in Brixton.

There were good times like Christmas, when the family would light the tree at Victoria Park, go to the pantomime to watch Miss Lou and Mass Ran and my Aunt Carmen—sitting in the royal box, which had two side alcoves from which Pardi and I would discreetly

drop peanuts onto the heads of bald gentlemen below. On Boxing Day we'd take a boat across the harbour to the women's prison
at Fort Augusta, and Mardi made me feel very excited and privileged to be there. I would feel embarrassed receiving small craft
gifts made by the inmates, having nothing to give them in return.
Mardi said they just wanted our company. Several gave me their
names and for a while they became pen pals. In the evening we'd
have our big family dinner with my father and his new wife,
Thelma, and Douglas and Carmen with Little Norman; and sometime later a new baby, Roy, who seemed to get sick a lot. Pardi and
I would share wishbones, and Little Norman always found the
florins in the pudding, which he'd located with a sharp knife
beforehand.

I was now facing longer separations from my grandparents as
they travelled up and down the Caribbean, championing the idea
of a West Indian federation. This new political entity germinating
in Pardi's mind was best expressed in one of his speeches to the
party.

"When we wanted to shine in the world as cricketers, we built up a West
Indian cricket team. When we wanted a university we built a West Indian
university because we were not big enough to build one large one for ourselves in
Jamaica. When we wanted to trade for sugar, for bananas, for citrus we
combined together in a West Indian organization. I negotiated not as Jamaican,
but as a West Indian for the future of those markets and those crops."

And so his thinking evolved from a self-governing island to a
group of ten islands governed as one.

Poetry was on Mardi's mind again as she was slowly collecting work—there was always another edition on the horizon—and
though not even a doting grandmother could claim I was ready to
be included in that rare company, she took a poem I wrote to
Trinidad and showed it to the great Trinidadian historian and
philosopher C.L.R. James, who had it published in a newspaper

there. She encouraged me to write and thank him, which I did, telling him a quite fantastic story I made up about our dog, Wrath of God, walking many miles from the vet to return home to me. To my chagrin, he published that too.

"There now," she said with satisfaction, claiming poetic licence for the fairy tale I was responsible for creating. "You're published, and in Trinidad!" as though, no matter the momentary sadness of their absences, much more was at stake; and somehow there was no chance of turning back, though back from what, I wasn't then quite sure.

I too had a stake in this thing called "federation."

I think at times I tried to live up to what I presumed were their dreams of what I should be, though I don't remember them ever articulating these or in any way pushing me. My letters to them, some written from Nomdmi to Drumblair or vice versa, some written in the house and just travelling from room to room, are scattered with promises not to let them down, and to try to do all that I did well. Mardi loved to start the day with a note to each of us, and these came to me with great frequency, praising me for finishing my homework or writing a poem, or helping wash the dog, or just not giving trouble:

"You're a brick!" she'd say.

But a feeling of doom was building over that time, my grandmother's sense of what I thought as a child was "ominy" about the coming second act in our lives.

First, Pardi had a heart attack in 1953, which, despite a few years of truce, signalled the beginning of his ill health. For me it provided a blessed time when I was happy to have him home, and Mardi gave me the welcome duty of helping to get him better. For a while he was propped up in bed with his baskets of On Her Majesty's Service files, with their lurid pink ribbons, and we'd play rummy, ludo, or Snakes and Ladders. I can still remember one particularly long, flat black snake that I dreaded landing on, because the slide down was almost to the beginning of the game and I would have to swallow hard not to cry.

Then as Pardi got stronger we'd go for quiet walks that always led to some new adventure or discovery. It was during this time that he arranged to have Mardi's studio moved from where it lay, within view of the house, deep into the grass-piece. We watched the wooden room with its peaked shingle roof as it trembled and swayed precariously on the back of a flatbed truck which struggled along a path cut by Batiste, all this so that Mardi could return to work at home in peace and be near Pardi.

I cannot name the dates when the other two harbingers of darker times began, but they were there in these years among all the glories.

There was the question of federation, which I always remember being part of their lives, its notion already planted by the time I came. At first it seemed to be a matter for harmonious conversation in our family. Pardi continued to travel to the islands for talks and conferences, and Mardi made it all seem so worthwhile and necessary, encouraging him, telling him it was what he was meant to do, wanting him to move onto a bigger stage, convinced that the success of federation would increase his prestige at home and abroad and prove to be the crowning achievement of his life.

Edna started travelling with him, and she'd arrive back with enthusiastic schemes to take our art and drama down the islands, and to bring their dance and music up to us. I'm not sure why we'd say *down* and *up* instead of *east* or *west*, but that was how we saw ourselves—at the end of a journey "up." Perhaps that in itself was a telling sign of things to come. I remember Beryl McBurnie arriving with her troupe of Trinidad dancers, and Mardi receiving a magnificent feathered headdress of an eagle, and saying with some satisfaction, to a group of horrified uptown ladies who had arrived

for an otherwise unmemorable tea at our house, that wasn't it wonderful to have the Little Carib troupe performing instead of the
usual awful beauty-pageant stuff. The only beauty pageant she liked
was the annual Denbigh farm show, where great sisterly cows were
paraded with garlands round their necks. In 1957 she even organized a competition for the best design for a new federal flag. The
winning entry depicted a background of aqua Caribbean waves
with a round orange sun in the centre.

But Mardi got something negative in her head about federation. She said she had a dream—a nightmare, really, about the ship,
the *Federal Palm*, sinking. I suspect it wasn't really from a dream but
her political instinct, which was as sharp as her nose, capable of
intuiting things around her before they happened, often making
her work prophetic. She had grave doubts about the decision to
place the federal capital in Trinidad. Because of a quirk of geography and colonial history, English-speaking Jamaica was separated
by distance from the other English-speaking islands in the eastern
Caribbean. Although Jamaica was by far the largest island, Pardi felt
that to have the capital of the federation in Kingston would place
it too far from the rest of the islands and disadvantage them politically. For all the logic of the decision, Mardi knew it would be
incomprehensible to Jamaicans so far west. She had encouraged
Pardi to run for the leadership of the federal government, which
most likely he'd have won, but he declined, probably knowing
that, being away in Trinidad, he would leave his back open politically at home. Bustamante would prove them both right. He
started to sow unrest by airing his doubts on the advisability of this
union for Jamaica, and what it might cost us, as the largest of the
ten islands. Mardi's unease had been justified. And that worry
continued in our lives, growing more tense with her doubts and
apprehension. Pardi would eventually call a referendum in 1960 to
decide on Jamaica's future within the federation. Our uncertainty

ended only when he lost the vote, and his political dream was shattered.

Finally, the vexing question of the family's finances loomed darkly over our heads, though we never seemed to dwell on it. This issue became more ominous in 1955 when we lost the Drumblair backlands. These were the acres where Pardi and I would walk, he with a thick stick, whacking the overgrowth like an accomplished bushman in between our long chats on the various possibilities of how the world began and who came first, the serpent or the man, the man or the woman. I reasoned that women had babies and men didn't, so surely woman came first, and he to tease me took the Biblical view that we came from Adam's rib, so surely man did. We talked about the use of salt in the churning of ice cream, why the poor were poor and how only education could really free us of poverty, why there were wars, and the secret of cutting a toenail in a small central V to counteract ingrown toenails "for nature abhors a vacuum"—while I picked off burrs from my sleeves with an irritable fastidiousness that he said I got from my father, that the countryman in Pardi couldn't fathom. They had to cut these blessed acres into house lots and put them up for sale. One would be kept for themselves, that would go one day to Douglas, and another beside it for my father.

As though aware that Mardi's work had recently taken a beating due to all the distractions, or maybe realizing they would need to generate more income, Pardi purchased a kiln that he had shipped from America. The first firing was of a terracotta mask, a powerful male face that introduced a brick colour and texture that would become as familiar to our lives as the glowing wood of her carvings. This first piece she gave to my father for the new home he built on his lot, which he called Ebony Hill.

In 1958 my brother, Joseph, was born. As my grandparents travelled more and I saw them less, for a while I spent time with my father and Thelma, until it was decided to send me to Knox College, a Presbyterian boarding school in the red hills near Manchester at the centre of the island, where Pardi was born. I was initially devastated, but those two years proved to be the most productive of my schooldays. I kept in touch with the family through letters, sending my poems, really small cries for attention, as though by doing so I'd continue to be a "brick." Most important of all was the note I received that, far away though I was, finally gave me some of the confirmation I had always searched for, which helped to ground me there.

"It has been a wonderful nine years," Mardi wrote to me, "and it is all just beginning. As the years go by we will live and grow in more love and understanding and I want you to understand—and I say this with everything in my heart—that nothing could ever come between us. So be happy and free and remember always what I have written."

In 1959, finally back at work again, she wrote me a note from Drumblair: "I want you to know that having you with me has been a great joy and comfort to Pardi and me . . . because it gave us someone to live for and helped us to forget the worries of political life."

When I got home for holidays, waiting for me was the second carving since she had taken back her studio. A small, joyously simple one, cementing the original pact between us: A Girl with Small Goat.

Pardi won a final magnificent landslide victory in 1959, as though a grateful nation had stepped forward and said thank you for all the work he'd done in modernizing Jamaica economically and socially, preparing us in the fifties to stand on our own with internal self-government, which he had partially won for us, and later on, when the British were finally gone. But then, despite Mardi's warnings and Rose McFarlane's growing premonitions, in 1961 he called that referendum on the federal issue two years afterwards, which he decisively lost. Jamaicans now wanted no part of the regional union they had joined, and their withdrawal would bring down the whole federal structure, which by then had been in existence for two years. Pardi felt he could not go forward into independence without a new mandate from the people, and he called an early general election in 1962 and narrowly lost that as well.

I have come to understand now what I couldn't then, that Jamaica in personality was really far more akin to the nature and philosophy and personality of Bustamante. They had admired Norman Manley and given him his chance. But what he wanted to create was complex and conceptual, far-sighted in a way that the present didn't seem to guarantee; it involved blindly ceding a certain amount of power while still only in infancy. And Jamaicans like the present; they like to live for today and count what is in their hands. What Pardi could not see was that, because history had given them no guarantees, they saw no reason to trust anything intangible or invisible.

We had all just bumped along through this period as though dragged behind a moving vehicle, and the one constant—like the moon, which Mardi thought moved and Pardi knew didn't—was Jamaica now casting a blind eye as Pardi tried to rescue her.

He would win his own seat, but never again a general election.

These losses I always considered to be Pardi's alone. What I didn't grasp at the time was Mardi's sacrifice. As she settled me, weaving me in amongst the many strands of their life, focusing all care and concern on Pardi and me, I was unaware of her struggle or the extent to which she gave of her own life to keep ours afloat.

In the private world of Mardi's imaginings, only a few things remain of that time—they include *Crucifix* and me. I couldn't know then the sense of loss she felt as an artist for the unborn works of that period. But she bore the knowledge of each one quietly and alone.

"I don't understand," I said many years later, staring at a picture of *Crucifix*.

"Maybe we are not supposed to understand. . . ," she suggested.

"But it's a blissful face . . . I see no pain . . . is it Christ's resolve?"

"It isn't resolve," she said. "It is resignation. And it isn't Christ; it is man."

The figure I would eventually see, its face once raised to the mountain light that would have shone through the glass at the Mona studio, and later dreaming on through the hallowed shadows of All Saints' Church, is said to be the face of Norman. It reflects much of Edna's anxiety and concern.

"What is holiness? Solitude? Closeness to God? I wrung that head out of my *heart*," she stated.

And she wrote in her diary:

If you believe in the concept of Christ you have to believe he cannot ever be unconscious. Rather his eyes are closed because I felt that he was basking. In the radiance. The radiance in which he believed. That is the rapture. The truly believing do bask quite literally at times in their faith and those around can't always see why they do. I am not sure about the figure. I wanted the arms to be like wings bearing him up— a floating figure. But I wanted his face to reflect his own terms because that is what his crucifixion is all about. It isn't a common execution but a martyrdom. I wanted that to be radiating from his face to us.

Perhaps she found her way to the figure of Christ, to the reality of godhead—a rite of passage through which all artists must pass, even if they are not counted among the faithful—through the men who had ruled her imagination. For while some glimpse Norman, it is the face of Harvey Swithenbank I see, just as she described it to me, when he was watching Halley's comet with unshakable faith and hope, at the end of his life.

10

Regardless

. . . and there is so much more there to challenge one than simply tears.
—Edna Manley: *The Diaries*

MARDI RETURNED TO WORK IN 1958, at about the same time that Michael and Thelma's son, Joseph, was born. I think she sensed, despite an electoral victory on the horizon for the following year, that in the longer run they would be returning to private life. She was resolved to cope with the consequences the only way she knew how, by moving back to where she found endurance and insight—the core of herself.

She knew she must make a choice, either to concentrate on her role as patron of the arts, offering energy and encouragement, or to return to the lonelier road, the more selfish one—to her own work—knowing any temptation to become materialistic and self-satisfied or vain and superficial, would get burnt away in the hard process of self-expression. Teaching her students, who still arrived at the studio for a couple of hours when she had time, she called it the lean road, pureness of heart—this single unflinching truth of creation would provide the yardstick by which to measure all values.

In between journeys up and down the Caribbean, she carved a large totem pole *Growth*, out of a tall, narrow plank of mahogany, a progression that began with two rows of three full-length figures, the first row drifting with their heads lowered towards their lifted arms bent at the elbow, as if in diffidence or modesty, towards sleep or prayer; the second row more energized, bent arms pushed back and heads thrust up as if awakening. Above them—evocative, shining—a torso of the horse of the morning, and uppermost an implacable mask, a godhead similar to the mask she had modelled for my father. I have often pondered its meaning. Was it her warning that despite many trials at unification of the islands, Jamaica was destined to stand alone as an independent nation? Did it signal her distrust of movements, her belief that the spirit of freedom must finally be solitary? Or was it simply a personal, prescient statement, written in chips, that no matter what, she would survive and continue even if quite alone?

In 1960 Edna held a one-man exhibition, at a Kingston gallery, of thirty-four drawings she had produced over the decade. She was stung by a review in which the writer referred to her work as dated. Whenever she received a bad review, it would throw her into the self-doubt that was always lurking. "It's time I stop this foolishness," she'd say.

But the imperative to work would eventually supersede her sensitivity, though this might take months, and we'd all end up coping with her injured demeanour—a lofty sulking that, after the initial rally of family support, could become both maddening and quite amusing.

The drawings mounted in that exhibition seemed to have floated back unexpectedly from a generally unproductive era, like lost messages in bottles. I thought many of them felt preparatory, but maybe that was because I was used to waiting to see what they would become in the round. Often the pencil lines, though on paper, wobbled as though pulled over rough wooden surfaces, or the black ink outlines overruled them emphatically as a child would trace a line. Many of these conjured up figures she'd met while travelling through the islands, and her old friend the moon returned as the face of several night-blooming cereuses.

Shaken by the 1960 review, Edna entered the comment that had stung her in her diary. For the next couple of entries she proceeded to dwell somewhat ruefully on the events of the recent past, recounting stories of the federal days, adding an artist's insights into character and history in a way no mere historian could—how Eric Williams, all affable and fun, was dining at Drumblair when the lights suddenly went out, and how deeply paranoid he became; and then when Grantley Adams had to move to head the federal government in Trinidad, his wife Grace refused to accompany him, small nuggets that helped explain larger issues of the time.

Unlike Mardi, after his defeat in the referendum in 1961 and the PNP defeat shortly thereafter, Pardi had great difficulty finding his way back to the central core of himself. In an act that over the years Mardi would see in different lights—sometimes as a heroic falling on his sword, other times as a wilful and vengeful act, and finally as something symbolic, a glorious funeral pyre to commemorate a life's work—he got up one morning, walked into his study, and took all his years of papers, legal and political and personal, his music reviews and his book reviews, his philosophical musings, the ones Mardi had not kept separately, threw them onto the garbage dump behind the kitchen, and burned them.

They had both evolved as very private people who were most comfortable in the world of the mind. In many ways politics didn't suit either of them. More shy and retiring than his wife, he was not a social being. He had the visionary mind of a political philosopher, the ability to envision and then institutionalize change. But although he could resort to his great gift as an orator and his craft of courtroom persuasion, he hadn't the rootsy, folksy, flamboyant personality of his cousin Bustamante. Maybe he had invested too much of his spirit in the party and the national movement. Although no ailment was ever diagnosed, over the next few years he visibly declined. Maybe it was just too difficult to start life again at sixty-seven.

Our family put on the best face we could for the Independence celebrations held in August 1962. We attended the celebrations, and Pardi did his official part and paid tribute to his country's magnificent achievement. But truly our hearts were breaking. It was hard to think that a concept largely born in my grandfather's head, and developed through years of speaking and work and teaching and fighting the Colonial Office and rewriting the constitution, was now to be presided over by somebody else. We had been battered by two consecutive defeats and the repudiation of much of what Pardi had stood for. The family was broke and about to lose the house that had made a home for three generations of Manleys.

Pardi went back somewhat half-heartedly to his law practice, opening a modest consultancy in Duke Street. Drumblair was sold for land development, the house finally torn down, some said for firewood but Mardi always corrected this, as though defending an old friend's honour: "No, for lumber!"

In April 1963 they moved across the gully to a small bungalow on the plot they had retained because Mardi had had the foresight to plan long before the sale, long before anyone expected a snap general election, much less defeat. It was an unremarkable place—just a square concrete building with two bedrooms and a bathroom in between, the living room the length of the house as though the space had been allotted this function as an afterthought, and a small dining room and kitchen on the far side. At the back of the house, facing the mountains, was a patio. As Mardi looked at the hills beyond the familiar town of Four Roads, they appeared to be younger hills than those she had grown accustomed to at Nomdmi. These were greener, nearer, more flawed by proximity. The hills behind Nomdmi that had consumed her life for eight years—she considered them to be the taller parent hills. They were grand peaks of the Blue Mountains, mountains that were blue from distance and distant from age. No geography lesson could have persuaded her otherwise. She believed that they had once looked as young and extroverted as these hillock grandchildren now before her, when they had appeared over the brow of the sea at the beginning of time.

She knew only one way to make such an upheaval painless. She treated the move like the ripping off of a Band-Aid, orchestrating the entire operation in one day while Pardi was at the office; she told him to pass by the new house after work and there he found his dinner cooked by Tildy, a domineering but tender-hearted descendant of the Maroons from Portland, waiting for him on the familiar Drumblair dining table with all its extra leaves taken out. Even their first in a series of Alsatians, a nervous animal called Whist, was now in the new house, scratching his fleas on a new lily mat. This time it was I who was given the task of finding a name; I came up with "Regardless." The house was next door to my father's Ebony Hill, where Douglas had moved in with Michael, since both brothers were now divorced and Norman, Roy, and Joseph were living with their respective mothers. I had changed to a Kingston day school and lived with them also. For the next four years I would drift between the two houses, veering between the child I still was with my grandparents at Regardless, and the difficult teenager emerging at my father's expense next door.

Michael's career as a unionist was now established in the PNP-affiliated National Workers' Union, where he was island supervisor. He had been voted president of the Caribbean Bauxite and Mineworkers' Federation and was already making a name for himself, regionally and beyond. Although he had not yet entered politics, he had worked tirelessly to help his father campaign for federation in the referendum, and then for the general election.

Mardi and my father always had the ability to turn their back on the past when it was necessary, as a lizard drops its tail. When Mardi was commissioned to do a work for Kingston's Webster Memorial Church, she built a little wooden studio with a shingled peak roof at the bottom of the garden, a sign of things to come and life going on. But Pardi seemed to have no stake in this new incarnation, no study, no tool room. Just his big leather chair, which now sat beside his latest stereo set, turned away from what he regarded as the maddening television set which, as Leader of the Opposition, he had been officially presented with when at Independence the medium was introduced to the island. He used the opportunity to support a dramatic workers' strike led by Michael at the national Jamaica Broadcasting Station, making a statement by sending the instrument back.

Mardi was commissioned to carve the bush that was not consumed. In that strange way that life and art can imitate each other, the church stipulated that Moses should not be in the carving, and Mardi was faced with an unusual challenge for her: to make an arresting work with neither man nor animal involved. It brought her face to face with all the real-life negatives with which she now contended: a fire that hadn't the power to effect its mission; a bush whose function was not productive but merely defensive, charged only with survival; a landscape in which Moses the patriarch, so intrinsic to the legend, was absent.

The little room rustled with lizards. She had made friends with the large ground lizards that dashed across the outside patio, tiny dragons coming in across the new lawn from the high, windblown grass at the bottom of Michael's lot. She wondered why Jamaican women were so frightened of lizards, especially the chameleon "croakers" who slithered so deftly on the roof above. They were always shrieking and flailing their arms when one emerged quite tactfully from behind a picture to say good afternoon, especially her daughters-in-law. Mardi didn't think the croakers beautiful, but they interested her. They were clever and could disguise themselves by colour, and they were nationalistic and had good taste, choosing only the finest Jamaican art, a Huie or a Parboosingh or Pottinger, for their home. And anyway they were useful; they ate the mosquitoes that distracted her in the late afternoons, saving her from burning joss sticks, which always made her cough. There had never been ground lizards in her other studios. At Drumblair the room was too high on its foundations—they would have had to climb stairs to enter—and at four thousand feet high, Mini was just too cold. She liked the sound they made in wood chips. They were busy company that never spoke, so she never felt alone. She saw their visits as blessings.

Edna solved the problem of *The Burning Bush*. She found a piece of wood out of which she could choreograph two flames, and carved them rising as alternatives, drawing them into Caribbean relevance by making the structure a ginger-lily plant shimmering under the fire of the right flame, the other branch standing pristine in front of the left flame as though appliquéd thereon, its main stalk and flower miraculously untouched at its centre. When she was pleased with it, she renamed it *The Bush That Was Not Consumed* and handed it over to Webster Memorial.

Edna then threw herself into a study of a Rastafarian head that she called *Brother Man*, after the 1954 novel by Roger Mais, a story of Rastafarian life. Many considered their smoking of the "holy weed" and longing for Africa as escapism, suggesting that in this it was no different than pocomania. She did not agree. She had been fascinated by the movement, seeing it as indigenous faith—faith rooted in the familiar. When the hurricane relief had finally ended and the Drumblair studio had become vacant again, some Rastafarians had moved in, installing the weather-beaten head of Samson, which they had retrieved from its human creator's angry act of expulsion, when Edna had thrown it with Delilah's head into the surrounding grass-piece. The sculpturesque locks—which in those days scared the middle-classes, who distrusted anything out of the norm—are a symbol of spiritual strength through their faith. Instead of evicting these visitors, Mardi befriended them. Several people warned her to be careful, insisting they were dangerous or mad.

"What we call madness is sometimes the pushing away of boundaries," she explained.

She talked to the Rastafarian brothers for hours, and was intrigued with their take on the links between Christianity and Africa; their sense of a natural connection with their original heritage. She was also interested in their lack of ambivalence about modern history and the prevailing anglophile culture, which they blithely ignored, most of all in their everyday comfort; they bent the English language as much as they needed to, to suit themselves, and their speech was as joyous as prayer, and never a burden. She loved their ease with the symbolism of the Bible, and when they left, politely thanking her for their time there, she was quite flattered that they took with them the head of Samson.

Brother Man now stared out over her new studio with inward confidence, his eyes bright with spiritual zeal, like that of a prophet of the Old Testament.

By October she saw the garden, which she had mostly trans-planted from Drumblair, begin to settle and flourish. The night-blooming cereus, rubbery and a deep, glossy green, thrived on the giant, fallen trunk of a tree that had been cut down to make space for the house. The ivy she had planted beneath the stark white outside walls to soften the austere cement lines and the bare small-ness of the modern house began to throw up lines from the earth, each looking like a house lizard. She had placed a bird bath in the garden and already knew the separate cries of the visitors, and would chase away the blackbirds so the smaller grass-quits could get a chance to feed. The pea doves she fed early in the mornings, when they called impatiently to wake her, and she liked to watch their comforting little waddled shuffles as they busied themselves, clucking their shortened, contented coos over the patch of corn she threw out for them.

Pardi had committed himself to getting the PNP geared up for the next five years, and he held the party together while preparing the infrequent legal briefs requested of him with his usual care and diligence. Mardi gently suggested that he might write a book on politics, an idea which he noted in a diary but made no further comment about.

But at home he often appeared out of place. Mardi had merely shifted her habits to the new house, waking to feed the birds instead of the cows or the horses, working in the mornings in the studio, gin and tonic at twelve, lunch at one, and a rest at two o'clock, followed by her afternoon bath—which seemed to take at least an hour in the only bathroom, leaving the mirrors fogged and the bathroom smelling of talcum powder—a cup of tea, and then receiving her drop-in guests for drinks and olives and cheese till seven, when we always sat down formally at the table for supper-time, even if it was a bowl of soup or a sandwich.

But Pardi seemed too big or too old or too weathered for the new place; not in size, really, but philosophically almost too exten-sive for this little house. He looked ill at ease and bumped into coffee tables and tripped over rugs. At times he seemed lost—not geographically, more as though he couldn't find his thoughts. In Drumblair he had always padded around upstairs barefoot, on ele-gant, slender, size ten feet with their twiglike bones and soft veins threading just below the brown silk of his skin. Now these feet were always housed in his socks and shoes, as though nowhere was private enough to undress them, or maybe the tiles were too hard or too cold after Drumblair's wooden floors.

By this time I had discovered Kingston's teenage social life, and I remember the time mostly for my battles about getting permission to go to parties, my endless rows with my father about how he con-ducted his private life, my insistence that he not interfere in mine.

Mardi, my father, and I had always shared an interesting tri-angular relationship. Where Pardi was god of my world, my father had always chosen to take a back seat and never tried to compete. Inasmuch as Mardi always promoted Pardi to me, perhaps without meaning to she demoted my father. Mardi and Michael often squab-bled over how the other handled me, and often within earshot. My father felt she indulged me, and Mardi felt that he didn't spend enough time with me. They were both right. But there was another dimension that came into this, that had nothing to do with me. They had always been close as mother and son; close in that, tem-peramentally, they excited and delighted each other. There was always an aspect of flirtation in Mardi towards my father—"Ah, Michael darling, come *sit* with me," she would coo as he walked through the door after a busy day, "come take a pew and tell us all about it!" They would share specially prearranged visits in the studio, where he would give her advice about some carving she was working on.

They never ran out of things to talk about—politics, union strikes, flowers (why did cows single out hibiscus to eat over any other bush?), books, music, track and field, boxing and cricket. Mardi loved to listen to my father's sports accounts, which always widened to involve some social aspect of the competition—whether it was the implications of cricket on the Caribbean psyche in its battle with colonialism, or the thrill of Jesse Owens annoying the racist Hitler, or whether the artistry of Ali was primary or secondary to what he stood for. She loved his passion for heroes and the way they came to symbolize important moments that needed to be mileposts. Many of her protestations about how little time he spent with me were really complaints on her own behalf. I think she liked having her family all within arm's reach again. My father went through several relationships, none of which seemed too serious, and Douglas, though he dated, seemed determined not to marry again, insisting he'd prefer to collect orchids, which demanded far less attention. I think Mardi felt both sons should take a break from marriage.

When she got a lucrative offer from a new hotel still under construction, the Sheraton Kingston, Mardi turned once more to a Biblical theme, this time from the book of Job, in which it seems that she again saw the conundrum of her life reflected:

Man that is born of woman
Is of a few days, and full of trouble
He cometh forth as a flower,
and is cut down
He fleeth also as a shadow,
And continueth not.

The large bas-relief carved out of purpleheart wood com-
manded our lives for months—from the patting of the wood for
good luck, to the days of cloudlike wisps of chalk marking shapes
on the flushed new roughed-out surface, to the appearance of
woman as mother earth—the land, surely, silently rising in the fore-
front—to the emergence of three patently human figures behind,
the woman holding a child who turns from the comfort of her
breast to reach for the man.

"Smells like life beginning," said Pardi as he breathed in the
nutty smell of fresh cut wood in our world again.

"*Man that is born of woman is of a few days...*," I joked to him,
remembering the chicken-and-egg discussions about who came first.

"Indeed," he said, but Mardi frowned and slightly shook her
head at me, worrying lest he see in this a personal significance I
had not intended.

I flounced out of the studio. In fact, I just generally flounced
in those days, taking umbrage at anything, finding fault with my
grandmother's irritating habit of making all things into stories or
issues or dramas, with my grandfather's slowness in moving and
bumping into furniture, with his miscalculations on the road when
he was driving even when he was kindly giving me and my friends
a lift, with his quiet sadnesses and developing old-age irritability,
especially when I sat for ages on the telephone.

From both my new homes the insistent beat of ska was now
booming, not just in the distance from the nearby Four Roads
sound systems, but from our stereos. Pardi and Mardi must have
felt under attack from without and within. It interrupted the classical musical evenings; it kept them awake at nights, when Pardi
would sullenly put a pillow over his head and Mardi would lie
there contemplating all the changes, probably trying to understand
why the little town of Four Roads, which they had befriended all
these years, establishing a youth club in Drumblair's backlands and

a clinic in their square, would repay them with such disregard, as though this tough ghetto enclave were one of her sons being insensitive. She sometimes phoned the police, begging them to be diplomatic because these young people, she explained, were her friends, but could they get them to lower the sound a little bit so Mr. Manley could get some sleep? And sure enough it would get lowered for fifteen minutes, and then as soon as the police had left, the sound would return exuberantly, full blast.

But there was nothing she could do about me. I belonged to the new world of ska, which was the sound of today, the sound of all my parties. My father and Mardi juggled me back and forth and tried to cope with what I had become—a difficult teenager. Pardi delighted in pointing out that "teenager" was the name given to the smaller cockroaches that were far more difficult to eradicate than the larger ones. Although we came up with a plan for Mardi to illustrate a book with me, I don't think I wrote a single poem in those years, but she did illustrate a children's book written by Aunt Carmen.

In 1963, Pardi, who liked the fact that I had taken Latin and now enjoyed hearing me roll my R's in Spanish (he could never pronounce R's which probably explained why he called Muriel "Mu," Vera "V," and me "Pie"), offered to send me for the summer to Mardi's old art school friend, Gherke, in Guatemala. The trip was arranged, with my school friend Melanie to accompany me, at great expense to both families. I think they all needed a break from me, but also hoped good would come of the change. I enjoyed a few months flirting with the farmhands in Esquintla, quarrelling often with my perplexed friend, learning to drive a Jeep on the glorious Finca El Zapote under the volcano Fuego, and buying gifts of silver and bright woven fabrics to bring back for the family I missed, especially my stepmother, Thelma, whom I unexpectedly discovered I loved only after she had gone.

When I returned home I was just as quarrelsome, and that first trip started a pattern whereby each summer the family let me travel "down" to Barbados with Kyk, another school friend, who came to live with us during term time when her parents were transferred to the eastern Caribbean. Looking back at it now, it occurs to me that a lifelong pattern of escape was being established.

My rebellion seems to have launched into full swing after Guatemala, and the time becomes a blur of trying to get my father's attention; complaining to Mardi; being embarrassed by both Pardi and Mardi, who seemed too old-fashioned to be seen with; resenting their explanations of poverty as I demanded more clothes, more records, more jewellery, gifts for my friends, lifts to here and there, a later curfew at night.

It didn't really matter what happened, I quarrelled. Once I discovered that an old friend of the family who meant very little to me had died and nobody had told me; I rounded on Mardi to ask her why.

"Because I know what a sympathetic heart you have, dear," she said. I lambasted her for being manipulative, telling her that she actually sought to control who lived or died.

I blew up because I came home one day to find no lunch prepared for me. "Dear, next time there is no lunch, take eggs and a little cheese and make an omelette."

"This has become a love-hate relationship," Mardi announced incontrovertibly one day, as though she were branding a cow. "I think there are issues of insecurities but also a certain amount of wilfulness and a refusal to be helped."

But this time I was in real trouble, for Pardi got into the act, and his opinion mattered to me in a way that no one else's did. He blew up at me on his Duke Street stationery, writing a firm letter about my intolerable behaviour and the disgraceful way I talked to people.

Soon after, talk began of sending me to school in England.

Most months were considered "bad months," which meant that Pardi wasn't earning enough money at the law and they weren't living within their income. Inspired by her new kiln and the relative speed with which she could turn around smaller pieces for sale, Mardi began a series of terracottas. Each month another figure would pirouette on her stand in the studio. She enjoyed the freedom of movement that clay allowed, and the flexibility it gave her to change her mind. It brought together earth and water and fire, she said. "The kiln when it is white-hot—ha! So like life, and what comes through has stood the test."

She did an owl with what she called "the owliness of an owl," and a seated goat majestic among stylized leaves, and then a female fawn, quizzical, wild, mischievously nude, and a pair of gossips, their white dresses, treated in polychrome, startling against the clay. A meadow bull she did for my uncle, a Taurus, and then, as though dealing with me in daily life had proved unsuccessful, she decided to use a medium to reach me that she knew even now I hadn't the will to repudiate. She sculpted me a *Tyger Tyger* that I could keep, and through which she hoped I would learn something about myself:

Ra Darling, I want you to understand something—The reason why I am turning and twisting and brooding so much over your tiger is that I feel I could do for you what I did for your Daddy with the horse— give you something that you would value and which in a sense is an expression of you—so that when you looked back over the years, you would see in it—some of the struggles of your youth. You see, to the world the tiger is a wild and cruel creature. But if one could get inside the mind of the tiger I do not think that this is how he appears to himself and I do not feel that Blake saw him like this. I believe that he is one of the most integrated of all beasts. Look at his colour and think of the gold light striking through the tree of the jungle, light and shadow, light and shadow and the deep red brown of the earth—the soft white of his under throat and belly with the ash grey of stones and fallen leaves.

He doesn't bellow or roar like a bull or a lion—to create fear—he has no horns or mane or hump—to assert his dominance—or to attract attention—He is silent of foot silent of voice—moving with the sureness born of his strength, protected by his marvellous colouring. Lions are nervous and fight more from fear—Tigers show coolness and judgment—and yet they have a far more collected courage. If you could get inside his mind—I think over the thousands of years that it took to create him what he is—you would find a greater understanding of the laws of life, of his needs and the needs of his mate, of how to move and live for greater safety and above all a deep unconscious urge to be totally at one with the deep emotional urges of his own being. Integrated with nature, hence integrated with himself and life, man cannot tame or train him as with a lion—because man is not part of the pattern of his life. He only becomes a man-eater when circumstances force it on him. So here is true beauty, true strength and in the world of the jungle— he is supreme. That would be a wonderful symbol wouldn't it darling?

This seems to have connected with me, for shortly after that I decided to turn over a new leaf. I would go to university, so the family made plans to send me to London to do my A levels. Mardi felt that an opportunity to get to know my mother who I had not seen for almost fifteen years, would help me lay some of my demons to rest.

I was being given a second chance. I left in October 1964 with youthful ardour, curious to meet my mother and determined to live up to my baffling, intriguing new challenge—to understand and come to terms with the characteristics and nature of my tiger.

Thinking about my grandmother's Dying God carvings, I have often wondered whether, just as one day must die for the next to dawn, the father must die before the emergence of the son. And I wonder if there are people so attached, or so fundamental to each other, that they can't resolve change or detach or say farewell, or cede as long as the other person is there. For in many ways I think Drumblair still remained in our hearts as long as Pardi lived. The world of the house, its deeper meanings, still existed in him. His presence was for many like history's silent reproach. Mardi kept working on her carving, and my father in the union, but both seemed to be biding their time, concerned and looking after Pardi, not quite able to gear up to whatever it was they would have to face when he was gone. His inevitable departure became a big unspoken dread that we tiptoed around even when he wasn't there.

If, as Mardi supposed, my mother had been the deep shadow of angst that haunted my earlier life, meeting her was relatively anti-climatic. She was a charming, witty, very pretty, sometimes prickly woman who was not given to sentimentality. She was used to brushing off worries, her own as well as her friends', and I think was often perplexed by the sense of do-or-die with which I treated most occasions. She saved the sort of emotional drama I was used to from my grandmother for the dog whose pictures were the only family portraits in her house.

Homesick and cold, once again I wrote letters, sending my poems home as peace offerings, flags of truce, small beseechments of forget-me-nots. In return the family wrote me their encouragements: Mardi talked of family news and carving and writing, moving easily between annoyance that Seaga, a government minister, had organized a function to coincide with her annual Drumblair

charity dance (which kept its name), and her deeper thoughts on
the poet Browning, and her description of Ethiopia's Emperor Haile
Selassie's terror on visiting Jamaica, when his plane was mobbed by
thousands of Rastafarians who had come to greet him, and throw
themselves prostrate on the tarmac before him. His Majesty was not
aware of their belief that he was the leader of a lost tribe of Israel,
nor that he was their Messiah. Pardi wrote about politics in Africa.
There were two African students at my school, one the daughter
of Ghana's Minister of Finance, Edusi, and the other the daughter
of Nigeria's finance minister, Ekotie-Eboh. The first was criticized
when his wife bought a golden bed, which Pardi explained resulted
from a different set of values in Ghana, where tribal chiefs were
expected to display their wealth, and the second was murdered in
a coup, the news coming over the BBC as we gathered with his
daughter one evening in the school's recreation room.

During these year Norman and Edna had taken a few trips,
some of them official with him as Leader of the Opposition, some
I suspect designed by Mardi to try to connect her husband's flag-
ging spirit to life again. They wrote me from different places—from
Israel on a postcard with a stained-glass window by Chagall, from
Mexico on a card with painted birds, from Florence and Rome and
Madrid, from Philadelphia and New York. It was difficult to imag-
ine them as tourists.

And Mardi would send me pictures of her work. She had
drawn at least three pictures of Moses parting the Red Sea. And
then she sculpted a terracotta of the prophet carrying tablets
down from the mountain. I told her he reminded me of a
favourite carving she owned by the sculptor Zadkine, a lyrical
bronze of the figure of Orpheus playing his harp. I always found
the smallness of both figures improbable, and thought I detected
an absence of any sense of moment or tragedy. But I think I grew
to love them for that. I saw in them the busy worker who has no

time to weigh the consequences of his vision, nor wallow in the possibilities of fate.

In 1965 Mardi got what she always considered the most important commission of her professional life. She was invited to sculpt a statue of one of our national heroes, Paul Bogle, to be placed in front of the courthouse in Morant Bay, on the east of the island. Only one photograph remains of Paul Bogle, and she was determined not to be guided by it. She wanted to find the essence of the man, a deacon from rural Stony Gut, a religious man of peace who would one day pick up a cutlass and chop the local Custos, His Majesty's representative, in the Morant Bay rebellion of October 11, 1865. She did not think she was likely to find that man residing in the neat studio portrait, where he posed with his deacon's collar. One of her letters to me discussed her trip to Stony Gut, where an old lady described him to her as "*a bold man*." She pondered the meaning of bold, deciding it took an awful lot of conviction, determination, and courage to do what he had done. In Stony Gut they wanted Bogle back alive, the villagers said, as though this commission somehow made her responsible for returning him.

"*The things he fought for are alive,*" she said, "*. . . what he died for—Freedom and Independence.*"

When finally the photograph of the dedication of the statue arrived in the post, an eight-by-twelve black-and-white picture kept safe between two sheets of cardboard, wrapped untidily in brown paper and string with purposefully re-knotted knots (for some reason Mardi could never produce a decent-looking package, and even on gifts invariably tied the clumsiest bows), I remember what struck me. There was this vast monument which had been cast from clay and finished in Ciment Fondu, rising from its plinth almost the height of the steepled building, its proportionally over-large head dominating the figure in the tradition of African art or the treatment by early Christians of the saints—shoulders thrown back, eyes implacable, arms akimbo holding his sword down flat on his chest, the arrangement like a cross. And below, not quite reaching even the top of the plinth, was the Minister of Finance, Mr. Sangster, and other ministers and dignitaries, like toy men under the giant figure that gazed out imperturbable from history over the crowd of country people gathered for the occasion. The official's speech was enclosed and I read of the need to honour our history as a newly independent nation, and the importance of this slave rebellion. The huge figure loomed over the small courthouse square, towering over the speaker and the old judiciary building, casting a long shadow over the antlike crowd diminished by distance.

And I suddenly realized the sheer magnificence of Mardi's contribution; the fact that possibly her work would outlive written history. Maybe that was the day this book began.

What I couldn't know was that while I was writing it in 2007, the courthouse would burn to the ground, its charred remains lying in an ashen pile behind Bogle, who wasn't even singed.

Mardi's small post-election family world split up after I left. Douglas got a job teaching with UNESCO in Africa; Little Norman went with him. Shortly before I left for England, my father had met Barbara, who would become his third wife. After a bumpy initial year in England, I settled down and produced the two distinctions in History and English that I needed to apply to university. I was accepted at the University of the West Indies.

Shortly after my return to Jamaica in the summer of 1966, my father married Barbara. She was an extraordinary woman, as bright and gifted as she was beautiful, as exciting as she was just and caring. I became close to her, alternately envying and emulating my new stepmother. Pardi grew fond of her too, but I think Mardi by now had learned not to invest too much in her son's marriages. "Every time I give them a piece of my jewellery, they promptly break up," she said, as her small collection of treasures diminished.

Again, everything had changed in our lives. For the only time I can remember in my father's many marriages, he seemed to become part of Barbara's family more than ours, and the gate between the two houses, which I hadn't realized was there because it was always open and hidden by shrubs, was now kept locked.

Pardi would win his constituency seat again handsomely in 1967, after a final flourish of joyous campaigning for a daring left-wing agenda that brought a welcome surge of energy back into his life again, while at the national level he suffered his final defeat. A year after that he wrote to his sister Vera, who had moved to England, "*So I have come nearly to the end of one phase of my life. I will not stand for election again. I intend to retire from politics in 2 years.*"

Soon after, Vera died in a car crash in Kidderminster.

Mardi finally persuaded him to try to write the book. A book about his story, his memories, about politics, about his role in fed-eration and the national movement. About his contribution to Jamaica. About things she knew he believed in. A political mem-oir. He was somewhat unsure of what he'd say, especially about himself. He also wondered how he should go about it, but some-one suggested employing some students to help him research the years. He'd meet with them on the patio and sit in a deep wooden chair with his feet crossed at the ankles on the low straw-woven footstool, his hands folded on his lap, and there I would find him some afternoons when I returned from university, looking captive, bored but obliging his wife, while these youngsters lectured him on what they felt in their youthful inexperience were the mistakes he had made.

And I was just as much to blame for making him feel fed up and unhappy. In the years before I went to university, my heart had been for Pardi an impregnable castle, a place, small and insignificant though it was in the grand scheme of things, where he would always be safe. I never doubted him for a moment. But my world was changing; Black power was all the rage, youth was on the march, and I was surrounded by my fellow students who were questioning everything I believed in—our modern history of nationalism, our Westminster democracy, the two-party system, most of all Norman Manley. I would come home angry at them and angry at my grandfather. I would show him the student paper, *Abeng*, which Mardi called a rag. I would say that I felt what was written in it was public and he had a right to know, but deep inside I really hoped for an explanation—wanted him to be able to disprove it all. They blamed him along with Bustamante for our nation's plight—its poverty and economic inequality, for the system that served the rich and the status quo, and did nothing about the poor. They blamed both parties for changing little after independence, as though it made no difference at all which of the two national leaders it was, as though their contributions had been similar or equal. What Norman had to offer of his elegance and integrity and renaissance thought, his disregard for anarchism, and his sense of history as a useful stepping stone, of life as a series of logical bridges connected and offering changes of heart and direction, meant nothing to the new generation who were hungry for immediate and radical change.

Pardi saw the Black power movement that the youth in Jamaica now embraced as an American concept, one born of an entirely different history of people who would never really own the land they lived in. But our history was different. Our colonizer was gone, we did own our destiny. The island now belonged to us. The music that Pardi heard coming through the distant sound systems late at night, an insistent pulse pushing away the order of life as he knew it, provided a deeper truth that didn't come from anywhere else; this truth he felt should have spoken more loudly to them than any America had to offer.

"*I think they will remember this as the age of lamentations . . . the music of lost Africa's desolation become the music of the town.*" Pardi resorted to sombrely quoting Dossie Carberry from *Focus*.

His increasing reticence troubled Mardi. Within a harvest of sadness his shadows deepened, and she wanted to shake him, dry him in the sun, rake away the dead, and let in the light. His mood affected her like the rainy season going on too long. I could feel a shadow of impatience at times, but she continued to do day-to-day things to keep it away; invite in friends, whom he would often hide from; encourage him to read and listen to music. She organized weeks by the sea, from Runaway Bay to Green Island, where they would try to replay younger holidays once spent with their sons or with me, but the loneliness of his disappointment seemed to darken even those shores.

Pardi had retired from the law, and in an article on the closing of his office the newspaper referred to him as "*The patriarch of the law.*" It seemed that what was left of him was titles—roads and schools were named after him, scholarships, a graduate degree from UWI planned in his name; he was even fondly called Father of the Nation by some.

Their finances were in such disarray that they were forced to rent out Regardless and move up to Nomdmi. Despite improvements made to the structure—an extra bedroom and a larger bathroom and kitchen—Mardi almost hated to live there now. It felt like being exiled to the past, as though she were locked away with so many ghosts. It was too far away, too lonely for one's final years, she said. With Pardi not himself, it made her feel hopeless and gloomy and depressed; although she knew this was not so, she sometimes imagined an ungrateful nation banishing her husband as though in disgrace. Feeling doomed to the past, she turned nostalgically to her diaries, with fond but wistful fragments of reminiscences about her children. She wrote to a friend something I had never heard her admit: "*Norman's illness has been coming on for some time.*" She watched and she waited, learning with difficulty how to keep throttling back.

My father turned his study, which he had built as an extension to his home when he married Barbara, into a flat for his parents when they came into town. By now the family, who tended to take a long time to let anyone into their deeper ranks, were getting used to Barbara. She was pregnant and spent most of her time in bed, not feeling well. We all put it down to morning sickness, and, out of sight, Mardi and I rolled our Shearer eyes and pretended to mop our brows at what we considered a self-indulged frailty—"oh, fragile flower," we'd say—till the baby was born by Caesarean section, and the doctor discovered the love of my father's life riddled with cancer.

Mardi's commission from Holy Cross Church in Kingston to carve Mary, the mother of Christ, came at about the time of Barbara's bleak prognosis. While Barbara lay in bed trying to survive radiation and early experimental chemotherapy delivered by doctors through injection directly to her liver at a hospital in New York, Mardi roughed out the relatively small figure. She said it was good to be back with a mallet and chisel again, to smell the familiar, poignant intimacy of freshly cut wood. She had just completed two small carvings—a torso of *Psyche* out of Belize mahogany, and a second one, which reminded me of the girl with the goat, of *Eve*, the mother of man, almost nestling the serpent that encircles her, their heads together, affectionately conferring.

Mardi was not interested in carving a Virgin Mary with some symbolic innocence. She was creating a grieving woman who had lost a son. I think she saw no heroism in sexual innocence but considered Mary an involuntary martyr, mother of the chosen, who must sacrifice the one she loves, whether to death or to the absence caused by a move onto a new horizon. In a way, she felt Jesus didn't belong to his family anymore. But Mary's sacrifice as a mother, though ennobling, was ultimately heartbreaking for one who, after all, had never chosen to be noble.

In *Mary* there is a resignation in the female figure that echoes her own as she watched Pardi battered by his mission. But the figure was also the mother who is always feeling riddled with some guilt or other over her children, over what she could or should or shouldn't have done. And the loss of a son was symbolic of the loss of all children who must leave the nest. Looking into the tomb to see if he is really there—hoping for resurrection—may be each mother's hope for a child's survival and success.

Crucifix came from one stream of Mardi's work: the rising of sons in the sun series, and the dying of their fathers, and the lonely journey of Moses returning from the mountain with his tablets. *Mary* came from another stream, where the courage women don't realize they have is lurking; where they are forced to discover that courage to cope with losing their men to their quests, with watching their sons overshadow their fathers, with witnessing their sacrifices. Mary looks into the tomb and she pulls up her shoulders, avoiding the pain of knowing that deepest of human dreads, to lose a child, and this pain she knows all along, before she gets to the tomb; but in her gesture, hands down at her sides in such posed quietude, she is keeping still so that something more wonderful may evolve. The original drawings had her arms over her face so she couldn't see. But Mardi realized that one has to see. One has to face grief. One has to face life. *"Tragedy is the individual's refusal to accept reality,"* she once wrote, and had often said as much to me. She had learned that reality had so much to teach.

By the time Mardi completed the carving in 1968—*Mary* leaning sideways, her arms straight down at her sides in a compliant, self-protective helplessness—Barbara had died. My father's sorrow was like an untamed element unleashed in our lives, and my grand-father one more layer sad for a woman on whose bed he'd come to sit many times to laugh, to be irreverent, to remember his luck by facing her lack of it. Before her funeral, Pardi and Mardi went to check the burial site. When Pardi slipped and fell down the raw-edged side where it was being prepared by grave-diggers, Mardi knew. She knew when we sang the hymns and my father—who, prompted by Barbara and the comfort of her by his side, had now run for office and narrowly won a seat—almost sobbed aloud as the coffin seemed to slide for a moment on its wheels gently towards him; she knew when her beloved sister Nora was dying of Parkin-son's in England and she couldn't bear to leave him. She knew when Pardi and I celebrated our final party together, when he was seventy-five and I was twenty-two, and we cut the cake, with me holding his tentative hand firmly below mine; she knew as he made his retirement speech at the party conference, and as he touched each thing at Nomdmi as if acknowledging milestones; she knew as his circles in Regardless became smaller and smaller, until he stopped venturing into the kitchen or sitting on the verandah. She knew when he finally went to bed and she sat beside him recon-noitring the past in her diary, aware of each hard-earned breath and wondering, since there was no difference between them, which would be chosen for last.

She knew in those two weeks of struggle, where he showed more determination to go than to stay.

He died on September 2, 1969.

She knew, with the resilience of the sound system still blaring from its resolute indifference in Four Roads, that the time had come to face life with renewed courage for the sorrow that was sure to be hers for many a tomorrow.

Part Three

11

A Ragged Cloth

I believe that a complete realization of life is only possible if there is an understanding and acceptance of death as part of the cycle. To refuse to think of death or to repudiate it is to deny the concept of infinity. Death is the un-illuminated side of the coin—it is not nothingness. I think to attempt to grasp what this implies stretches the imagination. It widens consciousness. It also accepts the reality that Life and Death are not two states but one.

—Edna Manley, in an interview with Easton Lee

WHEN PARDI DIED, Mardi didn't go to pieces, as everyone thought she had; she simply returned to them. She was left facing the person she had been before he entered her life—a collection of powerful emotions and impulses that battered her like surges at the mouth of a coral cove. He had taught her that once this energy was trapped in there, she could harness it to drive her work. With Pardi she had managed the appearance of cohesion, having enough to discipline herself beyond her work, enough to allow her to tackle life with a limited amount of reason and practicality. He had coped with the rest. Her life had been so sufficiently blessed by his generosities that she had thought nothing of giving some of this back and tailoring twenty years to suit his needs, even if he hadn't asked—and he never asked. She second-guessed what demands his life would have to make of hers, and answered them. In those years she lived by the rhythm of campaigns building towards polling day, electoral victories or defeats, and the crucial but ultimately fleeting intervening six years of official service when Norman was the head of government.

Douglas returned to his job in Africa, so it fell to Michael to see his mother through another campaign—her five years of grief. It was not the grief of the old, the tender nostalgia of the safe and sound who, having seen the other through, await their turn. It was a tortured time of someone very angry who now felt defied by her partner in his death, a partner who had been as deep and essential in her life as a solitary organ, as difficult to replace as a rare blood type.

On top of this—and most strangely—Pardi, Jamaica's incomparably finest lawyer, had died intestate. In the weeks following his death, after a thorough search was made of the house, my father tried every law firm and lawyer with whom Pardi had been associated over the years. There was no will nor any record of one. The house passed somewhat sadly from Pardi to Mardi, along with Uhuru, Pardi's last dog, a despairing Doberman, and the furniture and the garden and the view beyond. But Mardi had never dealt with the world of the everyday. Even her dairy at Drumblair had been for her just a joyous hobby, tending the cows along with the horses, naming each animal, studying their dispositions, predicting their outflow of milk and comparing the actual yield in the next column in a huge green accounts book. All expenses had been covered by Pardi, and she had blithely collected the payments when Wright, the dairy master, returned in the buggy with the empty silver churns, and in her buoyantly curling handwriting had neatly applied the amounts to the space at the end of the line for the total money for the day, pounds, shillings, and pence, and tallied that column at the bottom of the page at the end of the month. There had always been a profit. She had never been any the wiser. The dairy had remained her great triumph of enterprise.

But now, the practical things were messily tangled in bureaucracy, and Mardi couldn't believe he had not thought of telling her about them: accounts, insurance, license for the car—how to cope with these things about which she knew nothing, had been allowed to know nothing. My father stepped in to fill the breach, but found it all a perplexing instance of irresponsibility on his father's part, or at best, utter thoughtlessness. This lapse taught him such a vivid lesson that for the rest of his life he kept updating his own will, rewriting it to reflect changes in his wives, his fortunes and misfortunes.

I think there were times Mardi felt, with some bitterness, that death might have come in defence of Pardi, giving him a means of escape; he had been ready. He had believed that all people came to this earth to discover their mission. Some missions were long and some were short. Some were doomed to failure, as he may have believed his own was.

"I don't see how he could perceive his life as a failure," Douglas said to Michael when he returned from Africa for the funeral, and saw the moving public display of regret and grief.

"I don't know that he did," said Michael. "I think he had simply had enough. I think he was uninspired and bored."

Mardi knew that was true. Pardi always said that only a dog goes back to its vomit, and he felt the law was like a return to the past; he hadn't the interest or the energy to write a book about himself. She worried over his legacy: that it not be underrated, that he not be forgotten. My father—who had been elected to take over the leadership of the party in 1969 and was now deeply entrenched in the political fray, designing a campaign for the next general election, just eighteen months away—believed Pardi's legacy was safe. He knew that the movement that had begun in his father's head— a series of thoughts and considerations and calculations, sometimes miscalculations, a determination that things could be changed— would be a permanent inspiration. Pardi had transferred a dream to the national psyche, and then made it real, building brick after constitutional and institutional brick. That, he said, was Pardi's true legacy. Maybe what one considered one's mission was really just a compass point one walked towards. And Pardi had to have known that he was part of a generation that would leave an island forever changed, now belonging to itself, and that the people's choices, even if they differed from his, would be their own.

Had that comforted her husband as Mardi had wished it would? Probably not. Pardi had not seen life quite that way. He had not been a romantic. One did a job. He had been tired and bored and feeling ill. He had been ready to go. Going would have been a practical decision for Pardi, my father felt.

But Mardi, who had shared the end with him, could not stop thinking of him in his last days: his shuffling steps, his beautiful feet all shiny and swollen, his hands shaking as he tried to sign cheques, his loss of interest in Tildy's food, and the last heavy sigh she remembered before he was helped into bed for the last time. It led her to wonder if these nobler rationales were ever a comfort to the gritty everydayness of being older, less well and less well-functioning, slower, less good-looking—and that nebulous, blameless side-stepping of one, not meant to be taken personally but taken very personally, that left the aged, no matter their contribution, simply ignored. The sense that one had become stranded on the shore as the tide receded and life continued, keen and vital, elsewhere.

The archives had taken his papers away. Well, those he hadn't burned himself. And she spent many hours helping Rex Nettleford, who was compiling a record of her late husband's work, to be published by Longman's.

Late husband. Her mind bolted at the thought, which hit her soon after she woke each morning and, no matter how many times she came across it in a day, always managed to startle her afresh, so that she found herself, back legs blindly reversing like those of a horse being urged through a stile through which he knows his body cannot pass. Her, yes, say it, *late husband's* work—his important cases and speeches, his lectures, his diary entries and notes and letters and opinions. His fragment of an autobiography. He had written so much, and not a word should be wasted. And these were only the words that had been caught; the rest, like river stones, had shuddered under the weight of the water of time, tumbling along and rearranging themselves, each making a small dent in the riverbed and the shape of destiny. If she could only open a huge sack of them now and turn it upside down on the table, spilling out all over again each sentence, each word, every nuance of their extraordinary conversation, which had lasted over a period of nearly sixty years.

How could anyone imagine, from this small fraction she now offered, just how much had been thought and discussed and agonized over and theorized and devised, spoken and misspoken, gauged and regauged and instituted and constituted, lived and rejoiced and endured and celebrated, all that had emanated from that precious head?

His fragment of a story added up to only eighteen printed pages; he had gathered what he could, self-consciously and painstakingly as if for a school paper, the light all the while descending until he abandoned that fragment and wrote nothing but his last ramblings, even on the cheques she had given him for signature, or on the pages of his appointment book little stick men or amounts in gallons of gas that he needed for the journey he kept muttering he had to take—he must not miss that train—as though his ghost had left already, and all that remained with her must needs soon follow.

Pardi had chosen to die—he had even chosen the day, whose arrival he kept inquiring after. It was the day of a by-election to replace him as his constituency's Member of Parliament. Mardi was still angry with him. But the way he explained it, a time comes when it's best to go. He was so definite. She was left with no choice but to content herself with this brittle, vulnerable, paper-dry thing called legacy that one was left with after the breathing and burning of life were done.

She had sat in their room with him for the last weeks before he died. Michael had brought in a hospital bed and a nurse. Mostly she wrote letters or drew, intermittently checking on him, then turning to look with resigned detachment at the mountains beyond the green of their garden, a landmark to steady her equilibrium. She knew already that his quietly determined, defiant sleep was a struggle to unbreathe.

One morning she went into the studio for a few hours to make a small maquette out of clay, and left it swaddled under wet towels. It was the figure of an angel with one wing extended like a flame above, the other providing safe haven for a small figure of a man face down, asleep.

And then the morning of his death, when there was enough time after each completion of breath for her to ponder the ramifications if there were to be no other, she wrote in her diary that she saw the angel who left with him shortly after.

"It was an implacable face whose mission I knew was irreversible. I drew it that very afternoon, with its deep lines of resolve. The man was turned with his face into the wing, like a child nestling a pillow. He had turned his back on this world."

She struggled with a sudden urge of tears that seemed point-
less and inappropriate, so she walked down to the studio meaning
to pull herself together—whatever *pulling oneself together* meant—and
squeezed the unwelcome blessings from her eyes between thumb
and forefinger. Before her on the table lay her large sketchbook
open to an empty page, and she dragged those two damp finger-
tips down from the top of the paper, closing into a two-inch V,
leaving pressed frown lines that became those of the angel's face.

That afternoon, after the undertakers collected Pardi—someone
stealing the fob-watch lying on the table beside him—Mardi finished the drawing. It suggests each feature of the face in a separate
section; each surface—the nose, the cheeks, the jaws, the neck—
appears self sufficient and imperturbable as coexisting surfaces of
alabaster. The eyelids sculpted shut to us, the mouth resolute
beyond words, nothing to communicate with us here. She said she
drew the angel's face distinctly from memory, and she later referred
to it as too ruthless and too frightening to use in the ultimate carving, but its implacable power, eyes closed to appeal, was necessary
on his passenger's behalf. In that face I have always found the mysterious, unbreakable bond of secrecy that is eternity, and that
dependability makes me feel safe.

The small clay maquette and this charcoal head, thirty inches
high and twenty-four wide, would be the start of her work *The
Angel*, which took the better part of a year to carve.

And in that year she careered between the real world with its
practical problems and an abyss created in her soul, in which she
faced herself squarely and on her own again. Pardi had left her flat
broke. In all the years they had lived together, despite their having
to sell the backlands or both their homes, to buy back later when
they could—even knowing she had to sell her work to help their
finances—she had never felt the full impact of financial responsibility. Just as with the dairy, Pardi had paid all the expenses, and

let her run the house without ever being aware of his finances; she couldn't even write a cheque. My father, never known for fiscal acumen, helped her open an account and taught her how to keep track, and what she had to keep track of was at first a collection of unpaid bills that kept mounting, and two homes with staff who had to be paid.

For a while Mardi accepted kind invitations to travel from friends. At first nearby, to the home of an anthropologist Norman had been close to in Norbrook, then across the island, to acquaintances in the eastern parish of Portland. She even flew to Miami, to an old friend who had owned the gracious Jamaica Inn where we used to go for a fortnight in summers. She would sit for hours, unable to read or write or even think clearly, feeling confined by other people's lives and their routines and boundaries; feeling obligated and ill at ease with their kindness, ending up returning home a day or two early. She decided it was better she just stay put and battle it out at Regardless.

Friends in the island and abroad reconnected with her and, as she had always done, she spent a great deal of time every day answering letters. Whereas in the last two years she had reluctantly found herself having to live a reclusive life, either up at Nomdmi, or bound to Regardless with Pardi so sick, now she began to go out more—to dinners with friends, concerts and shows, and even to the races.

As long as she could get straight back home. Home was her anchor, the place where Pardi's clothes and possessions and shadows resided, the only place where through odd moments—something lost reappearing, some coincidence or unaccountable sound, she felt she might be able to find him.

My father made an effort to include her whenever he could— to movies, to lunches and dinners; he escorted her to exhibitions and concerts, often joined by his new girlfriend, Beverley, whom he had started dating shortly before Pardi died. And Mardi was grateful, accepting sometimes, and at other times excusing herself, withdrawing and then, in her renewed state of turmoil, fighting a sense of feeling abandoned.

Immediately after Pardi's death, I had taken my driver's test, getting a quick date by lying about having to drive my grandmother to the funeral. It was an official funeral and she was in fact escorted by a smart police detail, the army transporting her husband's hearse. It was the saddest funeral I've ever attended, and for the family it seemed at the time like an extension of my stepmother Barbara's. Yes, there was a vast crowd, but it had the same principal cast of our family and friends, except that we were now missing Pardi. The afternoon held such a silence. Thousands had filed past his open coffin in the days leading up to the service. Thousands came from all over the island to bid him farewell. And Jamaicans in their thousands aren't usually silent, not even at a funeral. I have always felt that the funeral reflected regret more complicated than simply for the passing of a man, even such a politically significant one. Sometimes I think that unconsciously the crowd may have sensed that his death might signify the end of an alternative for the country.

I have often heard it said that my grandmother, all in black, her face pale and very beautiful in grief beneath the drama of her wide-rimmed hat, seemed inconsolable. It's strange, but there was something about her that just didn't appear widowlike to me. She looked stark but she didn't have that quality of soft liquidity, the bruised vulnerability of a sorrowing wife who feels she is left irrelevant. I remember her looking very much detached, almost as she had the morning he lay dying—wide awake, like a soldier who has lost a limb and is pressing on the wound to avoid bleeding to death. Her eyebrows behind the distraction of her veil were lifted ever so slightly, in the way she had when she disapproved of something she wasn't prepared to comment on, as if this pageantry and appreciation were all very well and good but had come far too late. But perhaps I saw these things in her because I felt them in myself.

I spent a lot of time at Regardless in the year after Pardi died. Much to his pleasure, I had graduated from university with an English degree, and now went to teach English and history at Kingston College, a valiant old Anglican boys' secondary school. I shared a house with friends from the university and Little Norman, now grown up, who helped me help Mardi reorganize domestic life at Regardless, even repainting her room yellow over the blue as though by doing so we'd turn over a new leaf for her. I dropped in to see her daily on my way from school, in my first car, a second-hand Singer Chamois that kept breaking down, which Mardi assured me was a rite of passage. I spent many weekends at Regardless, my friends and Norman dropping in to play bridge or dominoes with Mardi.

She loved it when I stayed, and said the nights didn't threaten as so long or so lonely with someone there. I'd wake to hear the grille gates to the patio pulling open as she went to feed the birds. Even in those days, she never seemed sad in the morning, always anticipating the day like a new shot at life. Maybe she was just relieved to have another long night out of the way. We'd sit in the kitchen waiting for the ghost to rise from the kettle and she'd make us instant Nescafé with a teaspoon of condensed milk. She was very proud of the fact that she could boil water and make coffee, butter bread, and one day around that time she told me with pride that she'd learned how to boil an egg.

We became a lot closer. She was all I had left of Pardi. We started to share a lot more small confidences, things I expect she would have wanted to share with a daughter, like needing a more modern, effective cream for her face than traditional Pond's cold cream—I found her Elizabeth Arden's Visible Difference and Revlon

Touch & Glow Misty Rose foundation to cover the age spots on her face and hands when she was going out in the evening. I took on the job of finding her shoes, which were always difficult to fit. Her feet were long, size nine, with very narrow heels—a slender foot with the grimace of a bunion tugging any possibility of elegance out of shape. So it was a challenge to find a shoe narrow enough at the back and wide enough across the front. She liked low heels or flat elasticized slip-ons, and they had to be very soft so as not to hurt the bunion. She was delighted when I found her slingback shoes that also covered her toes.

Mardi was as ever selfless and adoring with me, but up close I felt her like a small boat rocking and tossing about in a stormy sea, tethered by her futile hope of finding Pardi in Regardless again. Her over-sensitivity reminded me of an electric lamp with a short, which sparks and shocks with no warning when you touch it in the normal way. She was often wounded by family criticism, however slight or unintended, imagining that she was being laughed at when sometimes we who also grieved, but less acutely, were just jollying ourselves along in a camaraderie we'd built to reinforce her. I must admit that at other times, as my father and I tried to build back a relationship, spending more time together—I'd accompany him during yet another of his hiatuses from romance, in lieu of a date, or as his partner in bridge—we did tend to side up a bit, laughing at amusing instances of her "high drama," which if viewed from a distance could be truly funny. But she took offence with us, with friends, often feeling slighted or derided, sometimes forgotten and discarded.

"It's the time of between from 2 till 5 p.m. [sic] which I dread even more than a sleepless night and Norman has gone—gone for always . . . ," she wrote in her diary in October 1969. She had always found her lowest ebb in the early afternoon, and had the habit of taking a rest after lunch to restore herself. But every hour of her life had now become that time from two till five, and she suffered from sleeplessness in the room she had shared with Pardi. She had moved one of the beds, her own, over to the spare room and now slept in the consolation of his bed. She kept the bed-table that had swung over his temporary hospital bed, and placed whatever book she was reading, and a writing pad and drawing book and pens and pencils beside her, things she could reach at night to keep her busy.

When she did sleep she had started to have vivid dreams—being ill and sent to live in the country; attending a terrible play that turned out not to be a play at all; being stranded alone in Miami airport; discovering her beloved carving mallet, as familiar and dear to us all as a member of the family, smashed into tiny fragments. Once she felt a shadowy figure in the room at night, not the way one senses an intruder but more as a hallowed presence visiting her, a feeling that for weeks after she could not shake. That was when I realized that she believed, was still hoping against hope, that she might see Pardi again.

Wayne Brown—whom they had met through me at the beginning of our lifelong friendship, which had begun at university—had returned from England, where he'd won the Commonwealth Poetry Prize for his first book, *On the Coast*. He planned to write a biography of Mardi. She was surprised at the time by this focus on her, as she was then consumed with safekeeping Norman's legacy. She was helping work on Norman's book, was keeping an eye on the progress of a statue of him that had been commissioned, and was in the planning stages of starting a memorial foundation in his name which would offer a yearly award of excellence. But after much thought, feeling that any story about her would quite naturally be Pardi's story too—and realizing that Wayne would do it anyway so it was better to co-operate, so she might have some control, and Wayne thought and wrote so beautifully—she went along with his proposal, giving him access to their papers and letters, to her precious diaries, and putting him in touch with key people he could interview.

Mardi had painted a small watercolour in which she placed her angel in the landscape of Pardi's departure. The angel is mov- ing along the horizon, one wing thrown back, the other lying below the sleeping figure of a man; there is a tenderness like that of a parent with a child, but the cradling is not in the wing but in the watchful compassion of the face, which is turned attentively to the angel's charge. They venture beyond a path that has led through the mountains from the setting sun, on through a darkening sky watched by the moon, the only presence of an open eye.

Soon after the watercolour, Mardi began carving out a large plank of mahogany. Although the project was a bas-relief, the wood was cut quite thick and gave her space to create a sense of the fig- ures above the recess created behind them, floating, no longer earth- bound. One day when she was still roughing out, I went to check on her and see how she was doing. She had outlined in white chalk *two* human figures lying along the angel's lower wing. I was seized with fear, realizing that she wished she were going on that journey with him. Recent experience had taught me that when people want to die, they can make it happen. I waited till later, when she was in the house, and then I returned quietly to the studio and placed the maquette with the single figure on the table at the base of the barely roughed-out carving. When I came in the next day, she had rubbed out the original chalk and returned the single figure to the composition.

When it was finished a year later, one wing extended the length of the carving, the other gently escorting rather than cradling the single small creature.

On August 20, 1970, she made a note in her diary that the angel was finished and *"like all great efforts it was a failure."* The carving, a hauntingly beautiful one, had transported her husband to whatever place of safekeeping there is beyond our capacity for imagining. He had left to take that journey, his naked soul sleeping peacefully under the inward gaze of the most compassionate presence. Behind the figures, which are carved so finely they seem to shimmer in light, the wood is deeper, the gouges wider rising like flames, she said, though they feel almost like a womb for a second birth. The carving always makes me think of her father, Harvey, lying there, martyred by faith, with the large upper wing narrowing to its tip almost like the light from the tail of Halley's comet shining down in an arc. And then one day I was reading an interview in which she had spoken of the angel: *"But quite subconsciously I carved the wing of the angel in this upward peak, and weeks into the carving I suddenly realized the wing was again this damn tail of Halley's Comet."*

A review appeared in the *Daily Gleaner*, along with a poem I wrote, still childishly driven to illustrate her work. It became in a sense a conversation, a link that kept her close to my writing and me to her art, but also kept us close to a world we had shared with Pardi. Years later, my father had the maquette bronzed and gave it to me one Christmas.

Her period of grief had just started. As though *The Angel* had placed Pardi in safe custody, Mardi returned to the chaos of what had become her emotional life. As if the completion of the carving marked the end of a season for me, I packed up my bags and left to spend three weeks in Malta, but didn't return till the end of the year. I came back from months of my own self-created chaos to find her beyond brittle; she was greatly relieved to have me home again, but often spoke of "neurosis and involvement," with no fur-ther explanation but the little shake of her head that I knew to be her way of showing impatience with herself.

She was tense about politics again, now worrying over my father, who was embroiled in the buildup towards the general election. She worried that another life in the family would be heartlessly broken by public service. She was worried about finances, and had rented Nomdmi to Wayne. She was worried about all the various projects underway for Pardi's memory. And—what worried *me* most—she had encircled herself with many a bird of broken wing, the daily stream of the poor up her driveway whom she could never refuse, the impoverished artists she was helping financially when she couldn't help herself, and some alcoholic writer from the *Focus* days, down on his luck, whose calls she rushed to answer on the telephone, whose lamentations I heard sometimes at night as he'd plead with her at two in the morning through the window to *Edna darling*, open the door to let him in.

I accused her of flirting, bringing these situations on herself. The truth was, though I wanted her to live forever, I just couldn't cope with the implications of her life having to change to go on without Pardi. In reply, she walked about her own house narrowly, silently, with a cornered, outraged look and the wilful silence she had skilfully honed as her refuge from us all. Years later I would read a note in her diary at the time about how awful it was when, for the first time in one's life, one came under personal scrutiny.

"You know you have become a perpetual worrier," I told her, but gave her no chance to stop. I went back to teaching for the January term in 1971, but at Easter I flew down to Barbados, where I met and married my first husband, whom I hardly knew, in a matter of weeks. My family was exasperated with me, and really, when I think about it, that was my design—to gain my father's attention. By July I was pregnant in London, virtually penniless, with my marriage falling apart. Meanwhile in Jamaica the first all-island remembrance services were held for Pardi's birthday, and his statue as one of our heroes was dedicated in Kingston's gracious Heroes Park.

My father was livid, and Mardi fretted: "*I know I am making myself ill worrying over Rachel and her future—and nothing seems ever to change the fact that I miss Norman—endlessly,*" she wrote.

Shortly after Pardi's second memorial tribute in September, the book *Manley and the New Jamaica* was launched, including his autobiographical fragment, "My Early Years." Mardi felt a peaceful sense of relief and satisfaction. One job well done. Rex Nettleford's moving preface placed Pardi in the context of history, and though reading it made Mardi sad, this was an important step towards safeguarding his legacy of thought and words. She was baffled when initially it was met by lukewarm reviews, not only from the newspapers but also from readers who had looked forward to a biography. She supposed they wanted to get to know him in the traditional way, through Jamaican "old story time." But she would live to see the book reprinted, becoming much referred to and quoted, an invaluable national treasure.

Now Mardi turned her attention to Wayne's book. His research was unearthing small moments of ancient family history she would have rather left forgotten—in particular her side of the family's opinions of Bustamante, which were less than flattering. She was shrewd and intuitive more than she was blindly partisan, and she knew causing offence in this way would do no good to the memory of Pardi.

She was also having long-distance disagreements with Mike Smith in England about which poems to use in an anthology of his work she had finally convinced him to have published. After the 1960 edition of *Focus* came out, he had suddenly stopped writing creatively and decided instead to concentrate entirely on anthropology—despite my grandmother's many attempts to persuade him to produce more poems, or at least allow her to publish those already written. Her efforts usually ended in fierce arguments from which she would withdraw temporarily defeated.

"He's a Leo," she'd sigh with resignation.

In October Mardi came to London to be with me when I had the baby, which was due on Barbara's birthday, November 10. She also hoped to settle her differences of opinion with Mike. I had already been lying in St. Mary's Hospital, Harrow Road, for a month with toxemia, and she booked into the modest Cadogan Hotel, quite close to me, to wait it out. I loved her daily visits; she would arrive with the *Guardian* newspaper, which she'd read to me, and her book of Rilke, and a pad to write on if I chose to have a rest.

By November the weather was very cool, and she'd arrive in her old Nomdmi sweaters and ponchos over woollen slacks, tall and slim, looking like an exotic yet elegant hippie and not at all the average seventy-year-old Londoner.

"That's why I like living in Jamaica," she said. "Winter clothes are like furniture. Caribbean clothes don't feel so heavy and permanent."

She liked to be able to choose to have life at arm's length, not to be hampered by things, I think, even something as inanimate as her clothes.

"Poets don't have to rhyme anymore," she said dreamily one day on closing an anthology of Rilke, and I have often wondered just what prompted her to say so at that particular time, but in the weeks I lay there dreaming on my back, I thought about that sentence quite a lot.

All the nurses seemed to love my grandmother, the Jamaicans who had known my grandfather, and even the English ones, who just enjoyed her interest, her courtesy and good cheer, and would bring her tea and an extra lunch or supper.

One day, quite out of the blue, she slapped the *Guardian* down on her lap and blurted out, "I *could* have remarried, you know!"

I asked her what on earth she was talking about and she refused to say any more, but she had a cussed look on her face that I recognized as her old rebelliousness, which now and then she liked to get off her chest. I asked my father about it later, and he looked mystified.

"Well, who's stopping her?" Maybe, he said, she thought Jamaica wouldn't approve, and we agreed that it might be difficult.

"Or maybe it's us?" I suggested.

We both found the thought uncomfortable, and decided we didn't know whom or what she was talking about, in that complicit way that family members dismiss what's inconvenient to them though it may be vital to another one. I often wonder about what she said that day.

The labour lasted thirty-six hours, a time in which she seemed to walk every step of the way with me, down the corridors to bring on the birth, to the theatre when they broke the waters, around the bed from one side to the other as the pains got harder and the time between them shorter, distracting me when they resorted to an epidural block, and all through that long last night of its numbing effect when we waited and waited in dumb mime as my belly rose and fell, as though we were watching a silent film in which the characters, even mine, mimed; as the nurses popped in to listen to my tummy with an iron funnel and open my legs to peer at progress; and then, exhausted, she kissed my forehead as they sent me into the theatre for a birth assisted by forceps.

"Remember I love you, Miss Pics. You've been a brave girl," she said.

It was a strange experience for me, because two strong emotions were happening simultaneously. I was bonding with my son, whom I recognized as soon as I saw him, and who I knew intuitively would be my anchor, my reason to be a better person if I could—but I also knew that, maybe for the first time, I had completely bonded with the woman who had become my mother. I think that November morning was the moment I truly accepted that this was who she was to me.

I wanted to call the baby Norman but, not wishing to hurt my father's feelings, I compromised, calling him after his father in the English tradition, and settled for the middle name Manley. But deep in my heart, as ten days later I left for the airport with Mardi and my infant son, I already knew my marriage was over.

I stayed with Mardi for the first few months, and she coped as bravely as she could with the endless feeds and sterilizing and crying and nighttime walking up and down, burping and soothing, but after a few days she hired a registered nurse and returned to her studio, where I could hear the familiar castanet of her mallet and tools.

She had been working on a piece with two young figures embracing, the male holding the face of the female. The carving is often ascribed to the mourning pieces of the period, but I think that's wrong. I think she started it after meeting my husband whom, in her often contrary way, she rather liked. So I think she started that carving when she thought there was hope in the relationship, and finished it knowing there was none. That was why she called it *Adios*.

I was there for four months, during which Mardi remained productive. She was gradually shaping a life around herself that my presence may have helped, for Regardless was filling with people again in the afternoons, a lot of them younger now. She was invited out to dinners and shows, and had started doing a number of public duties again, often sitting with Lady Bustamante, of whom she became very fond, as they attended official events where she claimed they were both trotted out as national relics.

She was working full-time again. First *Phoenix*, out of guango—a frenzy of large chiselled gouges, all rough cuts, part bird, part flames, as though in transition from death to fiery rebirth, and no doubt expressing her longing both for Pardi's return and for release from her pangs of grief. From a log of mahogany she carved *Woman*, a figure all alone with her head thrown back, basking in memory, her eyes shut against the present with its agony. As though she couldn't bear to leave it at that, she then carved what she considered a wiser piece, *Mountain Women*, three generations of women who survive with or without men; who bear such a heavy load and have to be resilient, grounded by the mountains of the land they belong to, themselves forming a range, the serene head of a grandmother presiding above the rest.

In December an exhibition of Edna's sculptures was launched at the Bolivar Gallery in Kingston. While reviewers praised the work and spoke of her remarkable contribution to art over fifty years as a sculptress, all she left on record of this time was a note to herself: "... *deep in the heart is this strange and terrible loneliness*," and a wistful poem, "*The moon is a piece of ragged cloth tonight . . .*"

But in time she began to feel overcrowded, and I ended up feeling almost jailed myself in tiny Regardless. One bad morning, after I had beaten her in the race to the phone, both of us lonely and yearning for the call of a friend, I got there first and no one would answer.

"Are you having an affair?" I demanded rudely. She did what she had taken to doing in those days, announcing it was time to die and withdrawing, sulking, to her room.

It must have been that night that she wrote in her diary: "*Can't you understand that as the light fails and the great depression descends, some men reach for drink, and others reach for a telephone for a moment's brief communication with a friend?*"

My father put his foot down. "You are a married woman with a baby. It's time you lived on your own." And so said, so done. I got a small flat and a job nearby, and Mardi drove Pardi's old Benz to visit us every day. She was pleased that I had brought out my first book of poems, self-published and illustrated by Wayne's wife, Megan, dedicated to Mardi. She returned to rereading Rilke's *Elegies*, which always steadied her, brought her back to some place of equilibrium through beauty. It seemed to be a brief respite for the family, all of us in the same country and things at peace, with my father enjoying a brief political honeymoon after victory at the polls in 1972, the first few months an extravagance of goodwill from all sectors of Jamaica. It had been a tough few years, with the perception that not enough had changed since Independence, and the country seemed to be a nation only in name. Jamaican youth were on a radical march, and many felt my father's platform of change had averted a real showdown that might have led to revolution. He had already published his first book, *Politics of Change*, and it spelled out quite clearly his beliefs in a democratic socialist system.

Mardi was reading *Save Me the Waltz* and studying the Fitzgeralds when two huge meetings in Montego Bay and at Race Course in Kingston kicked off the final weeks of the campaign, with the election date announced for Mardi's birthday. My father said victory would be his present to her. She knew he was going to win, and so he did: a magnificent victory at the polls, becoming Jamaica's fourth prime minister in 1972, before midnight on her birthday.

I remember, as we all celebrated at my father's house, watching a growing incomprehension alter Mardi's quietly radiant face, and shortly after that she went home.

Douglas, who had returned from Africa at my father's invitation in time for nomination day, had also run for office. Though initially he narrowly lost, he won on a magisterial recount and became Minister of Youth and Community Development, which Mardi thought to be quite a mouthful. She had her two sons back, and it was both gratifying and oddly upsetting to her to have them doing the job that Norman had done, that she wished he were still here doing. The limelight and praise heaped on my father made her privately uncomfortable, and every now and then she'd get defensive about Pardi, correcting some person who attributed something to the son that she felt was due to the father. When Michael's first official portrait as prime minister was taken, the well-meaning photographer created a picture with a photograph of Pardi as premier placed beside my father as prime minister, which he presented to Mardi. She shivered when she opened it, and put it in a cupboard, leaning up, facing the wall. She said she found it eerie to see them side by side, both as older men. He was, after all, their son and junior. And this ambivalence, a reluctance to compare two men whose jobs might be similar but whose relationships to her were quite different, would remain.

Shortly after my father won, he and Beverley, who had been beside him throughout the two years on the campaign trail, decided to marry. My son, Drum, and I had just moved out of Regardless when Beverley came to live with Mardi for the weeks before the wedding; Beverley says Mardi coached her on the little-known job of being a first lady. A small private reception was held at Regardless, and the bride's parents stood in a circle with Mardi, Douglas, Aunt Muriel, Norman, my new sister, Sarah, and me flanking my father with Beverley in the middle. None of us was told about the wedding until the last minute, for fear word would get out, as a result of which my brother Joseph, who was away at boarding school at Munro, his uncle's old alma mater, missed the event.

Once more alone, Mardi started dreaming again. She kept dipping into books on Jung, searching for their meaning, as well as a copy of Ann Faraday's *Dream Power*. She even thought she saw Pardi looming at the end of the drawing room one evening while she played Debussy's *Afternoon of a Faun*. He was tremendously tall, and she said the presence frightened her, so we decided whatever the figure was, it couldn't be Pardi, just a deep fear unsettling her at night. She went on playing that haunting music often, perhaps hoping the nostalgic piece would lure him again from the shadows where she felt he hovered, and in the studio she carved *Faun*, a ter-rified figure peeping around the leaves of its forest tree at the world, its hand to its mouth in alarm. It reminded me so much of her.

"It's all about having to face the night by yourself," she explained.

By August, when Pardi's last dog, the intelligent Doberman who had never recovered from the loss of his master, started los-ing the use of his back legs, Mardi had to have him put down. With his death, the last tangible vestige of Pardi seemed to be gone, and despite herself, she knew she had to have the courage to let go—to let him travel on.

And it was at this time that there began to form in her mind the stirrings of perhaps her most extraordinary carving, a mahogany bas-relief—*Journey*.

By now she had looked at Norman's death and at death itself from many angles. I had given her a copy of Carlos Castaneda's then popular *Journey to Ixtlan*, which she read more than once, refer-ring back to it, and she said it had made a deep impression on her for what she expressed as its capacity to free one to think "other-wise." She needed to find a way to express the paradoxes whose sides argued against one another in her mind. There was the par-adox of death and life, which, though totally divergent, seemed to make each other possible. There was the imperative to go and the imperative to stay. In her mind she always left room for questions about an afterlife, because of her father's faith and her mother's question posed to her as a child: "Just suppose there was . . . ?" But was the afterlife what remains—what we were left and what we left as legacy—our children, the change we brought the earth, the mes-sages we left in art and in buildings and in books and in knowl-edge handed on? Was rebirth just tomorrow's flowering from the mulch of our care—the flower from the humanness of us? Finally there was the question of how to separate the vital memory of a life from its shadowed grief and mourning.

Journey went through many incarnations of drawings, the first as early as Easter Sunday in 1972 when, soon after the excitement of my father's victory, she had woken feeling *"as if I were hanging, floating above life, unable to move away on a journey, unable to detach myself."* As though she realized that, for the first time in a life together, neither Pardi nor she was able to take a separate path. After a hiatus of a year in which she considered the piece of mahogany she had chosen for a bas-relief, she kept worrying that the wood might not have the depth to provide the hollows and lurking shadows she needed to offset the form. Maybe she should do it in the round. But David Boxer, a friend and artist and curator of the National Gallery, was sure it could be done, and egged her on to tempt its depths. And so she started carving.

There were times when, following the track of the chisel's furrow, and seeing the gouges lengthen like the spill of tears, she found herself dwelling on doubts and guilts. Should she have stopped Norman from going into politics? Could she have? Probably not. By giving him twenty years of support, had she abetted him? Had she made his final disappointments possible? Her unease about federation was proved to be correct, but that hadn't saved him. Maybe most of all she had let him take himself too seriously, allowed him to miscalculate.

Out of her fret and worry came a face used to suffering; as though the thought of death might be a relief. The head leaning back in a small shrug against one shoulder had appeared as long ago as *The Beadseller*, and later on in *The Dead*. This face had none of the radiance of *Christ*, more a nothingness born of disappointment and maybe longing or loneliness. The body was almost concave with movement, as if a heavy wind were billowing against it, as if it were held almost against its will by feet that, unlike *Christ's* tethered by nails, were tethered instead by life here on earth; by what she hoped was the paradox of his wanting yet not wanting to go. Tethered by her.

The first time I saw it, the carving seemed to look down from a great height, from the very skies, although on its stand it was only a little above eye level. Sometimes I had the impression that the tilted head could have been carved separately and placed there at not quite the correct angle, but of course it wasn't separate. The face seemed to float underwater, the skin of its surface like withered scar tissue, below which lay its steady features void of all expression—". . . it's the inhumanity of it that's difficult," she said. The body was still in the rough, but I had a sense of it drifting upwards, a figure encased in the pod of a fruit. It had an incubated, cradled appearance, almost as though the figure were back in its womb; the face was likewise a small embryo sheltered in its body, in a series of inversions. The face compelled me to look, yet made looking almost unbearable. And the more I looked at it, the less I knew what lay behind it.

"The night he died I felt him being taken away," she told me once, and I remember wondering why she often referred to it as "the night," for it was in fact ten o'clock in the morning. Because the polls were open for the election of his constituency successor that day, the news was held back till they closed in the evening. "I hardly noticed that at the time, for the trouble was that I felt he didn't struggle to stay. I was so mad with him. I felt that way for many years. Till I resolved it."

I must have asked her how, because she answered me in a letter:

You see, it was a very old rage really. Remember my father had died when I was very young. Very unnecessarily I thought. He got soaked one night and developed pneumonia. In those days no antibiotics. But

*the thing was, I remembered all my life so clearly Halley's Comet
shining outside his window and the almost mysterious sense of this
Christian man beholding his own resurrection. I wanted to scream out
and tear up the sky and put out the light of the damn comet. It was
no bloody resurrection. I wanted Father to stay.*

*It took me four years from carving Angel to get to this, to arrive at
Pardi's point of view. To see it from the other side of the argument, and
in a way it has helped me to understand my own journey . . . and,
when it comes, departure. But again these journeys have stops along the
way where you have to reconnoitre, and build up understanding. I
did the whole series in wood, and this will be my last carving.*

*The young can't bear anything to end, to be final. But that's what I
mean about getting there. It has taken me a career in art to know that
I have come to the end of a stage. It isn't a choice. I have just reached
what is a boundary. As Pardi had when he left politics. You know
when the time comes.*

The wood was pink, as though it had come out of an oven too
soon, and was still warm with her grief. She wasn't finished with
it yet. Wrestling with it night after night, as if only the evenings
could produce the shadows of unbeing, she deepened the cave of
the chest, deepening the hollow, creating that trough from which
the figure emerges.

"Guide my hands, Norman, guide my hands," she found herself beseeching at one point, her knuckles being smashed against the
wood as she tried to get deeper, her left hand clutching the chisel
bent almost into a claw by the awkward angle.

"*Your shadow standing behind me & saying deeper and deeper shadows
has been driving me on!*" she wrote to David Boxer, who had become
a fellow traveller in her quest.

When she was finished, only the feet yearning for the earth kept the floating figure back.

After that big bas-relief, which was really seeing Pardi off, she was left with herself. And there she was facing her old demons, getting old, having lost her mate, and he hadn't been just a husband, but her island, her backbone—but in the most democratic and voluntary sense, two separate life forces very independent but very supportive, subterraneanly linked. She admitted that for her, in many ways, he had taken the place of God.

True to her word, she packed up her carving tools and gave them to a young sculptor. She then returned to terracotta and, as though in a last act of defiance, created a final, tortured *Grief*, an exquisitely tiny figure running with her hands up covering her face, edgy, neurotic, even the sweeping folds of her skirt desperately trying to escape.

There they all were—*Angel, Adios, Phoenix, Woman, Mountain Women, Faun, Journey,* and *Grief*. Broke as she was, she wouldn't sell *Angel*. She eventually gave it to Kingston Parish Church, where everyone had told him goodbye. *Journey* was sold to David, where it rightly belonged. The knowledge that the money she earned from the sale would see Pardi's only remaining sibling through to her end gave Mardi solace. The charcoal drawing of the angel's implacable face, which she left for me, hung on the wall at Regardless over the dining table for the rest of her life.

12

Ancestor

Leaving you is
Knowing in me deep
Flowers of you . . .

—George Campbell

We all see ourselves as either having to smash the past. Or as taking
great strength from it.

—Edna Manley: *The Diaries*

BACK IN THE DAYS when we were struggling against the empire, our fight seemed noble. We had been David against Goliath. Violence—sticks and stones, even broken glass bottles—had seemed unavoidable. But things had become quite different. Within a year of the PNP victory in 1972, Jamaica was back in an angry mood. Local elections were marked by a new kind of violence. Illegal guns had been a growing phenomenon since the battles of West Kingston politics in the sixties. Pardi had seen them as a scourge that might forever change our way of life. Mardi had difficulty understanding why we were now fighting ourselves. Unlike many who, scared of the violence, fled to the States or Canada, there was no question that she would stay put.

She was commissioned to create a mural for the outer wall of the Little Theatre, which had recently been built to provide a well-equipped modern building for a bursting exuberance of local drama and dance; leaving her mark on the wall seemed to her like casting a vote of confidence. She had to enlarge the studio to accommodate the work. As always, her art brought distraction and rescue. When she was modelling *Bogle*, a room had been erected outside the house, just beside the kitchen. One had to approach it from the patio, through the garden that circled the back of the house, and that was enough to give her the feeling of separation she needed, even though the room was only a few feet from her kitchen window. The walls and roof were of cheap grey corrugated aluminum sheeting that sounded like gunfire when the rain came down. There were several narrow windows with glass louvres to let her blessed sunlight in.

Rainbow Serpent was a vast bas-relief, over seven feet tall and nearly twice as wide, framed by the heads of Adam and Eve staring towards though not actually at each other, and gazing out between them was her familiar masklike godhead; encircling the carving with its head squarely facing Eve was the serpent, its body passing behind the place where the godhead had no mouth. When asked about its absence, Mardi said, "God needs no speech." But I often wondered if subconsciously she intended the serpent, bringing us the only possibility of procreation and thus continuity, to be the mouthpiece of God.

The irony of this work, and the voiceless way in which fate gets decided, would not be understood for years to come, but *Rainbow Serpent* would plant the seeds of Mardi's undoing, its innovative material having a negative effect on her health that would characterize her remaining years.

Knowing that the bas-relief had to hang on the exterior wall of the theatre, and trying to find a material that was both durable and comparatively light, Mardi decided to cast it in a new material for her, fibreglass. But the drawback to her aluminum shed was that by eleven in the morning the studio felt as if it might burst into flames. Mardi would be sitting in there, fanning herself with an old paper fan with Japanese flowers that smelled of sandalwood, her fair skin almost transparent, with no expression on her face, which she always tried to keep neutral in heat so as not to use up too much energy. As the summer approached, my father tapped his limited resources to help buy a small air conditioner, which she had installed in one of the windows. It cooled the room, and though she disliked the droning and shudder caused by the machine, she willed herself to concentrate on feeling rooted to the firm concrete floor, and kept her mind on the composition before her. When the work was complete, she was glad that the casting in fibreglass could be done right there in her studio.

Rainbow Serpent wasn't unveiled on the theatre's wall till April, but on February 8, 1975, twenty days before her seventy-fifth birthday and seventeen days before the birth of her second great-grandson, Michael Luke, she noted in her diary with joy that it was finished. In 1974 I had met and married my second husband, a cheerful, down-to-earth builder and developer who seemed to contain my craziness, and welcomed both me and my son. My family liked him—he was a likeable man—and we were married at Jamaica House in a chaotic but memorable ceremony, the guests like two different tribes of the island, his the right-wing businessmen and their conservative families, mine mostly left-wing politicians and artists. Mardi, who just wanted me to teach and write, was somewhat skeptical about the speed with which I'd remarried, but said she had a good feeling about him.

Life continued to have its interminable complications for her. Despite the unsettling sense of continually having no money, she tried to be creative about it, writing charming, almost coquettish letters to the newspapers or the electric company or whomever she owed when she had to delay payment of a bill. This didn't stop her attending to the needy who continued to walk up her driveway each day, meeting each one spirit to spirit with her unique concern, each leaving with a letter of request, referral, or recommendation, some money, or at least a bowl of Tildy's soup. Nor did it dissuade her from buying the occasional painting from a starving artist. Nights she spent coughing, but in the mornings she found the breath to phone a friend "having a hard time," and to send her interminable notes—of offered solutions, of inspiration, of appreciation—*You were a knight in shining armour.* She cheered, she soothed, she inspired, she amused, she enchanted people.

Doctors said she had developed bronchial asthma, and she was placed on steroids. She made every effort to avoid allergens—dust and pollen, though not animal dander, as she now had the pride of her dog-owning life, a magnificent black Doberman called Johann who, unlike so many of their dogs before, was not neurotic and made a fine watchdog. She even stayed in town for fear the cool at Nomdmi would bring on attacks.

My father had offered Mike Smith a contract to work in Jamaica, preparing reports for the new government—a study involving what could be done with various old, unused estates, and a civil service review. He stayed at Regardless, a help to Mardi not only as company but also through rent money. I would sit with them having lunch or dinner, in a harmonious circle talking about art or music, politics or history. Mike had wonderful stories of living in Africa with the Hausas, whom he had studied, and stories of academic life in America, where he had taught anthropology at both UCLA and Yale. He had a mischievous sense of humour, and it was good to see Mardi laughing and enjoying life again. She always saw to it that he had a small saucer of finely chopped bird peppers, and he'd eat these blistering little firebrands as though they were nothing more than HP sauce.

My father's position had brought Mardi renewed eminence in public life. The real pleasure in this for her was an opportunity to travel. She escorted a national art exhibition of Jamaican works on tour to the United States in 1972, attended the newly formed regional cultural Carifesta in Guyana, and visited Germany shortly after, at the request of that government. She asked her young friend Rose McFarlane to accompany her. Rose by now had worked at the government information service and had later joined the diplomatic service as press and cultural attaché. They remained close, working on various committees and social promotions together, which entwined Rose in all the highs and lows of Drumblair and Regardless over the years. She found in Rose a companion with whom she shared an irreverent sense of humour, the younger woman bringing out a naughty, sometimes delightfully light-hearted side of Mardi, who trusted her and loved to sit down and hear all the local gossip and say what she really thought about so-and-so. On the trip to Guyana, Rose helped Mardi to escape the formal arrangements made by Forbes Burnham's government, and one afternoon they set off to make a secret side trip to Mardi's old friends, the Jagans. Cheddi Jagan had been Guyana's Communist leader who had backed federation. His wife, Janet, maybe even more political than her husband, had over the years sent Mardi logs of purpleheart wood to carve. They found the Jagans living simply—"they lived as they were," commented Rose—and spent a rich time with them remembering the triumphs and tragedies, already shadows of the past.

In Germany they spent an inspiring month visiting galleries all over the country, and the studios of many artists. Mardi returned with her spirit full of energy and a harmony of hope nourished by new ideas. But once again their most memorable experiences were not found on the official calendar. One night their young guide persuaded them to go to a casino in Baden-Baden. They went reluctantly, but when Rose began winning some money on a slot machine, she got so caught up that she never really noticed Mardi till she started losing. She turned round to find Mardi visibly shaken, looking almost horror-stricken. Gambling was forbidden in Jamaica through all the administrations, mainly due to the influence of the churches. It was felt that the way out of our national struggles should be not through easy money, but through hard work. But what Rose saw in Mardi was not idealistic disapproval, but something more visceral. She wondered if it was the old Methodist ethics of her father. But I have seen that look of hers, and I think it is a horror of a world given over to the mercenary, of mindless greed for its own sake.

They also took a trip to the Black Forest to see a maverick artist, HAP Grieshaber, in whose work Mardi was very interested. She was warned that he tended to be reclusive and could be eccentric and difficult. But she charmed him so utterly that he didn't want them to leave, plying them with gifts including his drawings and two peacock feathers. But since they both believed the feathers were unlucky, they discreetly left them out of sight by the roadside after their departure.

The newly established Chinese embassy in Kingston was making overtures to the West, and had found a welcome in Jamaica from my father's socialist government, which had been encouraging untraditional relationships as Jamaica sought new sources of aid from left-wing countries. The Chinese ambassador was enchanted by Mardi, who often went to their embassy's parties to

represent my father, and she and Mike enjoyed the amazing variety of cuisine from various provinces as the offerings spun around
on a Lazy Susan. Mardi was invited to pay an official visit to
China, taking with her whomever she pleased. So in May 1975,
after careful planning, she set off for China with great expectations,
accompanied by Douglas and Mike.

Mardi's diary entries on this cultural journey through China
are continually interrupted by both small and large irritations. Her
excitement when they arrived in Peking to be met by a large dele-
gation from the Association of Cultural Relations is followed by her
frustration trying to organize her habitual cup of hot coffee, which
led to her visit at five-thirty on the first morning to the hotel's
kitchen, where she and the cook couldn't communicate. Then came
a tour to see a monument whose coordinated artwork, shared by
as many as six different artists, baffled her.

"It would make me feel like I was working in a straitjacket," she
explained to me. Socialist as my family was, they all seemed to stam-
mer back from leftist ideology as soon as individual freedom in any
form felt threatened. That entry was followed by an agitated account
of a visit to a hairdresser who permed into tight curls her mane of
short, mildly wavy hair, which she felt made her look like an old lady.
Then she records staying in bed for a whole day, feeling wretched.

She was suitably impressed by the splendour of the imperial
palace, where she noted vast crowds of people, mostly men from
the rural areas; she recorded their amazement at her height, and her
great irritation at being escorted with the reverence accorded to the
aged of their culture, firmly removing her elbow from the grasp of
a well-meant supportive hand as she bent to make the relatively
easy manoeuvre of getting into the car. She not only looked ancient,
but also was being treated as if she were.

Her visit to Tatung was interrupted by a terrible period of
coughing to the point of blood, and what she interpreted as a show

of indifference from Mike and Douglas, neither of whom probably knew what to do. Whilst she could enchant, she could also exasperate, and inquiring later about the trip, I knew by the resignation of their sighs that she had done the latter.

But she ended on a high note when she became the first woman taken to see the unpacked marvels of the pottery soldiers recently unearthed in Shensi province, long before their existence was made known to the Chinese people.

She returned home, plump from the steroids and with a most unattractive mop of frizzy hair, to receive four pieces of news.

In England, Barbara Hepworth had died and was being hailed as "the greatest woman artist in the world." Although she didn't know Hepworth, and found her work somewhat cold though dedicated, Hepworth was a fellow sculptor from her own era. The death must have struck a chord, for she noted it in her diary.

But she also found two announcements in André Deutsch's publishing catalogue that gave her special pleasure: Wayne Brown's *Edna Manley: The Private Years, 1900–1938*, and Michael Manley's *A Voice at the Workplace*.

The fourth piece of news came from me. My husband and I were packing up that summer with the children and moving to Barbados, where he intended to build a low-income housing development. Although this reason was true, she knew how scared I had become of the violence in Jamaica, how confused by the endless criticism and hatred I met in regard to my father's politics. To make matters worse, my father and I had entered the latest low in our relationship. My sister Natasha had been born in 1972 but I had hardly seen her. It was now I who felt he had no time for us, tightly wrapped up in his own world with what, despite knowing the public pressure he was under, I glibly and jealously decided was a glamorous new life with his new family.

By November Mardi was back at work, and she did one last

piece in fibreglass, a river god, *Rio Bueno*. She also promised to spend Christmas in Barbados, by which time, she felt sure, the perm would have grown out and she would not embarrass us, a consideration that hadn't crossed my mind. She was still plagued by her cough at nights, dragging on her asthma puffers with what seemed like endless bronchitis. A lung specialist at the TB hospital sent her to an allergist. After wide-ranging tests, they were able to pinpoint the source of her problem—fibreglass particles. The dust from sanding of her sculptures had caused early emphysema. She always used a mask when she was in the room, she explained. Nevertheless, the small, eternally durable chemical splinters from the casting material had got caught in the air-conditioning vent, and every time she turned the system on, it exhaled them back out into the air, an invisible pollution she unknowingly inhaled.

She never worked with fibreglass again, but the damage was done.

Mardi rallied valiantly to keep balanced in 1976, another year of rolling waves. In addition to emphysema, she was now diagnosed with diverticulitis; both were probably made worse by the tension around her. We had sent letters backwards and forwards as she helped me compile and edit a second book of poems, but my new marriage was falling apart in Barbados, and my father and I were almost not speaking. Aunt Muriel was getting frail and forgetful. She lived next door to Regardless, in a small cottage built at the bottom of my father's lot. He had sold his house, which Mardi felt had too many bad memories, with the breakdown of his marriage to Thelma and then the illness and death of Barbara. It had never brought him luck. But my aunt remained there, and was badly shaken up by a frightening break-in by several gunmen one night while she was alone at home, after which her health rapidly declined. A comfortable old-age home would have to be found. This would take money.

National elections were called, and despite the relief of a land-slide victory for the PNP, the mood in the country was divisive and the campaign marred by more violence. Mardi had begun to notice her friends leaving Jamaica, some saying goodbye quite sud-denly with polite excuses, others disappearing like thieves in the night. She always found it perplexing that Jamaicans could get up and leave an entire lifetime and identity because of a rough patch for what would surely be a relatively short time in their lives and in history. I think she interpreted this as nationalism not having taken root, and felt that people didn't have a real sense of identity. This made her almost as sad as if they had lost an election. Poli-tics had not been Pardi's cause. It had been a way only to achieve a state that defined what being Caribbean meant—to make it pos-sible to truly be Jamaican or Trinidadian or Barbadian or Kittisian. Politics was just a means, and we were all Pardi's cause. The fact that politics led to intolerance and violence, that a generation of male youth seemed to be lost to guns, and violence had caused people to abandon their homeland, seemed to unravel everything his life had been about. Added to this was the excruciating impli-cation that her son was responsible.

In the midst of these pressures she created *Manchild*, a boy turning from his mother to the traditional Jamaican grandmother, sculpted and then cast in Ciment Fondu. It was the culmination of many recent studies of older women, whom she depicted as strong and enduring rather than diminished. She sold it to an architect, himself an artist, and was furious when she heard he had sprayed it with bronze paint, claiming it looked dirty. For her it seemed to sum up a certain middle-class intolerance that she felt was in man ways at the root of the exodus—though, to be fair to him, the owner of *Manchild* never joined it.

After the election, things continued to fall apart politically. Mardi could feel an agony in my father, who was caught between forces. He had legislated huge change that would alter the social landscape of our island forever, outlawing each injustice and invoking a new order with each stroke of a pen: outlawing the "bastard act"—a relic of British law that legally and psychologically disenfranchised Jamaican children born out of wedlock—and invoking a minimum-wage law, maternity leave, and free education up to university level for all. Most of this was of course costly, and he could not have known that OPEC prices would rise and bring the Third World to its knees economically. If he should have predicted the effect that reaching out to his neighbour, Cuba, supporting the liberation struggle in Angola, and embracing the socialist world generally would have, he didn't.

Out of this time of political chaos came Mardi's *The Message*, a pair of resilient women, the older one charging the younger with a secret. The bodies, crouched in a mound, pull one into the immediacy at the centre of the sculpture, where a finger of warning cautions the scared younger figure, and in that composition are the years of caution from slavery days, the resilience of our women, the tradition of word of mouth that saved lives and passed down history, and now was probably saving the embattled sons of feuding Jamaican tribes.

Mardi's social circle had dwindled until it was just a backbone of loyal well-wishers. Her original artists, painters, and Cecil Baugh the potter were growing old but some still visited, and she enjoyed David from the National Gallery and Pam from the School of Music coming to talk art and listen to music. Some of her older friends who had remained in Jamaica tended to complain about either Michael or their aches and pains, so she preferred those to stay away. But slowly she made new friends—young writers and artists and poets and teachers, like Olive Senior, Hope Brooks and Christopher Gonzales, creative people who saw her as a beloved matriarch and mentor—art critics and book reviewers, lawyers and fashion designers—an animal husbandry expert who had created a new breed of cattle, the Jamaica Hope, which would be of great interest to Ramón Castro in Cuba—illicit lovers, heartbroken poets, actors and playwrights, an occasional musician and a conflicted priest. I don't remember any athletes, but diplomats came, and foreign dignitaries. She still created ripples. A U.S. diplomat, a regular visitor to the house, brought her a photograph taken at an official function, with the Queen wearing a silver gown and Mardi a blue one. His attached note read: "Frankly, the lady in blue looks more regal." Echeverría, the President of Mexico, was so beguiled by her that he never noticed the time and was late for an official meeting. Her visitors all brought their work and their thoughts and their arguments to share, discussed their world in new ways, and the wider one beyond. They invited her to their plays and readings and launches, often escorting her to opening nights of dance and theatre, sometimes to the movies. She loved their energy and curiosity, the audacity of courage she remembered from her own youth. The whole world lay ahead of them, and even the purity of their foolishness and rashness at times rejuvenated her.

Mike was still at Regardless, and his eldest son, Danny, had come to manage an agency that sourced food at cheap prices to be made available to Jamaicans. Danny and his future wife, Sarah, befriended her. When Mike's job came to an end and he returned to England, the young couple moved into the void left in his wake.

As though challenging the storms, Mardi created a couple standing holding hands under a wave: *The Wave*, a bronze signature of her endurance.

Fate would again prove itself fickle. In 1977 the government commissioned a seven-foot recreation of *Negro Aroused* as a monument to mark the spot where Pardi had stood to address the striking workers in 1938, and where they had later listened to Bustamante after Pardi secured his release. Mardi felt the figure could work on a larger scale, and Mike's son Pete, a sculptor (Mardi loved the coming full circle of this connection), along with some young local artists, came to assist. First she had to raise a portion of the studio's roof for the sculpture to fit. Christopher Gonzalez, the sculptor to whom she had once given her carving tools, came to create the plaster. It was a time of joy for Mardi, being in their youthful company as she fed them and watched this crazy, energetic group of men who spent no time pulling down governments or whining about life. They just got in there and worked with their hands, grey with the blessed clay, making shape of something they felt to be meaningful.

When it was ready, the cast was carefully crated and stored at a local shipping agency awaiting transport to New York. There it was planned to be bronzed eventually, at a foundry. But that was not to be.

In early August Michael called to tell his mother that Bustamante had died. The old man had been ailing for a long time, and Mardi would hear news of him from his wife, Gladys, whenever they attended functions together, representing the two national heroes. In the public mind they were already myths. But the greater portion of Norman and Edna's life had been so affected by this cousin that when she heard the news it was a shock. A tug-of-war that held both sides in a state of uneasy balance had suddenly lost one side of its equation. The very spot that she had just commemorated in her work, which she had returned to many times in the past few months with various government officials, seemed suddenly to evaporate into a ghosted mist of history.

"*He did Norman and Jamaica many things I never forgave,*" she recorded in her diary, "*he never saw a new image that was waiting to be born. One couldn't hold him responsible for that, he had never seen it in those terms—but all his life he did look out for the cause of the poor and the needy, and in his own vain, arrogant way he was kind.*"

When a year later she got a call one morning telling her that the plaster mould, along with the warehouse, had burnt to the ground in a fire, in her mind that massive work was somehow already gone.

Castro made his official visit to Jamaica and according to Mardi "*came, conquered and departed.*" Some think his giant rally in Montego Bay was the largest crowd in Jamaican history. Michael thought it a resounding success. But unwittingly this passionate guest, despite immaculate diplomacy and sensitive restraint, brought along with his visit a high price. The U.S. State Department watched the events with rising consternation. The Americans feared the presence of a second island going communist in Florida's backyard. Washington turned on Michael, expressing its wrath socially and politically through the CIA, and financially through the IMF and the World Bank. The CIA moved into high gear, and the use of its destabilization tactics during the Cold War is now part of a well-documented history. In Jamaica, tensions rose with the violence that stemmed from the CIA's not so subtle interference in our politics, combined with the consequence of an unfavourable rating by the IMF that threw our economy into a rigid austerity program. The daily newspaper attacked my father ritually, and a columnist, once a friend of the family, actually accused him of ruling by torture.

The party's left wing became loudly confrontational, reminding Mardi of the early PNP and the 1930s party purge. But there would be no purge. My father just did what he felt he should do, and let the right and left go on slugging it out, convinced that every step made towards social justice was a step in the right direction; that the point of independence was that a country made its own laws and decisions on foreign policy, and that the idea behind democracy, and of a democratic political party, was that everyone should have a right to speak.

On the home front, Michael now took over Muriel's cottage, after Mardi had found her a caring old-age home. He planned to move out of the official house and live in the cottage as soon as he had enlarged it. Something about the *Daily Gleaner*'s vitriol and the country's mood made him hunker down, made him defensive; made him not even want to live in the public residence he was entitled to.

The last two years of the seventies dragged on with increasing violence, increasing flights of immigration, increasing hostility to Michael, especially from the conservative *Daily Gleaner*, to which Mardi eventually cancelled her long-standing subscription. Now my father's marriage to Beverley was on the rocks, and my uncle had lost his ministry after government 'downsizing and a Cabinet reshuffle made necessary by IMF fiscal conditions. This last debacle affected Mardi deeply. She felt caught in the middle between two sons, torn apart at the deepest level and not able to express any opinion.

As young men Mike Smith and George Campbell were friends who quibbled over semantics, but as Edna grew older they seemed increasingly intolerant of each other. In the family we joked that they were both jealous and squabbling over her. This intolerance was displayed whenever their paths crossed at Regardless. If Mike arrived, George would become possessive and demanding of Mardi, behaving like a spoiled child. This would infuriate Mike, whose eyes would become piercing and he'd seethe in quick sucks on his pipe. After a while, their visits to Jamaica to see their muse were carefully planned by her *not* to coincide.

So in 1979, after Mike had returned to England, George came back from his long exile in New York, fragile and extremely nervous.

He initially stayed at Regardless, his company—especially given Mike's departure—a welcome rejoining of the past for Mardi. She at once set about arranging a reprint of George's poems, encouraging him to start writing again. Mardi had become aware of a growing industry in rural wood carving displayed at the side of the road for passing tourists. Some of this work was original and worthy, and she planned with George to locate the finer artists and compile photographs of their collected work into a large art book. But George's neediness would eventually wear her down. They seemed to have a baffling relationship in which Mardi was always mothering him, and he was always playing up like a naughty child. He drank too much, and Douglas got so angry one day when George was nagging Mardi that he decked him outside the front door, George landing in a flower bed. My uncle returned inside, firmly locking George out, whereupon, to Douglas's chagrin, Mardi exploded not at George but at him, letting her guest back in and sending me for the witch hazel to bathe his bruised face.

Visiting Mardi one afternoon, Wayne, whose insightful book *Edna Manley: The Early Years* had been published in 1975 amidst some temporary ill feeling that had now abated, was sitting with her on the verandah having a drink when suddenly a taxi drove up and an indignant poet from her *Focus* group walked in and hurled a heavy black typewriter the full length of the living room, shouting, "Edna, I can't be bought!"

It was amazing; she still had that energy and power—at almost eighty—to mesmerize and infuriate; as Pardi once said, they were all in love with her.

But "still" was a word that Mardi totally ignored. Mardi was infinite. She had always worked and always engaged life at every level of her being; the thought of anything else had never occurred to her. "Still" was what she would be doing when most people became pot-bellied and bald, belching and attending the funeral of friends, survival their only solace. She would be "still" what she was, that extraordinary force that was feline and witchy and wanton, whose thoughts when shed on an island rose as monuments.

Once, I asked my father if Pardi had been safe with her, wondering if she was dangerous for men to love.

"Oh, his vulnerability made him safe," he said.

Like all good waifs, when she was at her most undefended, her wiles made her impregnable as a fort. She knew when to protect herself and when to leave her defence up to others.

Just before her eightieth birthday, when it was decided that a nearby road and traffic circle that she had been travelling for nearly sixty years should be turned into a one-way system, Mardi declared herself too old to tolerate any direction being dictated to her, and sold the Benz. "*So life begins at 80*," she wrote triumphantly of her decision.

She began taking taxis. This was a new challenge. Not only did she have to organize herself once a week to do all the chores, setting out with carefully drawn up lists, but also had to search for a suitable taxi driver she could depend on. One day on the way to a dressmaker she was treated to a vociferous attack on my father from an unsuspecting driver. Only when she got out and turned round to pay him did he recognize her, and he was so filled with remorse that he chastised himself because, as he said, a mother was, after all, always a mother.

The National Gallery planned a gala retrospective exhibition to celebrate Edna's important birthday, coinciding with her receiving Jamaica's national honour, the Order of Merit, second only to National Hero. She wanted no more than a modest show to exhibit her carvings of the seventies. Knowing these were for the most part on desolate themes of grief, she set to work and completed some exuberant pieces. A terracotta *Old Ram*; two trees whose branches literally danced in rapture, their trunks pressed together in desire like lovers: *The Trees Are Joyful*; and a precious piece, *Once upon a Time*—a bas-relief in forest-green Ciment Fondu—a secret pastoral world within a frame, two boys with young kid goats among the trees, a piece she created, she said, for all the children in Jamaica, and those in our family—my father's young daughter, Natasha, and my two young sons. Just before the exhibition, she agreed to join in a project to have six of her finer drawings turned into silkscreens by two Puerto Rican artists, experts who came to Jamaica.

But to me the most moving piece in that exhibition was a bronze she had sculpted in 1978. With her chronic and severe asthma, her health had been wearing her down at a time when she most needed her strength, and she was learning to stay calm, learning to conserve energy, training herself to make the most of every increasingly difficult breath. She felt a need to be strong for her family's sake, especially Michael's, and for all the people who hung in there, determined to have faith in their little country.

As though for them, she created an extraordinary composition of a woman, the sum of all her older mountain women and grandmothers for the last decade, standing tall, her bearing serene, her face distressed but resolute. Standing in front of her a full-grown man, though in proportion to her no bigger than a child, turned in to her skirt, his face hidden in her stomach as though in shame. There is something both immeasurably consoling and ultimately enduring—*The Ancestor* is probably my favourite of all her work. In it can be seen the struggle of her final years to remain balanced, to remain hopeful, to create some kind of faith and touchstone that the future could turn back to; something that could be relied on to be there—a history that, though it shades and comforts, is not a fairy tale or Anansi story, but real and true and solid.

This is the piece that most evokes for me the pain of those years when, after the most violent period in Jamaican history, and my grandmother's deep sense of foreboding that haunted her on her son's behalf, my father lost the 1980 general election to the JLP under Edward Seaga. Mardi, who knew only too well that familiar heartbreak, wrote how "*the knowledge pressed through my brain that we had lost,*" and we all had to dig into ourselves as a family and a people to find meaning and strength. And here was *The Ancestor*, mother-tall by centuries, there if we needed her, to whom we could all turn.

13

The Garden

It's a process. By the time you get through it you have become it. You aren't looking at the knowledge, you are looking through it. It is part of you.

    —Edna Manley, in an interview with Easton Lee

A beauty too of twisted trees.

    —Philip Sherlock, *Focus* 1943

LIFE WAS ALWAYS ABOUT SO MUCH MORE THAN ART, and art was less about art than it was about life. Besides, what was so interesting to talk about if it wasn't the whole, how one thing touched on another, and how some things shrank when you put them next to something else and others just thrived and bloomed? Life was about that interconnectedness.

When Mardi was young, even though she was by nature a rebel, she thought life was a series of finite things. Symbols. Actions and feelings and relationships that had rules of engagement. Tasks that were performed for neatly specified objectives, rewards that would be commensurate; disobedience had consequences. Growing wise was perhaps discovering and admitting that one's neat presumptions, which were presented like a guidebook by parents and schools and laws and churches, in fact were a great conglomerate of mixed-up shortcuts and assumptions—a lowest common denominator that regulated every possibility that any person might reasonably expect to meet in a completely balanced and airtight situation. That was what parents and churches and policemen could teach you. It was a start, a movable framework with which one could leave home.

But life wasn't exactly like that. It was never airtight. How could it be with three hundred and sixty-five days in a year, and twenty-four hours in a day, in a world of hundreds of countries and millions of people, and seasons and landscapes and the mood swings of weather and personalities, not to mention the animal kingdom and the germs, which were nowadays smartly separated into things like viruses and bacteria and parasites and God only knew what else. No. There was no way anything could ever be airtight. One had to be flexible.

Mardi had no patience with those who passively succumbed. But I think in Pardi's case, she rationalized that he had been an active participant in his own demise. He didn't complain, he didn't drag it out. He decided that he couldn't be relevant anymore, said, *a pox on it all*, and did his best to simply bring things to a stop.

Mardi viewed manifestations of old age as irritating lapses in effort or concentration, treating each sign of wear and tear as a challenge. As she became hard of hearing, she struggled to master the complex art of using a modern hearing aid, which required adjustments for any change in situation or tone of voice, my father getting in on the act by chasing through stores in America to purchase some new model he'd found in a catalogue. She knew that this little piece of equipment could be strategically turned off if guests became boring, or if the Four Roads sound system was protesting away across the gully. Her eyes were giving her endless trouble, one eye partially clouded over, so she made her drawings bigger so they were easier to see. She made her sculptures gradually smaller so she didn't have to climb. When she could get someone to accompany her, she'd go to the Mona dam, circling its peaceful track for exercise. She kept a strict diet of non-pappy food, avoiding all nuts and small seeds to prevent the little sacs in her large intestine clogging and becoming infected, eating bran and drinking her Metamucil. As her lungs got weaker and there were repeated emergency visits to the hospital that ended up in expensive bills, she installed an oxygen tank and mask for emergencies and worked hard at her breathing exercises, blowing and inhaling the newborn air in the early mornings on the patio as the birds chattered and rejoiced in her garden.

Arthritis, she felt, was a metaphor for a state of mind—a refusal to become more flexible as one grew older and discovered just how much more fluid life really was than one's youthful conceits. Rheumatism and lumbago—a word so unfit to rhyme with her beloved blue plumbago—all these words she saw as signs of a person's spirit having become moribund; having given up and turned to salt. And she knew that people did give up; she saw it all around her in old friends. They'd wake up one morning and decide they'd arrived at a town called "old age" and they'd stop. Just stop and wait for death to send its transport to collect them, mumbling in irritating complacency, "We're in the waiting room now." And if you suggested a way to treat their ailment, they'd literally lay claim to it, possess it with all their might till, had it been just a rumour in them before, it was now part of them, bestowed with a name, certain and solid.

She had times when she railed at life's refusal to just stand still long enough to get things fixed, for it seemed as soon as one thought one had solved one problem, there were many others to take its place. Even the good things that happened which did take root eventually became irrelevant as life's dynamics changed around them.

The eighties had opened full of foreboding, with prices and violence soaring. As she'd read the foreign news she had decided it was the same everywhere in the world. By 1986, after six years of the JLP government under the leadership of Edward Seaga, things were if anything more divisive, more violent. The inner cities were seething—the youth with their rage fuelled by drugs, and their guns fuelled by the trade of those drugs—and what had begun as party tribalism seemed to have taken on a life and culture outside politics. Uptown crime had become a daily occurrence, the terrified middle classes taking solace in the fact that these were hits within the lucrative drug trade—a deal gone bad between bad people—but knowing deep inside that a dike built over the years to protect the status quo was insufficient to safeguard a lifestyle that had always been based on an unjust system. Beneath a scattershot of random criminal acts, subterranean and inevitable, lay a much deeper threat. So you either left, or you added more burglar bars and alarm systems and guards at the gate and spent your life as more or less a prisoner, hoping you'd come through the violence unscathed. As the handsome Doberman Johann got older, Mardi had added a small golden boxer, Nansi, for her protection. But she soon discovered that Nansi was no guard dog, being hopelessly sentimental.

Yes, after the food shortages of the seventies, one could now buy anything, but at a price only the very rich could afford. We were back to the old days of privileged rights: *It's okay to be middle-class and wealthy—hey, who's stopping anyone from working hard and making a buck?* Reagan and Thatcher had made privilege acceptable over there, so why not here in the Third World? The Reagans had been

Jamaica's first official visitors, weeks after the JLP return—a sure sign of changing times. We were back to imported Kellogg's corn-flakes and American apples, and somehow Mardi thought the most significant and regrettable return was that of beauty pageants. She had watched as the years of work of first her nationalist husband and then her socialist son had become irrelevant, as a new gener-ation embraced the tough-minded economics of a world fast reshaping itself into huge trading blocs. Now one simply offered oneself up as the cheapest, most convenient form of labour and raw materials if one wished to survive. No more leeway would be granted through imperial conscience for the misdeeds of history—it was going to be each man for himself.

Life at Regardless now meant coping with the battle to get a bath or a hot cooked meal, as water and electricity cut-offs became a daily occurrence and sometimes Mardi was without water for as long as four days. One learned to store water in large plastic con-tainers or even the bathtub, to wait till it was crucial before giving the toilet that precious single flush, and she bought herself a small two burner gas stove and brought down some of the old kerosene lamps from Nomdmi. Tinned sardines, sausages and soups, and dry crackers became her standby foods, and the cupboards were permanently stocked as though for a summer hurricane.

On the home front, the family was completely unsettled and seemed to lurch from crisis to crisis. Michael's marriage ended and he grieved for his two smallest kids, Natasha and David, who had lost that sense of certainty he'd come to realize guaranteed chil-dren their innocence. Michael and Beverley had been both to blame, having in many ways behaved with reckless disregard for one another and their family unit. David, my father's last child, had been born premature during the agonizing run-up to the 1980 election. It was a miracle he lived at all, but not even this managed to heal a family whose central premise had long ago gone awry.

Mardi ached for them all. Michael was on his own, trekking the coasts of America on a lecture circuit to talk of his failures and mistakes, with an occasional meeting with the growingly dispirited Socialist International, of which he was a vice-president. Like his mother, he suffered from diverticulitis, at one point so dangerous he had to have emergency surgery to remove many feet of his colon.

Douglas, for his part, was out of a job. Mardi had had to relocate George Campbell—ever more frail, nervous, and contentious, in and out of hospital—so that Douglas and his younger son, Roy, could move in. Douglas had got a Fulbright scholarship in New York, which rescued him for a year, but when he came back, still unable to get a job at the local university, he was again forced to stay with his mother. Norman was in and out, seemingly bent on self-destruction, though it appeared to elude him. Roy became a permanence at Regardless, his company providing Mardi with unexpected comfort and happiness. He had lived stoically with severe health problems from birth; he was extraordinarily kind in his quiet, rather ponderous way, and with him Mardi found a quiet camaraderie based on what she described as their "two great lonelinesses." Again she learned flexibility. When Roy had the TV blaring, which was a lot of the time, she simply turned off her hearing aid. When Norman played Marvin Gaye full blast on the stereo, she bought him a pair of earphones.

Mardi was cheered when Douglas went into business with a wealthy friend in May Pen to grow green plants for shipment to foreign florists. At the same time my father, who had built his own holiday home on a piece of the Nomdmi land, began growing flowers there, especially roses for export. Other than my father winning an international prize for his black rose, both ventures lost money, and my uncle's flowerless flower farm soon went into bankruptcy. Again my grandmother felt perverse pride in the fact neither of her sons was any good at business.

But nothing in my life could have offered her comfort. It was chaotic. I was divorced again and had lost custody of my younger son in a wrenching battle that left me totally bereft, grimly aware that whatever the reason I'd been separated from my mother, the cycle was repeating itself for another generation.

Mardi, increasingly frail herself, had become the hub of what felt like a rickety wheel.

She had spent half her life trying to get everyone to write or to paint or to carve or to think bravely, or to be necessarily reckless, or to calm down. In many ways, as her daughters-in-law would no doubt have said, she had spent a lot of time interfering. But she felt we all seemed to get bogged down by life, and she just wanted us all to be free to dream our dreams and exercise our talents. Insofar as her care had affected the family, she must have had her misgivings. But on the wider front, despite the turbulent political scene, the cultural life of Jamaica seemed to have taken root. All around her it grew and flourished—in dance, where every year new companies formed, each with its own unique style, and there was no time in Kingston when at least two local plays were not on. Galleries emerged everywhere, and though the rich got richer, they always bought Jamaican art for their offices or banks or hotels or homes; even people running away from Jamaica in the seventies felt it safe to take art instead of prohibited currency, knowing its value would only increase. Jamaican reggae and the message of peace from Rastafarianism had throbbed through the entire black world, and the Third World; just as it had helped the PNP win in 1972, it became a heartbeat throughout Africa in the fight against apartheid, through the war in Angola, through Mozambique, as though a distant pulse, a small but determined legacy that had strayed across the world all those centuries ago, was returning with its instinctive repeated contraction.

She was learning that hope always stood beside hopelessness.

Mardi took comfort from the things that did go well, and turned to themes that were rewarding and materials that were safe, creating *The Dancer*, then *Drummer and Dancer* in Ciment Fondu; a shepherding, evangelical presence, *Brother Levi*, and then, as though these were more about the surety of mission, she turned back to the unique spirit that, though still sometimes repudiated and often misunderstood, lay behind modern Jamaican culture. She created a powerful Rastafarian—head thrown backwards as in *Negro Aroused*, mouth partially opened—which she alternately called either *The Word* or *The Voice*. It was often referred to as *Marley's Redemption Song*.

In 1982 she willed herself to tackle *Negro Aroused* as a monument again. It was not as large as the first doomed recreation, but it was larger than the original carving, and travelled with the Exhibition of Jamaican Art 1922–1982, which was viewed in eleven American museums; one of its casts was purchased by the Wadsworth Athenaeum in Hartford. The original came home to stand at its historic spot on the waterfront where in 1938 she had fed the strikers from the back of the truck, and she was delighted when a postage stamp came out commemorating that watershed moment with a picture of the work, sending me the first-day cover.

Despite moods of annoyance and unhappiness in her diary— "*It is quite unbelievable to be living in this world with all this murder and bitterness and brutality*"—the world recession, the Falklands War, which strangely disturbed her, and her expressing peevishly again and again that she had "*no wish to live any longer,*" she would ultimately divert herself—"*the only thing to do is to have FAITH*"—with hope. Hope when my father's book *Struggle in the Periphery* was published, hope when advance notice of the republication of George's *First Poems* arrived, hope in my brief new effort to return home and teach and, when that was abandoned, hope in the invitation to attend Carifesta in Barbados. She had been officially invited to be honoured alongside the famous Trinidadian calypsonian, the Mighty

Sparrow. There she would see me and, in the way life connects and guides us if we let it, she would receive from Mike two books that would inspire a huge new work. They were on the sculptor Käthe Kollwitz, whose sculpture *Seeds for Sowing Shall Not be Milled* would make a vivid impression on her. Hope also in George Lamming's suggestion that she write her autobiography, which she toyed with for a while before deciding instead to become more diligent in recording the past in her diaries.

And then, in her eighth decade of a life that lately had come to seem impossible, she set to work again on what was perhaps her most ambitious piece. She worked as though she were not old or biding time between asthma attacks; as though all the disappointment and confusion hadn't surrounded her, and friends and acquaintances and strangers in houses around Kingston were not building walls around themselves and pulling down shutters to block out the reality of violence in the inner cities, where a mother was afraid to let her children walk to school or even lie in their beds at night for fear stray bullets would come through the dusty air or a closed window or the insubstantial walling to shatter their unspent lives. She worked as Jamaica evolved into a country where an old-age home was deliberately burnt to the ground, where violence was so horrific that a house was set on fire and escaping children were thrown back into the flames through the burning eyes of its windows. And from all that she created *Ghetto Mother*.

In Kollwitz's drawing she had found a universal language, an allegorical icon for mother-suffering, and the Jamaican woman emerged as a massive, squat torso with shoulders like a broad mountain plateau, embracing four small children who look like stark, open-mouthed, featherless nurslings shrieking from the nest. Above them she lifts her head, and faces whatever enemy is out there in a grim beseechment of outrage, terror, and frustration.

Coming from Edna, it was somehow unexpected by the public,

because despite her often prophetic and always revolutionary voice, nationalism was now the norm and in many ways she was by now seen as part of the political structure, whichever side was in— whereas this was a work that came from the voiceless outrage of the disinherited, and demanded a reckoning of both warring parties, pointing an unswerving finger at the entire system.

But in truth the genesis of *Ghetto Mother* reflected so much more than just the bitterness of the 1980 campaign, which had left over eight hundred dead. It was also a prophetic piece. There is something stunted and squat about the sculpture. Its shape isn't just about people but about imploding mass. It can also be viewed as an island, a lone atoll hunkered down, protecting itself from the onslaught of vaster powers, both economically and militarily. It is a culture and a people protecting its self and its ground, its history and dreams and future, protecting the very things for which Pardi and she in her own way had led the fight for over half a century.

In the preliminary drawings of *Ghetto Mother*, the woman stared straight at a gun held by a man towering above her. But she eventually left the source of the fear to the viewer's imagination, making it even more menacing. *Black Sun*, a black head of Ciment Fondu with the dreadlocks of the oppressed and defiant inner-city youth, derived from the head of that absent gunman.

As though *Ghetto Mother* had spent Mardi's dark night, she now reached again towards hope in her work, which was restored to such buoyancy, as though lighter, ready for rejoicing. Having wrestled demons, she was ready to tackle angels. Despite a note in her diary that in truth she couldn't afford the wood for the new work, and intermittent periods of coughing and asthma, she turned to *Jacob and the Angel*, a theme she had flirted with over the years. She had always pondered the myth of the blow to the thigh (and it makes me remember one of my father's favourite, dramatically rendered quotes: "*smote them hip and thigh*," the little "*hip*" so tight it caused his upper lip to slam shut with a fillip, of air and the "*thigh*" to come out with the release of a sigh, when any victory—a grand slam in bridge or a century by Rowe—caught his imagination), and wondered what the angel really represented. I think that as she worked on this carving, the process became her own battle within, between the temptation of darkness and a willingness for light; between the negative, self-sorrowing tendency to give up, and the positive instinct to rage even to the bitter end. The bas-relief was cast in Ciment Fondu.

I used to long to come to Jamaica for holidays, bringing Drum up with me to meet Luke for a few precious weeks, seeing Mardi and my father and Douglas and the siblings and cousins, surrounded by family again. It became a happy ritual. I had recently met Iz, a Canadian journalist who'd come to give a course with the newsroom of CBC in Barbados, where I worked in the advertising department. His assignment was over but with the help of my boss, Vic Fernandes—the unofficial but de facto voice of Barbados, my great friend, and an incurable romantic like my father—he was making arrangements to return for a longer stint. I came "up" to visit Mardi for Christmas in 1983, bringing Drum and to be with Luke. We would stay at Regardless where Mardi, usually tolerant at a distance with children, developed a growing connection with her great-grandsons with each holiday, settling them down to draw or to paint, taking them for walks in which she would bring the landscape alive for them in much the same way she had done for me. It became a great a hiatus of peace and happiness for her and for me. In return, the children grew very attached to her, and Drum would write her complaining notes from Barbados when he felt I fell short as a mother, which was fairly often.

That was when I first saw *Ghetto Mother*. I hadn't been in Jamaica for the 1980 election; it had become frozen in time in a phone call from home as I sat alone in my Barbados apartment, a huge dance floor from the old Club Morgan nightclub, my phone in my bedroom, which was up on what had been the bandstand. It was my father's tired voice, as ever consoling even when the bad news was his, telling me gently and matter-of-factly that he had lost. "We must all keep an eye on Mardi," he said, and he emphasized "*Mardi*" as though she, and not he or I, was the point of heartbreak that would need protection and consolation.

And so, looking at *Ghetto Mother* in the new downtown Kingston gallery, I didn't associate it with the election, which was narrowly filed in my head without its violence and wider implications. I saw in it the small body of islands that huddle in their oceans nurturing their own, resisting both the natural hurricanes and the human storms that arrive to plunder them physically, economically and politically. I see in *Ghetto Mother* now, created a full two years before the invasion, the island of Grenada shrunk in terror, unprotected, opened up to its terrible fate by the indecision and rivalry of its politicians, and the inability of its sister islands to mediate a solution. Washington's self-righteous invasion of a commonwealth member and Caribbean entity, was, I believe, a milestone of failure in the region's history.

I had been hovering near that story, as I worked at the CBC and our station became the de facto voice of Grenada. We called numbers at random from the Grenada telephone book, and fearful residents breathlessly explained to our anchors over the airwaves what they knew.

My father and I had flown to Grenada for a day just six months before, when he had met with Prime Minister Maurice Bishop. We remembered now how tense the lunch had seemed when we joined Bernard Coard, his right-hand minister, and how that evening a frantic Jamaican woman had tugged at my sleeve and whispered as though lives depended on it that my father should warn Maurice to watch his back with regard to Bernard. We also remembered the first place we had visited that morning, when Bishop met us and took us straight to the new airport under construction. He beamed with obvious pride, explaining how the ability to land a large jet would increase their tourism, from which this jewel of an island would prosper greatly. My father, a trained air gunner, had been certain that what we saw there was a commercial and *not* a military airport as the United States would claim. And the island *was* a jewel. Flying in, we saw the brilliant green hills sloping steeply to the bluest, clearest water; it shone there pristine and experience-young; love child of the Caribbean. It felt unjaded, like the Jamaican north coast of my youth.

The U.S. invasion of Grenada had shaken not just Michael but also Mardi. Whether it was to rescue the American medical students, or to stop a Marxist rebellion that had swallowed up the moderate Bishop, or the meddling hand of a foreign "*agent provocateur,*" or an effort to stop the spread of Cuban Communism in the region, in the long run of history the motive didn't matter. What mattered to them most was the vulnerability of our sovereign region.

Things nearer home were falling apart too. Mardi saw my father every day, when he walked over from next door, using the gate we had once used to visit Muriel. They had become very close again, as they always did when my father was alone, and he complained of rattling around like an old bone in what was now too big a house for a single person. It had been substantially enlarged, and Muriel's peaceful aura had been replaced by so many bad memories—the last rocky years of his marriage to Beverley, the loss of the election, the separation and departure of his two small children—as though that burglary in my aunt's time had broken some spell of cosmic goodwill. Beyond the empty rooms of the home, the unused guard hut at the gate stood like a haunting reminder of a bygone state of grace.

My father had decided to sue the *Daily Gleaner* for the vitriolic articles they published, which he considered libellous. He became embroiled in the time-consuming and arduous process of preparing his defence, but could not afford to pay the lawyers, many of whom put in long hours gratis. Defending his reputation in a political climate hostile to his recent administration, which was still fresh in people's minds, made it difficult for him to find credible character witnesses who were not afraid of the consequences to themselves.

"The damn cowardice of people," Mardi railed over the phone. "This—more than anything else—" she hesitated as though overwhelmed by the implications—"has broken his heart!"

Eventually the former prime minister, Hugh Shearer, and Olympian Herb McKenley—both members of the opposing JLP party—came forward to speak out for him. But Michael, plagued by bouts of ill health and demoralized by defeat and disapproval, seemed to have lost his nerve. Who knows which disappointment was the final straw? One of his lawyers remembers how, during a long session in preparation for cross-examination, he seemed to flag and lose the will to go on. The case was settled out of court.

He still travelled on his lecture tours to earn his living, often unwell—diverticulitis, a growth on his thyroid, repeated attacks of flu and bronchitis, and the onset of emphysema—and in between, he'd visit Mardi and confess how much he missed all his children, how lost he felt without a meaningful relationship.

Mardi loved to hear Douglas and Michael on the patio outside her bedroom window in the afternoon, chatting and laughing peacefully, and sometimes took longer to join them, not wanting to interrupt their reconnection. Whereas Douglas seemed to be finding peace as he settled into Regardless, Mardi felt Michael rocking around without an anchor. They were so alike, he and Mardi. He reminded me now so much of her after Pardi died, the professional life undiminished while the private person one dealt with day to day had become needy and uncharacteristically accessible.

As for Mardi's work, her instinct to rage again won.

Praise was inspired by words from Isaiah: *". . . give him no rest until he makes Jerusalem a theme of endless praise on earth."* A small, exquisitely lyrical bronze, the torso of a young nude woman with her clasped hands thrown upwards, her long hair rising like a flame above her head, her face turned to heaven. Its companion piece, *Orpheus*, a fig-ure rising on notes of music, his arms tenderly cradling his harp like a baby—which, as was astutely pointed out by ten-year-old Natasha, he was listening to rather than playing.

In late November Seaga called an election, before the electoral office had completed the new voters' lists. Michael decided to boy-cott nomination day and thus the election, touring the country and holding meetings to explain his stand for "the sanctity of agree-ment on which all civilized societies base themselves."

"*He's a great fighter,*" Mardi wrote to me, *". . . he's faced everything win or lose and is at peace with himself."*

But she must have felt as though it never ended, crises after crises, the world hideously bearing down on one at times. Over Christmas, when I visited, she gave me a drawing, one of many preliminary sketches of Orpheus. Over a globe—maybe the world, or maybe the sun—a thin figure, naked, rather like Orpheus float-ing, almost swimming, as though the sky were his ocean, but the angle of his head was bowed as if in a hopelessness or shame that was uncharacteristic of Mardi's work. She had signed it, *"For Rachel, who understood."* It was titled *Fallen Angel*.

Years later, I would find many diary entries around this period that toyed with the suggestion of ending it all, as if she were a teenager making light scratches with a razor on her wrists. On my father's birthday, shortly before I arrived, when something more than just the world out there seems to have upset her, she registered a soulful *cri de coeur* in her diary with a tremulous hand: "*Tonight I know there is nothing worth going on living for.*"

But there still was.

In one final exhausting act of bravado, she decided to do something for Pardi that she hadn't been able to do before, because of the technical difficulties it had posed in the thirties; she recreated *Tomorrow*, his favourite, for casting. Her work had saved her again, this time from a great descending depression. And then she put away her modelling tools, all wrapped in their well-used, soft, stained cloths, in the studio cupboard, and decided that the time had come, at eighty-six, to turn over a new leaf and tackle painting.

I last saw Mardi in December 1986. I had been living in Montreal for six months and returned to Jamaica before Christmas. My father and I were on much better terms; as usual, we seemed to grow closer when I was relating to him one on one. I think, too, that unconsciously we were drawing together, knowing we might soon be left alone in a relationship that we had always shared three ways with Mardi. I had married Iz in May of that year, in my father's garden. My father and I had mapped out the course of our walk side by side, my arm slung through his, to the makeshift altar on his patio under a magnificent vine of trailing white flowers. Mardi watched us from his patio, where she still looked regal and upright though vulnerable as she perched on an uncomfortable iron chair, hugging her crossed knees, regarding us sentimentally, as if *we* were the loving couple. It was my third wedding, an unextravagant, homey affair. My father had a new girlfriend whom he invited to the ceremony. The atmosphere in the family was tense. My siblings stayed defiantly on the sidelines, looking resentful, loyal to

Beverley. My father and I both noticed that Mardi looked thin, unsteady, and exhausted.

A week later, my bags filled with placemats and tablecloths (our guests having decided these were the perfect gifts for travel), I set off less than happy for a new life in Montreal, with a promise to return for the holidays. As comforting as my marriage should have been, I was distraught at having to leave my younger son back home with his father, and my elder with his in Barbados to finish his last year in high school. Also, I had a great fear in my heart that I might never see Mardi again.

But for the next few months Mardi kept busy. She wrote me often but her large, curling handwriting, preciously familiar, got weaker, even the ink from her detested ballpoints seemed to be fading. "*Last heard from, you and Israel were opening 120 parcels!*" "*It's early Monday morning—the sun isn't up yet but there are streaks of light across the sky . . .*" "*I have just finished* The Color Purple *. . .*" She was reading D.H. Lawrence again, which opened up such a torrent in her soul. "*Oh Lawrence, why did I have to meet you again?*" she wrote. "*One had lived the best one could, but so often one has compromised with the naked truth. How else to survive?*" But she reopened her spirit to what she described as his genius of perception and awareness: "*This man who could make a whole landscape take on the palpitating life of his own body . . .*"

I noted with relief that, despite her eyes giving trouble recently, she was still able to read. She sent me a cheque from the sale of her work to a Canadian, a well-needed gift, and she was delighted and I think felt vindicated when I shared the news that I had finally got an offer from a real publisher for my latest poems; the previous two collections had been self-published.

When I arrived for Christmas, my father took me aside and warned me that she was fading. She was in that quietude of the old who concentrate to rise from a chair or reach for a book, or cross a room to fetch a glass of water, as though they have already left here and this is just a visit, a borrowing of someone else's element. But her mind was as sharp as ever. She explained that her latest picture had gone off to be framed, but she had a small photograph of it, two women, an older and a younger, looking up, their faces bright, their hands as if held in prayer, in that joyous way that people hold them when they clap their hands. There were no shadows, nothing sombre, no "ominy" here.

After my father left, she took my hand and I followed her over the lawn to the series of flat, rough cement tiles that passed through the overhanging trellis of Douglas's orchids, then bent round the side of the house. The earth lurked muddily around stones that had been laid as a path approaching the studio, and one was always careful to shorten one's gait so as not to overstep and land between them. "Left, left," I muttered, taking the lead for these last steps, and guided her to the door of the rough zinc shed.

Mardi unearthed the key from the deep pocket of a bright, loose-fitting shirt and unlocked the padlock that she always left hitched to the chain, the key dangling from it, and we went in. The glad-earthy smell of clay was mixed with that of linseed oil and kerosene, beeswax and acrylic and something chemical and acrid, and the smell of old clothes soaked and dank as they had once shawled mounds of clay sleeping on their stands. It was a world where no two planks of wood fit perfectly, no cupboard door shut without light shining through an uneven in-between—nothing was straight or flush, no louvre shining, nowhere swept; every movement displaced something valuable, some space that contained her moments, her movements, her breath. She could stride through, sense every nuance, every grief-stricken reference; she knew the room like an old dancer you set on a stage, a blind Maria Alonzo counting, marking her steps through *Swan Lake*, each ruffle of feather, each third position, each plié and relevé, the tiny tiptoes of her boureé safe.

Art is a conclusion of so many arguments in the artist's head, and on the walls, on the bathroom mirror, even on the floor. Magpies ravenously gathering and pilfering life for all its small gems. I looked at Mardi's nest. Clay maquettes stood on one table under the window, and on another there were countless cardboard scrolls, and in the corner a stack of flat picture-holders and drawing books. Life around her was always something like this, something that only she could sort out. Even though retrospectives of her work showed her astonishing achievement, the story wasn't really about what she managed to do in those years, but how she kept the spirit alive despite everything.

She had spent the last year drawing mostly variations on a single theme, *The Ocean My Mother*. They were all over the studio—flat on tables, under paperweights on the floor, tacked to the doors of cupboards, or lying in scrolls. She explained how one morning it came to her, a huge drawing of a young woman emerging naked from the sea, from the aureole of a wave, and rising up from her hair the heads of three white horses, their manes of spray flying— spray that her chalk and these wisps of white paint knew over and over, as if they were tatting between her fingers. She showed me a reproduction, for the original had already been sold. It was tacked to a canvas on the easel. Looking around, it was hard to believe how feverishly she had been working, seeing her now so tentative, so carefully applying her will to the smallest task, so conserving of her energy.

And we got through Christmas with Mardi deciding who should sit next to whom, and whom we should make a fuss of, and who should or should not have another drink.

The day I was due to leave, my bags packed and waiting, I sat in the garden at Regardless talking to her. It was December cool, and ginger-lilies peeping round the corner from under her window were bravely soldiering on. Two square plumbago beds of blue faced the mountains with their tiny, diligent blooms. Douglas had staked out the left of the patio beyond the dining-room window with a white lattice trellis that supported his wide variety of waxen orchids, flowers he praised for their uncomplicated needs as opposed to *some* whose needs were far more taxing. And the way he said "*some,*" as he looked at Mardi or me, left no doubt that he was alluding to women, probably us. The almond tree had continued to spread its shade wider and wider over the family, over so many strangers and friends and conversations, celebrations, heartbreaks, and rescues.

Although Mardi worried that my new husband, whose hand she perused for his fortune, had no lines in either palm, she was relieved that my life seemed nonetheless to be taking some kind of shape that might provide security for me. After Iz explained that when he met me he had been surprised by what he called the depth of my poetry, assuming at first that it would be sentimental schmaltz with flowers and smiley faces doodled in the margins, she hoped that as a journalist he might provide the sort of supportive influence and understanding—most of all, the practical help—needed to keep me writing. She talked about my new book, and said we would have a big party at Regardless when it came out. We discussed who should make the speech at the launch.

And we chatted and laughed about my odd little wedding six months before, then worried together as we always had about Michael's and Douglas's and Little Norman's futures, and as I was about to get up and go, she said out of nowhere, "You know I am leaving my diaries to you."

She had told me this on numerous occasions, so it was certainly something I knew, as I knew she was leaving me Nomdmi, and *Angel*, which hung over the dining table. In fact, I think she used this information as a form of good-humoured, not so subtle blackmail—she'd remind us about Douglas having Regardless,

Michael the Zadkine—whenever she was not somehow getting her own way. We never took it too seriously.

I got up and walked over to her, seated in the deep wooden slatted chair.

"Why are you telling me this?"

I may have sounded a little fierce, but I looked at her imploringly, for I felt it wasn't a note I dared to leave on. But she wasn't backing down. She pulled me gently to sit on the little straw footstool that Pardi used to use on the verandah—the one that had come all the way from the days of Drumblair, when he'd used it to tie his shoelaces.

She told me a story about her last visit with her mother in Neasden. Edna, sensing it would be the last time, had turned back to look at her mother from her gate. The older woman was feeding the birds. She looked at Edna and with a sense of all-knowing finality told her that it was late, and she should leave to catch the train.

I think I told her I remembered how sad she was when she heard the news that her mother had died. I was just a little girl, but I never forgot her sorrow that morning, all I then knew of my great-grandmother Ellie.

"Mardi, it's so hard for me to go. . . ," I explained. "I dread you dying and leaving me." I was tearful, but this was not a new conversation; I said this at some point before every departure.

"But you know you have to let me go one day," she answered. "I am really tired. Every breath becomes such a wearying effort." She dragged out the "wearying" as if to provide an example of this. "So if, just *if* I ever have to go, I want you to remember Mother and me that day. For you're *my* little firebrand."

As soon as I got to Montreal, I sent her a poem I had written on the plane, called "The Garden Gate." She wrote me back saying that she thought it was the best poem I had ever written, but that the name was all wrong. The point of the story, she said, was not the gate but the garden; that boundaries do not kill, they just contain, as do the words "The End," a story.

14

The Gate

But if I can live to do my Lazarus . . . I want there to be a joy of reunion as Jesus summons Lazarus back. . . . It tore him to pieces to do that miracle and the Marys watched—one in supreme, painful confidence—the other, unconvinced . . .

—Edna Manley: *The Diaries*, October 1986

ON FEBRUARY 10—eighteen or nineteen days before her eighty-seventh birthday, depending on whether it was February 28 or 29—it was her grandson Roy who found Mardi dead. He hadn't heard her wake for coffee, and he peeped through her keyhole and some shape he thought he saw bothered him. He opened the door and went in, and found her lying on the floor with a foot extended, trapped in the tucked-in sheet. He couldn't tell whether she had been reaching for her asthma medicine or trying to get out of bed to get to the bathroom. When he checked the aspirator, which he had filled the night before, it was empty. It had been a very cold night, and before she went to bed she had asked him to bring her a stole while she sat on the verandah talking to her granddaughter Sarah, who had come to warn her that someone was forging her work.

"Oh my, haven't I arrived!" she had said, amused.

After they left she went to bed. Douglas came in quite late that night. He said her door was closed.

When Roy found her, she still had her Walkman over her ears.

The funeral parlour thought she might have died of a stroke, because they saw the telltale pooling of blood on her temple in a listless bruise. Or maybe her head could have hit the floor when she fell. We would never know. Whatever it was, it was believed to have been sudden, and the doctor who saw her at seven figured she had been gone only a few hours.

Many thought she had died in her sleep like an angel; one eulogist actually printed it so. David, in the foreword of an art book, quoted:

Like a fallen rose
As quietly as a gentle wind dies at sea . . .

For me the generations link, and I remember her as she wanted me to, looking back at me from her garden as her mother had looked at her, in that safe place where continuity is assured and people have lived their lives well and on their own terms. A place from which I hope my sons will one day retrieve me.

On the day before Mardi died, my father dropped by to see her. He had brought her an early birthday present of a Walkman. A friend had given her a cassette of Quincy Jones's "Amazing Grace," which she was anxious to play. She liked to listen to music late at night or in the early mornings, when she couldn't sleep and didn't want to wake the family.

He found her in the studio. He took a moment not so much to accustom his eyes to the gloom, as his senses to the intimacy of the woman he had known for sixty-two years, even before he had memory. In this room he probably smelled her more privately, more surely, than any man would if she had undressed and taken him to bed. She stepped back from the far wall on which, improbably perched on a stool, she had been deftly and deliberately applying charcoal.

"I can't get Jesus to raise the dead," she said matter-of-factly. And she looked across the room at an easel in the far corner, where a doll-like, cocooned figure of Lazarus rested quietly, diagonal across the page, wrapped in his shroud.

"I have had to call on the good old Almighty!"

A pencilled Jesus pointed helplessly at Lazarus from another easel.

From an adjacent wall, the cement one built during the studio's extension, the face of an Old Testament figure opened his eyes wide, his arms in the air, rays of light rising overhead.

"I see what you mean, Mother," Michael said. "I do see *exactly* what you mean."

Douglas walked in for a moment as though he had forgotten something, looked at the figure on the wall, and said, "Oh dear, yes, I suppose you do need some more paper."

And he left.

Michael helped her down off the stool and gave her the present. She was excited and hugged him, then sat with him for a bit, discussing this and that. She told him she had the family Bible to give to him for safekeeping, and then he walked her over to the house, for it was lunchtime, and he too left.

The family now took the liberty of tapping Mardi gently on the head as she sat through the low energy of late afternoon with a book, a book she must continually blink at to see its words in focus. Reading her beloved Lawrence again was an effort—just sitting there and lifting her back from some low pain or other, or twisting her ribs a moment to make sure they could still twist and take back a fraction of the original height of her spine, while at the same time mentally holding maybe three important things, things that might matter because she had set them there as a test, as something she was determined to keep faith with: the note to Michael to ask him to drop by after work to collect this ridiculously heavy family Bible, the call to Cecil Baugh to ask him to make a new birdbath to replace the old broken one—oh, how mad the birds were, dashing in to land and complain and tearing off again—and the third, to get dear George to take a taxi when he was up to it and collect her new glasses from the optical company. Douglas she hoped would remember the drawing book. Now, that was four!

Her contemporaries were dying, leaving their family Bibles to their children and their children's children and *their* children. More and more generations. What was this now? People her age were becoming great-grandparents! This was ridiculous! It was time to die when one had to add so many adjectives to one's relativity.

Yes, it was certainly time to let go.

As she reached and surpassed Pardi's age, she too found herself seeking consolation from their life. What were the things that comforted? Knowing that her sons belonged to a country with its own passport and flag and anthem, despite the mountain of problems it would take generations to solve. And every time she went to the new open-air theatre instead of the ornate old colonial one, or opened an art exhibition, or attended a poetry reading or book launch, or heard the popular local rhythms of ska or rocksteady or reggae—music whose beat drove her mad at times but that she celebrated for the fact of its existence as ours—or attended some school prize-giving where a child was reading a Jamaican poem instead of an English one—she knew how worthwhile it all had been. She'd look at these children standing there all dressed and tidy, their hair braided or in a proud Afro, swaying as their hands clasped a book, and think of her own youth, and wonder if they knew how long life lasted, how long one would have to be practising good behaviour. Hopefully, dying was just going back to being one's own self again, regaining one's own sweet time.

But under all this lay the worry of her sons' personal happiness. Michael drifting in one tide after another, never seeming to be able to settle emotional roots. Douglas, who had circled Africa teaching and learning, as though his father's journey hadn't gone far enough and he needed to open curtains further back into the past, to strip off deeper layers of historical skin, back home as though he'd never left. She felt he was being victimized by the university here, which wouldn't rehire him. After she'd gone, he would go on living in Regardless, and Michael living next door, the two families slowly drawing closer she hoped. This gave her comfort. But how could she tell what personal happiness meant to each of them? Michael seemed to snatch it in quick forays from so many aspects of life. A fibrous root like her, he was capable of renewal, and the kiln of life had fired and burnished him the way he was, made him more joyous and less considered—more spiritually squandering. Douglas was very like his father, a taproot plant, with the need to keep balanced, to walk in a straight line looking ahead without looking down. All three men had suffered from what she called nervous ulcers, but in his quietly determined way, Douglas would probably be the more enduring.

But this was the mulch; the humanness from which we flower. When all was said and done, just that flowering is left. Michael was writing yet another book, this time a history of West Indian cricket. Douglas was planning to write a humorous novel on rural politics. Her two boys had taken so much that was entrenched, left over from a bigoted colonial system, and shaken it up in the seventies. Whatever the problems, we could be free of the past. And I had found a publisher for my next book.

And what of her own work? Not a day, an hour, a minute passed when some new idea in her mind was not jostling a myriad of others for her attention.

Someone had asked her recently in an interview if she had ever been tempted to give up her art. In those years when Pardi was premier, were there times when she found the celebrity glamorous? Though she'd been too busy to undertake a carving, she used to make herself draw the way one enters a guilty line in a diary, meaning to come back and fill it in properly one day. But she always knew she would return to sculpture. It was what was real to her. She could not have convinced herself to give it up simply for Pardi; it was his work that she found compelling. Strange how far away and small that period seemed now. Maybe as you got older things passed by faster, as time was running out and somehow the details mattered less so you didn't remember.

Over the past ten years since she had given up carving, she had sculpted mostly for Ciment Fondu. Michael joked that her work grew instead of diminishing, and he'd open his not very big eyes in mock astonishment. It was easier to raise it all onto a larger plane. The thing was this—she had found that she could compensate for any problems with her eyes, with her arms and shoulders, with her wrists and hands. The muscles remembered, as long as you didn't tie them down to anything too specific, anything too small and constricting. The greater problem was the risk of falling off the stool, mis-stepping on the ladder, tripping on the descent of a flight of stairs. She wasn't good at judging depth, and one didn't like to move too slowly. The young showed such impatience, being ignorant about it all. They'd look at you as if you were a fool because you were slow, but they didn't know how your body in all sorts of ingenious ways, was busy compensating, one thing for another, a progress far more complicated and demanding than the extravagance of their mindless speed.

Recently she had felt like the last leaf on one of those temperate trees that hangs on into winter trembling stubbornly, its hold increasingly tenuous in the grey wind, the last to fall. The effort to pull in air till her lungs cracked like kindling; the wanting, unfinished yawn of her breath; the freckles now cancerous, which must repeatedly be burned off; the abscesses requiring the extraction of her natural teeth one by one, her two long front incisors boldly ignoring fate. "The day they go, I go," she had decided, and so they stayed.

All her brothers and sisters had now died except for Ralph. It was strange that none of them had ever had children. She was probably the only one whose childhood dreams hadn't included a life with children. Ralph was still in Cornwall. The thought crossed her mind that she was also the only one who had returned to her mother's homeland, and maybe in there lay some karma, an obligation as the family's lone representative.

Ralph had written to say that the local church in Callington had sent him the Swithenbank family Bible. Being childless, he was making arrangements to send it to Douglas and Michael, in the safekeeping of the two remaining vestiges of Swithenbank blood. No doubt they'd send it to the institute.

Swithenbank blood. Her sons were that too, but she had chosen, and they lived as Manleys. She had no regrets at all about living her life here. This was her land, she had known that, though her English father was her friend and her first hero; her link to him was like the touching of minds and hands, even now. Not knowing what it was, she had felt the blood of her mother in her, like her own temperature—sometimes a silent, sullen tide, sometimes an angry rising flood, but mutely and limitlessly, intimately her own.

Michael, seeing her light on, came in for the second time that day for a moment's visit to collect the Bible he'd forgotten to take that morning. He rang the bell, and she went to meet him at the door where he stood breathy and lovably catastrophic and in his usual hurry, and she placed the heavy gold-edged tome in his hands.

"The weight of your maternal ancestors, my dear!"

"Indeed!" he said.

His shadow had faded into the dark long before she heard the faint clunk of the connecting gate.

The end of an evening. The end. One always came to the end. To the end of everything—days, carvings, stories. Everything was owned by an end.

⚌

How will I go when my time comes? How will I meet it? Lying in crisp white sheets in a hospital bed, surrounded by pretty young nurses telling me their love stories, with a dry martini in my hand?

Will I be up on a ladder constructing some huge piece that I can't see anymore, that my shoulders can only sense through imagination, these old hands narrowed to a single trembling intent as they clutch the piece of charcoal or chalk?

Will I be here in Regardless, lying in Norman's bed, trying to find my puffer in the dark? Tildy always tucks in the sheets too tightly, so I may be trapped, gasping for breath, unable to pull the damn things out enough to reach the night table. No, I usually find a way to ease them out with my hips just enough to stretch over. But maybe, as I lean over, my elbow will give way and I'll fall. Will Douglas or Roy be able to hear me? Will Ra phone, and let the phone ring till one of them wakes? Will one of them discover me in the morning, lying half-sprawled between the bed and the floor? Or will Michael drop in to tell me about some speech he has made, or the new love of his life, and find me stuck there? Or dear George turn up unexpectedly, looking for love, always looking for confirmation?

I bet that lying there, waiting for something to happen, instead of dreading death or worrying what it feels like cooped up in a dark, dreaded coffin with awful little worms, I'll suddenly remember some silly thing not very grand, something funny. I'll imagine my funeral, maybe a few friends with the usual weeping and wailing and gnashing of teeth, George there as one of my pallbearers, probably a nervous wreck with all the stress, and maybe needing to stop for a quick pee on a tree at the side of the road; and dear Mike—he'll probably make the journey home for me—he'll be longing to return to the welcome treadmill of his work. Michael looking solemn but thinking about some new girlfriend; Douglas longing for a stiff drink. Little Norman restless, fed up with all the fuss. And Ra. Dear Ra getting all worked up.

Or, like Mrs. Moon, will I just replace my book on the shelf and follow the stones in the path to Norman? But suppose there are no stones? Then I'll draw them. No. Stones are stone. They are supposed to have a rough surface. So I'll have to get out my old Bouchard hammer with its clawed head, and carve them, one by one, till I reach him.

Acknowledgements

For their generous assistance: The Guggenheim Foundation, The New York Public Library, The Pierre Berton Foundation, The Toronto Arts Council, The Hawthornden Writers' Retreat, Canada Council for the Arts—Travel Grant.

Heartfelt thanks to:

Wayne Brown for his generosity in sharing his research.

David Boxer for his catalogue of EM's work, and Easton Lee for his interview with EM.

Denise Bukowski, my agent, who rescued the book.

Linda Pruessen, my editor, who lovingly adopted it and helped me reshape it.

Marijke Friesen, Jennifer Fox, Daniel Rondeau and the caring and talented members of my new Key Porter family.

Gena Gorrell, the finest word mechanic I know.

Katherine Sterry for meticulous assistance on the early manuscript and recognizing that the story could not be written as a novel.

Orlando Patterson, Austin Clarke, Shelley Tepperman, Jacob Larsen, David Whiteside, Tony and Rachel Bursey, Rebecca Federman and Desmond Brodie for their kindness and help along the way.

My astute readers, Christina Shea, Katherine Russell Rich, Dorothy Prosser, Eileen Mais, Bev Hunter and Joan Beckford.

Gordon Robinson, whose wise opinion I can always depend on.

Ainsley Henriquez for support and encouragement too many times to list.

Rose McFarlane, for help in so many ways, and for reminding me to "trust life."

My bridge clubs and book clubs—you all kept me sane.

My beloved sons—Drum, who read and helped me edit, and most of all gave me the premise of the book when I was at a loss; and Luke, whose care and gentle "hush" whenever I needed it kept me steady.

And to my unique and wonderful family, who let me pilfer their stories.

To Israel, who makes it all possible.